EDUCATION

VOL. II
and
VOL. III

EDUCATION

by

OSTAP E. ORYSHKEWYCH, Ph. D.

VOL. II

THE GENERAL PRINCIPLES

OF

EDUCATION

and

VOL. III

THE PRINCIPLES OF MODERN

CURRICULUM IN THE CLASSROOM

with a Foreword by

RONALD M. PATTERSON

SECOND EDITION

ST. JOSAPHAT'S PEDAGOGICAL INSTITUTE
and
SEMINARY
Washington, D.C.

© 1977, 1982 Ostap E. Oryshkewych

Library of Congress Catalog Card Number: 79-64937

ISBN 0-9601414-1-3

Printed in the United States of America

TO
MY MOTHER

FOREWORD

In recent centuries, particularly in the last few decades, pedagogues of different ethnic origin have come to the firm conclusion, when teaching theory, that it is most useful and expedient to follow certain principles in the interest of better understanding, and also that each principle be explained and motivated. The principles help, above all, to systematize the knowledge of the student, greatly facilitating not only his understanding but also his powers of retention.

It is, therefore, my firm conviction that properly assembled and appropriately published didactic-educational principles will prove of great benefit not only for the student but also for the teacher. Young teachers will thereby broaden the scope of the knowledge of their profession, and have a greater opportunity to test the validity of their pedagogic efforts. More important still, the teacher, equipped with these didactic-educational principles, will stand on solid ground, and be in a position to substantiate the demands made on the student for performance in study, or even conduct, with greater confidence. Moreover, the publication of such principles will vindicate the teacher in the eyes of the students' parents or of the students themselves, in confrontation with any dissatisfaction.

It is for this reason that, even in days long gone, every pedagogue has felt that the educational system needs an educational code which would embody a collection of didactic-educational principles that would be cited frequently in the classroom and in educational literature. Nevertheless, over the course of the centuries, the great desire for publication of didactic-educational principles has resulted only in scanty, fortuitous references to a few pedagogical principles and their related motivations in the works of a few pedagogues. In all the pedagogical literature I have examined, I did not find one single work that contained at least a significant portion of the conglomerate body of educational principles. It is only now that an important pedagogical work in two volumes has come to my attention which includes, if not all, at least an impressive number of pedagogic principles with excellent interpretation and in-depth motivation.

In reading this profound work, one recognizes immediately that its author, Dr. Oryshkewych, is truly a specialist in his profession, through his accurate classification of the aforesaid principles, their logical structure, and his systematic approach to them. His keen pedagogic expertise makes the book easy to read and understand, while its contents are easily committed to memory. However, since I do not want what I have written to be interpreted as exaggerated praise, I would call the reader's attention to the table of Contents. One cannot help but admire the pervasive logic in the systematic arrangement of the subject matters listed. The reader will also observe how, in addition to educational literature, the author has availed himself of methods which he has applied in his own pedagogical activity.

In writing this work, Dr. Oryshkewych has drawn on the most reliable sources in this field, and has not overlooked one single serious pedagogical work. I can say this because I, myself, have read all of his works on pedagogy, including those still unpublished. It is my firm conviction that all of us here today—and also those who will come after us—will be grateful to him for this genuinely scientific-educational work.

Ronald M. Patterson

CONTENTS

VOL. II

CHAPTER I

CHAPTER II

CHAPTER VI

CHAPTER VII

CHAPTER VIII

VOL. III

CHAPTER I

CHAPTER II

CHAPTER III

THE PROCESS OF
CURRICULUM IMPROVEMENT................. 267

CHAPTER IV

CHAPTER V

PREFACE

The General Principles of Education, and *The Principles of Modern Curriculum in the Classroom* are sub-titles given to the second and third volumes of a seven-volume work under the general title, EDUCATION.

The basic educational subjects: *The Philosophy of Education* (one volume), *The Principles of Education* (two volumes), and *The History of World Education* (two volumes), are located in the first five volumes of EDUCATION. The next two volumes are additional. The sub-title of the sixth volume is *The American Schools in the Past and Present,* and the sub-title of the seventh volume is *The Modern Method of Teaching Foreign Languages.*

EDUCATION, Volumes II and III, are designed for students of education, for high school student-teachers, and for high school teachers. It highlights the basic educational principles that are important to every teacher.

While attempting through his choice of suggestions to recognize that high school teachers work in a variety of situations, the author has tried to be as consistent as possible in his interpretation of educational principles, which he has presented and illustrated with explanations, interpolated with his point of view, and has described a sound educational philosophy and practice of teaching.

The book has been written with the hope that it will serve as a basic guide in student-teaching seminars or general methods courses for secondary school teachers. In preparing this book, the author has carefully re-thought the topics encompassed in the original choice of chapters, keeping in mind the problems of teaching adolescents, and the typical administrative and curriculum organization of the secondary school.

The third volume examines the curriculum subjects and organization, and the processes of curriculum evaluation and development. At times, the author points out the directions in which he thinks school programs should develop.

In the text, along with the footnotes, there occurs a "see also" reference, which will guide the inquiring reader to additional sources where a given problem is discussed.

At the close of each section, there is a "Summary" which condenses the salient points developed in it.

It is no wonder that many educators believe the time has come to take a good, hard look at the secondary school curriculum and reappraise it. It is my conviction that this book will help students and teachers make such an examination and appraisal, for it is designed to describe the substance of the primary and secondary school curricula.

I hope that this book will be found useful in understanding both the theory and the practice of modern teaching.

O. E. O.

INTRODUCTION

There are a number of different types of high schools in the United States. In many school systems, the arrangement is what is known as "6-3-3," in which a three-year junior high school plays an intermediary role between the elementary school and the three-year senior high school. In the older pattern, "8-4," a senior high school course of four years follows eight years of an elementary school.

The American high school has just come through one of the most intense periods of public criticism in its history. The field of secondary education is today embarked upon a new era of innovation and improvement. Scholars and researchers are engaged in a renewed search for knowledge about the processes of education. The present secondary education in the United States is unstructured and unsystematic. It embraces a broad range of phenomena; but the interrelationships among these phenomena are matters of conjuncture, rather than of logical formulation.

The characteristic features of the traditional high school are: local initiative under a central authority; a liberal or general orientation, rather than a vocational one; provision for the masses, rather than an intellectual elite; and a comprehensive curriculum designed as preparation for college and for work.

Now a new era has arrived. Machines are rapidly displacing human labor. Some individuals claim that such advances argue for a highly specialized, highly technical high school education. There is ever-increasing pressure being exerted on the high school to match selected individuals with selected fragments of knowledge. Recent inventions have resulted in considerable consternation. Educators are confronted with decisions as to what should comprise the substance of learning at the secondary level.

The current movement in secondary school improvement is a new spirit of cooperation between the universities and the secondary schools. The cooperation between public school teacher and distinguished scholar has recently expressed itself in new ideas for the sequence and the method of presenting subject matter to learners. New questions are being raised about prevailing concepts of teaching and learning, with renewed interest on the part of psychologists and educators in the whole problem of how learners acquire knowledge.

A number of schools are deliberately scheduling small-group discussion classes. They are identifying teachers with unique talents in this teaching device, and they are providing special facilities for effective group learning. There are many aids which enhance individual inquiry. Many of the technological devices now in use are employed to increase the effectiveness of some specific teaching procedures, and the search for an ordered and disciplined view of the entire field of education assumes increasing importance.

The professional educator must be concerned at all times with fundamental questions; he must also be something of a philosopher. He must have his own value orientation, his own sense of purpose and direction, his own philosophy of life, and must also be a scholar in the traditional academic discipline. Secondary education is an extremely complex and demanding field of study. It requires philosophical orientation; it requires a knowledge of the art, the science, and the method of education.

Learning takes place in a wide variety of situations. The essence of the teacher's role is understanding the complex nature of learning situations, and being able to employ the most effective measures for enhancing the process of education. It must be admitted that educators have not yet had much success in appraising the efficiency of the educative process. Formal education may be best conceived as the process of facilitating one of man's most natural and fundamental drives: the search for knowledge and understanding. The process becomes even more ordered as the learner acquires specialized methods of inquiry. Education is a continuous and active process of inquiry and/or discovery. The purpose of formal education is to develop to the fullest the potential of each individual student. Each learner during the secondary phase of education should experience some contact with all of the major areas of knowledge.

It should be recognized that change and improvement in secondary education must be regarded as a continouos process, and that establishing the conditions for change will be our major task.

EDUCATION

VOL. II

THE
GENERAL PRINCIPLES
OF
EDUCATION

The
Principles with Their Interpretations
and
Suggestions

CHAPTER I

BASIC PRINCIPLES

The significant products of learning for living are attitudes, appreciations, skills and understandings, not facts and information for their own sake. Facts are useful only as they form the basis for thinking through a plan, idea, or problem, or for understanding a process.

Education, as such, at first glance, can be of no interest, attracts in no way to itself, but seems rather a dull routine. But in looking into it more deeply, we immediately become amenable to the educational process because we see definitely that education places a person in his proper place in all situations. The application of principles based on modern developments in the psychology of learning is found most frequently among teachers genuinely interested in keeping up with new developments in this field.

The teacher is not able to foresee all possibilities with which the child will be confronted in the future, but he does have the means of defining the direction along which, if followed, the child will be able to guide himself on the pathway of his life.

The principles discussed here are concerned with the more lasting types of learning, not with those which have no permanence or social significance. They are stated in the form that may readily be applicable to teaching - learning practices.

The Fundamental Purpose of Education

The fundamental purpose of education is to help an individual to discover himself and the world in which he lives so that he may live a happy and useful life. In other words, education has *two* basic purposes: to enable each individual to realize his full potential so that he may enjoy the greatest personal happiness; and enable him to develop to his fullest capacity for citizenship. All of the aims of education can be organized around these two purposes.

General education for the grammar and secondary schools provides, in simple terms, a learning environment where the varied needs of students can be nurtured. It is an educational program designed to provide experiences by means of which youth can learn to meet life's needs effectively.

The educational program should help every individual to realize his full potential. Experiences which develop an awareness and responsiveness to human values should be the constant concern of the school.

Democracy is based upon mutual respect for differences in social or racial groups, and strives to elicit the unique contributions of all to the common good.

The school should provide experiences which demand novel adjustments to situations, rather than those which emphasize routine and repetition (developing creativeness).

All experiences should aid in the process of "growing up", by which is meant the gradual development of mature relationships with others.

All students should have opportunities for leadership at their level, and all should be able to cooperate with leaders.

So long as the effort is mainly to improve methods of teaching, particularly by making subjects more alive to the students, progressive education is on the right track. But if progressives think that interesting the student is the main thing, rather than how substantial might be the knowledge he acquired, such a movement will be regressive education.

The principal goal of a good education is the perfection of a person.

The teacher must always show himself a thoroughly upright person who, at the same time, tries to implant all his qualities in the child, just as a painter wishes to make clear on canvas the image conceived by him.

The true perfection of all education is the full realization of the ideal of personality. In no case can the teachers denote the character of this ideal as physical, biological or psychological features, but they must search for the highest quality terms which would denote accurately the importance of education and would also take into consideration moral and spiritual criteria.

A good education always takes into account the inborn and acquired emotions in a person, and does not try to destroy them, but makes every effort to place these emotions under the full control of the reason of the individual and the opinions of society.

The task of education must be to make full use of the natural longings which are aroused in young people.

The pedagogue is first of all bound to recognize the aspirations in every individual psyche; to direct him to the above-mentioned goal. If teachers pay no attention to these aspirations or directly contradict them, they will thus prepare the soil for anarchy. The task of the school is to help children in their creative work.

The conscientious effort to understand the breadth of the life situations in which children and youth must become competent is one basic guarantee that provision will be made for balanced development.

The potential educative values of all life situations should be appraised by the teacher. The specific experiences through which situations are studied are determined as teachers and learners together investigate the immediate problem. Here the teacher plays a major part in determining what will be the focus of the year's work, what situations to expand on, what to deal with briefly in the course of daily classroom living, and what new experiences to provide.

Balanced development grows out of the teacher's best insight into the real problems with which the learner is trying to deal. Providing balanced development requires consideration of ways to acquaint children with new experiences which will enrich the total pattern of living.

Growth in ability to deal with life situations depends on how clearly teacher and learners see the relationship between present problems and those which demand similar competencies.

Insights into new situations are often achieved with comparatively little additional study.

The teacher can also find what types of concepts from past experiences he may be able to draw upon in helping learners deal with a present situation. The teacher builds upon the present and toward providing a sound basis for dealing effectively with the more complex situations of the future.

In the situations with which all individuals must deal with reasonable competence lies the scope of general education.

The general education experiences provided for the learner in a rural community will not be exactly the same as those provided for the child or youth in an urban community. The problems, as seen in the light of the talents, needs and experiential background of the particular learner, or group of learners, set the goals of general education.

Specialized education provides for greater depth of understanding of certain aspects of general education and development of particular understandings and skills needed by the individual.

Even at the level of grammar school, some specialized education must be provided for unusual ability and talent, such as in hobbies and unique interests.

Decisions regarding what knowledge is of most worth are complicated by the speed at which our world is changing.

Advances in all areas of human endeavor are coming so rapidly that what we teach as fact today may have to be modified tomorrow. To make our task even more challenging, interrelationships among the various fields of inquiry are more important than ever before. One cannot understand physics without some knowledge of chemistry and mathematics. All areas of knowledge today are significantly interrelated in one way or another.

Teachers must provide adolescents with the experiences that develop fundamental understandings within subject fields; they must also help them to become aware of the ways in which many areas of knowledge contribute to the solution of human problems. To meet this responsibility successfully, there are a number of problems the teacher must be prepared to face:

1. He must know clearly what his ultimate goals are.
2. He must decide how to deal with many opportunities which will help learners grow in their understanding, which topics to treat lightly, which to explore deeply, etc.
3. He will have to provide the experiences that guarantee that accurate concepts and generalizations are the result of learners' explorations.
4. He will have to make decisions on how and when to work through individual and small group projects, if he wants his learners to be active in acquiring and using new information.
5. He must be prepared to help pupils develop the reference skills they will need to locate new information for themselves.

Each learning experience must be appraised in the light of its use.

Since the pupil learns in terms of his purposes, much depends on whether or not he sees that the problem he is facing outside of school is similar to the school situation. Conscious efforts are needed to help learners draw parallels between what they are doing in school and related out-of-school experiences. Repeated contacts with varied aspects of a problem are important if learners are to adjust effectively to a new situation. The learner operates more effectively in a new situation when he has reached generalization about the old one. Teaching that leads to generalizations encourages pupils to experiment, to discuss, to reach conclusions. There are differences both in learners' ability to generalize and in the quality of the generalizations likely to be arrived at by youngsters of various maturity levels. Younger children and children with limited intellectual ability will not generalize as readily nor will their generalizations be so comprehensive as those of older and more mature learners. The child who grasps the partial generalization that the hands must be washed before eating may not see the need to wash before preparing food for others.[1]

The chief task of the school is to develop individuality properly.

The goal of education lies in awakening the spiritual resources in a child with the aid of instructional processes and in developing the child into an active and useful citizen. The most popular slogan of modern education emphasizes the demand for the independent development of the physical and spiritual powers of the pupil. As to the question of educational ethics, it must rest on the completely natural tendencies of the individual. By these natural tendencies, we must understand the corresponding psychical qualities which the educator can never destroy or increase but, at best, through his wise conduct, can guide and perfect.

The exact nature of learning is determined by the purpose of the learner.

Purposes can also be developed jointly by teacher and learners in a planning session. In helping learners develop new purposes, teachers should realize that learners are not always going to sense immediately and accept all the goals an adult foresees in an activity. It is desirable to start with the purposes that learners do see. Every suggestion for school experiences is based on the assumption that what is learned will apply to life situations.

In any learning situation, the individual should accept the goals as worthy ones.

We must criticize that trend of education which overloads children with a great quantity of knowledge without taking into consideration the fact that the children themselves cannot see how it will be of any benefit to them in the future. A mature individual, if he does anything, does it from greater or lesser necessity or from interest; the activity of children also must proceed from these reasons.

---

1. Stratemeyer, F.B. and others, *Developing a Curriculum for Modern Living* (New York: Bureau of Publications, Teachers College, Columbia University, 1957), p. 76.

The schools are undertaking a large number of activities that aren't essential to education at all.

The educators began to get very confused about the fundamental purposes of education. *The real purpose of a school is to teach how to use the minds effectively.* What schools are really doing is pushing the fundamental subjects aside in favor of other things. The *object* of education is to raise the intellectual level of the students. The teachers can raise it by teaching the fundamentals (languages, science, mathematics, history) to all groups of students.

The schools' greatest contribution lies namely, in helping learners to define more clearly the nature of their problems, and to provide materials and environment for a systematic attack on these problems.

Teachers deciding to utilize student interest and concern about a current problem introduce relevant material to students who are asking for experiences of a more contemporary and meaningful nature.

The first and chief aim of instruction and education is the properly good existence of an individual in all aspects.

With this goal, there is a strong basis on which teachers can rest their teaching and educational activity. In principle, this means that the object of every person is first and foremost his own existence. Parents and teachers have a greater possibility of arousing interest in children to ever-increasing limits of self-awareness in themselves when they produce in them the goal of revealing themselves in their work.

Turning to the question of the importance of awareness in education, and taking the position that consciousness is the basis of personality, education must deal the best that it can with this question, for otherwise it is not education but training. Teachers are bound to take into account all the conditions of awareness which usually show the trend of each child's natural inclinations.

Compulsion should not be applied in education.

Modern education asserts that complusion distorts the soul of young people; that it very often makes children shut themselves up within themselves, and then their natural inclinations turn in completely opposite directions.

The teacher desiring to urge the student to conscious activity must make the children aware of the value of their activity. Self-understanding develops proportionally with increasing age.

The school must give students a theory of life.

The teacher and the parents can transmit this theory in frequent conversations which can even be of a private nature. These private conversations can either be with individuals or with groups, i.e., with the children collectively. They can be in school or outside it, on various occasions and on different subjects, but chiefly on those themes which most interest the students. Such conversations refresh each child's mind, which too often is over-burdened with dry theory.

Private counsels and conversations awaken ambition in the students, as well as the desire for self-education. In private conversations, the teacher realizes his goal, because he can more concisely indicate to the students their ideal and the routes by which they can reach it.

The primary function of education is the development of the rational man.

Education asserts that its chief purpose is the development of a common orientation and point of view. Although it may granted that the development of the common is the first purpose of education, still it must be said that the development of individuality is also a major purpose of education.

The first duty of education and its greater contribution to the development of intelligent citizenship is to concern itself with the mastery of principles and with the cultivation of the rational faculties. The study of ethics, as a normative science, has a legitimate place in the educational program. For the education proper to man is that which unites man with man, rather than that which stresses the development of individual differences.

A false pedagogical assumption is that the acquisition of information ultimately produces intelligent thinking.

It is highly doubtful, however, that the information so acquired would be translated into genuine knowledge. The information they absorbed, since they did not learn it in the context of practical problems, would rarely be functional in their daily lives. The modicum of knowledge in each of the various disciplines to which they had been exposed was too fragmentary to be really usuable in the solution of practical problems.

Repetition aids in retention.

Learning not used tends to be forgotten. There are procedures that help to reduce forgetting. If facts, skills, and generalizations are important in the learner's daily life and he continues to use them, his retention is likely to be quite high.

The many means used today to heighten insights and meaningful relationships also tend to contribute to the permanence of learning.

Studying a foreign language is an essential part of learning.

When we study other languages, we study the literature and culture of other peoples and therefore begin to understand them.

A school program that meets individual needs must provide for the special problems of students with a special talent.

The student with a special talent in music, art or mechanics faces the problem of how to secure the specialized education he needs in order to make the most effective use of his talent. The gifted student has persistent problems in human relations, vocational competence, use of leisure time, and other such areas, just as do all students. But, because he is gifted, and is intellectually able, other pupils may regard him as "different", and may develop positive or negative attitudes toward him. His skills and knowledge make possible certain kinds of learning experiences which, while desirable for all students, are essential for his further development. The talented musician, for example, must practice on his instrument daily. This raises certain problems in his relations with others. The gifted student should develop the ability to make a realistic evaluation of his own strengths and weaknesses, and should be able to offer suggestions regarding experiences that will contribute to his own growth.

Physical or intellectual handicaps call for different answers to problems.

The methods of achieving goals for the particular learner are different. For groups of slow learners, the patern might more nearly resemble that of a primary grade with more definite guidance, simpler activities. In addition, there would be other times when small groups or individuals would have an opportunity to pursue special activities of a simpler nature, and the general classroom organization would be such that the teacher would have time to give individual help. Many schools are not yet making full use of the potentialities of the regular classroom to meet individual needs. Specialists are needed to help learners to explore problems as deeply as desired. All appropriate resources of the community should be used in extending and enriching the experiences of learners. The learners' problems determine the type of specialist help needed, which would then be sought at the point where the classroom teacher's competence is insufficient. The classroom teacher and the specialist plan jointly in the interest of learners.

The school must give extensive attention to the quality of its functioning as a social group, to the extent to which personal and group needs are satisfied.

The psychological and social sciences indicate that character and personality are, first of all, the products of group atmosphere and behavior and of the ways in which the physical and psychological needs of the person are met. The school must concern itself with the factors of family, neighborhood, and institutional life. Teachers are members of the society in which they teach. Where a society is united and certain about its major premises, teachers would share the common faith as a matter of course.

The educator must carry a substantial majority of his community with him; he must broaden his concept of education to include adult education in all its forms.

Education may be defined as the absorption, into the individual's personality, of the arts and sciences, and the moral attitudes.

The social structure, of course, is a product of learning; but the learning involved in the formulation of folkways, mores, customs, and institutions is social rather than individual learning. It follows not the rational method of thought, but the method of social evolution. The study of social trends is an indispensable aspect of any educational theory that holds that the school should be an agent of social reconstruction.

The primary purpose of education is a continuous reconstruction of the ideological and institutional structure of society to make it a more perfect embodiment of the democratic way of life.

The school may play a significant, or even a decisive, role in shaping the attitudes and the perspectives that will govern the conduct and behavior of persons in the face of problems and issues of social change and reconstruction.

The chief task of the school must be to develop self-control in the children and to harden them so well for life that no difficulties on their life's path will be unsurmountable for them.

Such an education acquaints the student with his intellectual, psychic, and physical powers and develops his self-confidence and responsibility. It is true that strength of will is also dependent on heredity. Thus, one man from birth has a greater power of self-control, and a second has it to a lesser degree. Yet, in every person, this capacity acquires active strength only with the aid of development. This is one of the chief factors which makes every person more or less valuable. The teachers must believe in the power of development and the possibility of a change for the better through the path of development.

Chief attention must be directed to independent work by students in school in the field of all intellectual subjects.

Involuntary, imposed tasks performed without any interest do not have a good influence on a child. The first and main task of every teacher and educator is to comprehend the soul of the child and to understand it; this will facilitate the work of the child and will arouse his creative interest. In other words, educators must seek the beginnings of their work in the child and not outside him. The teacher must first theoretically and factually convey the connection of definite information with the vital needs of the student. There are teachers who pay no attention to the children whom the program is to serve, but place all their stress on the program which the pupils must complete.

The school must first be based upon psychology.

It must always follow the path of the natural process of recognition, i.e., beginning with the need a person feels toward the utilization of knowledge as the chief tool without which he cannot perform his task.

Furthermore, the school must take into account independent creativity, the good mood of the students, and the self-confidence which is customary in every person, especially in a child.

The school must not treat instruction and education superficially.

The passive acceptance of knowledge, as well as the constant, senseless sitting in school, not only damage the physical make-up of the child but also cause equally harmful psychic damage. The teachers must at all cost apply a variety of methodological devices which quite naturally appear in the process of instruction. The school is unable to give the child well-rounded and full knowledge, but it must awaken in every single student his independent drive to learn and must offer the method for this learning.

The school must stop believing that it can so arrange the program of instruction that it will simultaneously teach and educate, and refuse to assign a definite time for education.

There is really no time assigned for education in school because, if the school program of instruction takes education into consideration, it is very superficial and does not allot definite time for it.

All the teachers must occupy themselves with education and, on all occasions, in various circumstances, and even during instruction periods, the teacher can insert his observations which pertain to education. In addition to the efforts of the teachers, the school organizations, which are regarded in the secondary schools as subsidiary educational institutions, must also occupy themselves with education, unless they are merely connected with the school, i.e., that the school program does not allot them a definite time. For work in these organizations a special time must be assigned; otherwise, it will collide with instruction time in the school.

Experimental background, abilities, interests, and aptitudes combine to make an educational experience meaningful for significant learner.

The skillful teacher accepts the spontaneous question, remark, or action of the learner as a clue to an interest, need, or problem,—not as a spurious phenomena of immaturity. The teachers should respect their hypotheses on how to solve the problems, and the materials and activities they propose. The scientific approach to problem-solving supplies the context for learning which places a premium on the teacher as an expert who can assist the student in clarifying the problems and providing him with means for solving them.

The learning situation should provide for continuity of experience.

Learning experiences need to be sequential, not merely repetitive. Only if by previous experience a pupil is prepared for a new experience can there be any continuity for him. The teacher should begin teaching a person where he is, rather than according to where he thinks he should be.

Learning is guided to help children use previously developed concepts in meeting new situations, and to extend these concepts as needed in dealing with new aspects of problems.

As the situation recurs in a new and more complex setting, it is the responsibility of the teacher to help students acquire new insights. The teacher has an obligation to appraise the potential value of each new experience in terms of possible contribution to growth in dealing with life situations.

Children of any age can become interested in a wide range of facts if these are presented in a way that suggest something new or different. Gifted children are more likely to need and to benefit from such experiences than are slow-learning children. As the learner matures and situations calling for the use of a given skill change, his competencies will have to be developed and extended.

The purpose of organizing learning experiences is to maximize the cumulative effect of the large number of learning experiences.

Understanding the basic principles of science and to use them in explaining the biological and physical phenomena about us requires a variety of related experiences. If the development of such complex behavior patterns is left to unrelated periods of learning, adequate achievement is impossible. Hence, a major phase in building a curriculum is to work out an organization of the many learning experiences required so that the student develops these complex behavior patterns gradually, day-by-day, and relates them to others so as to have an increasingly unified understanding.

The major objectives of instruction can be accomplished, but any significant accomplishment demands planned and directed efforts.

It is possible to develop in children the ability to recognize and apply scientific principles, to think critically, and to use rational techniques. The most effective methods will differ, depending on factors such as the age level of the students, the topic being studied, and the personality of the teacher. A *variety* of teaching methods seems to be of greater effectiveness in achieving the objectives of science instruction than one method alone.

The developmental approach suggests that all students should be brought to a standard of achievement which is appropriate for the abilities which they possess.

A program of instruction should be provided to meet the needs of the individual pupils concerned. For those who are not doing as well as their ability permits, some special instruction should be given to help them improve in the skills in which they are deficient. This instruction should be given only as long as it seems appropriate in helping the student conquer his learning deficiencies.

The main purpose of the schools is to prepare students for purposeful life, to help the individual to discover his own potential and help him to develop it.

More and more the individual is called upon to do fewer things that require greater knowledge. The school must look to new techniques; it must study more closely the means by which the human mind masters facts, ideas, skills. A child has a firmer grasp of a subject if it can be related to his own experience.

The difference between education and indoctrination is that, while indoctrination depends upon preconceived viewpoints, education is open-minded, appeals to our rational capacities, and tends to be an objective process, seeking complete knowledge. Education is incomplete without the enjoyment of the arts and humanities. Its task is to give students a balanced view of science. Moral and spiritual values cannot be excluded from the educative process. Development of creativity should be stimulated. The teacher can aid creativity by stimulating students, by uncovering hidden talents, and by respecting the individuality of students.

Science should be studied in terms of its implications for contemporary society and its role in human affairs.

Science-teaching should be directed toward human betterment, not only materially but culturally as well. Every effort must be made to introduce systematically the concepts and ideas of science which are essential to human adjustment. A primary purpose of science-teaching is to provide the type of experiences which will help students solve the personal-social problems encountered in contemporary living.

Modern education is concerned with the development of desirable behavior patterns.

Modern education is concerned with providing every student with the facilities that encourage and open the way for learning. It is important, however, that the work be so well organized that the pupils have as much significant experience as is possible. The teacher must guard against a too automatic sequence of movement from one phase of work to another, however, lest a sense of monotony develop.

It has become necessary to determine the most desirable attitudes the student should have, and the extent to which techniques and skills in the solution of problems can be mastered while the student is in school. The most effective way for the student to acquire such adjustment is by *precept* and *example* that require a similar adjustment within the school to that demanded outside.

Modern education is committed to the policy of creating the most favorable conditions possible for learning activity.

Enthusiasm, alertness, and a radiant spirit, so necessary to the success of the teacher, are concomitants of good health and pleasant working conditions. The new school buildings are constructed to facilitate a modern educational program; rooms are larger; lighting is plentiful and properly blended; and the freedom of the workshop atmosphere of the rooms makes it easy for teacher and students to adjust their activities in such ways as to take advantage of all lighting possibilities. The temperature and humidity are controlled and some air movement assured.

Each lower school is a preparatory school for the next higher one.

Recognizing the facts of individual differences, the high school education not only accepts, but expects pupils from elementary schools to vary in their capacities and attainments. Another source of difficulty in the relations between the high schools and the colleges clusters around the practice of the higher institutions to require a prescribed set of courses for admission. Whether or not with intent, this practice places the college in a position of powerful control over the curriculum of the high school.

Since the colleges and universities include more mature students than the high schools, select intellectually superior students, and have responsibility for the production of intellectually disciplined practitioners in various professions, they appropriately take a more intellectual approach to education.

In selecting students for admission to college, multiple, rather than single, criteria are proving to be more useful. A combination of overall grade average in high school, scholastic aptitude, recommendations of school officials who know the pupil well, and entrance tests has yielded the highest results.

The minutes in the school day are limited; time spent on one concept cannot be spent on another.

However, there is a firm belief that, for any one individual or for a particular group, the most effective basis for selecting what is to be taught is found in the problems actually faced in daily living. There is also a firm conviction that experiences so chosen will acquaint children with broad cultural resources and help them become skilled in using them in meeting life situations. There is a conviction that, in this changing world, it is important to educate for change; if necessary, to treat some of the past in less detail to make room for a look at the present.

Mechanization of classroom procedure tends to blind acceptance of procedures without question.

Creativeness cannot thrive under too rigid a classroom routine. Where all must work alike, the spirit of creativity is effectively discouraged.   Students must understand and accept whatever routine is required.   To require all to study the same materials or write exactly the same type of theme within the same time limits would sooner or later be destructive of individual needs and cramp creativeness at its best.   To require a certain standard of work for all as a minimum with care for varied interests, to require that the work be completed on the same uniform paper, with a standard pattern of arrangement and a maximum of time in which to complete the work, would involve both conformity in broad catagories and freedom for individualization of work within resonably extended limits.[1]

Separate secondary schools for boys and girls reflect the conviction that intellectual studies are most effectively conducted without the distractions of boy-girl relationships.

It may also reflect the viewpoint that educational objectives for girls are different from those for boys and demand different curricula.

Coeducation means that boys and girls work together in classrooms, in school plays, in getting out the school paper, and like activities, in which they learn to understand and appraise one another on bases other than sexual attraction.

Another possibility is that coeducation may be better for some aspects of the school program than for others.   The values claimed for coeducation might be equally well served by having boys and girls in the same school, but not in the same sections of the classroom studies.   It might make possible more concentrated attention to the classroom studies.

The school as an institution cannot accept some needs of society

---

1. Bossing, Nelson L., *Teaching in Secondary Schools,* (Boston: Houghton Mifflin Company, 1952), pp. 447-448.

as aims.

All educational aims are social; but not all social aims are educational, for the schools do not accept all social aims. Aims of schools are expressions of what society wants. Since educational aims are social aims, as society changes, the aims must change. The schools must constantly change their aims, for institutions themselves are constantly undergoing transformation.

The school as an institution cannot accept some needs of society as aims. There are four principles for determining objectives: 1. they must have the approval of society or at least some articulate groups; 2. they must be susceptible of being achieved through instruction; 3. they must suggest activities that are within the capacities of the school population; and 4. they must be actually accepted and undertaken by the school.[1]

Taken together, these four aims constitute the social aim of secondary education in the broadest sense of the term.

The importance of learning through understanding has been a big issue in modern education.

The emphasis on understanding stems in part from a rebellion against drill and rote learning which were so paramount in older educational practices. Bright children can learn very effectively through freedom for individual exploration of subject matter, and drill is less important to their learning and understanding.

One must see himself as worthy and educable in order to strive, to seek meanings and to solve problems.

If an individual sees himself as being able to achieve a certain goal, his chances of achieving it are enormously enhanced. On the contrary, if his self-image leads him to doubt whether he will succeed, he is literally beaten before he starts. This self-concept affects all life. It is a positive fact that one must see himself as worthy and educable in order to be able to strive and to solve problems.

1. Wesley, Edgar B., *Teaching the Social Studies,* (Boston: D.C. Heath and Company, 1950), pp. 118-119.

*The Adaptation of the Young to the Social Order
is the Primary Task of the School*

*Job analysis is essentially a theory of curriculum determination,
not a statement of the methodology of teaching.*

The job of the curriculum-maker is *first*, to discover exactly
what functions the adult citizen is expected to perform; *second*,
to ascertain precisely what attitudes, information, and skills
are involved in the best existing performances of these functions;
and, *third*, to develop, with due regard to maturation and abilities
of children, a graded curriculum designed to produce the indicated attitudes, knowledge, and skills.[1]

The curriculum must not be confused with the course of study.
The curriculum denotes that which is to be learned; the course of
study is the sequence of courses by which the learnings are secured. The curriculum is universal and constant, but the course
of study will vary both with the form universal institutions take in
a given society and with the pedagogical knowledge and practice
in that society.

Particular social orders or societies are going concerns based
upon estimates and expectations. These expectations and estimates are the folkways and the mores hammered out in the
daily processes of group life. They are reinforced, and enforced
by those modes of group behavior that we call customs. The
social structure, of course, is a product of learning; but the learning involved in the formulation of folkways, mores, customs,
and institutions is social, rather than individual learning. It does
not follow the rational method of thought, but the method of
social evolution. The study of social trends is an indispensable
aspect of any educational theory that holds that the school should
be an agent of social reconstruction.

*The primary social purpose of education is a continuous recon-
struction of the ideological and institutional structure of society.*

However, that reconstruction is limited to an adaptation of
the character and personality of the young to the social reality

---

1. Smith, B.O. and others, *Fundamentals of Curriculum Development*, (Yonkers-
on-Hudson: World Book Company, 1957), p. 613.

defined by a projection of existing social trends. It is true that even this form of the theory recognizes that the continuation of these trends will create certain technical and social problems, which demand examination and criticism in the classroom. But the trends are taken as immutable facts.

The purpose of education must include that reconstrution of ideas and institutions required to make society more perfect.

The core of the curriculum of school should consist of a careful study of the significant social problems.

The core of the curriclum, although of first importance, is not the whole of it. A well-rounded education should result in several types of learning products: skill in the manipulation of things; skill in the manipulation of ideas, in the sense of logical analysis; skill in the processes of group discussion and co-operation, and in personal relations with others.

The primary task of the school is to ensure that pupils learn the facts and principles warranted by established knowledge. Critical thought does demand some capacity for theoretical analysis, as well as comprehension of relevant priciples and facts. But critical thinking is not the typical result of prolonged practice in the assimilation of other people's thought. When students are encouraged to think for themselves, even to the extent of assisting in the selection of problems for study and in the organization of learning activities, they typically respond to the challenge with vigor and intelligence. Even in the teaching of number combinations, understanding gained through experience and problem-solving has been found superior to sheer drill. Indeed, there is evidence that memorization of number combinations does not readily occur untill the child has found meaning for them.

The selection of issues for study, the choice of methods of study, and, above all, the atmoshpere and discipline of the school represent subtle but significant ways in which the school inevitably shapes the mind and personality of the young.

What is important is recognition of the need of curriculum material based upon personal and individual needs, interests, and capacities.

Scheduling aspects of the school program should be planned with the overall problems posed by the community in mind.

Flexibility is always necessary if the program is to be balanced, both in range of life situations and in variety of experiences provided to meet group and individual needs. The school day should be planned in relation to the needs of learners. The school may take the leadership or cooperate in securing better community provisions to meet the problems. In some cases, the school can make its best contribution directly and will provide for the extended program.

A curriculum designed with concern for all-round development of the student requires a different length of school year for different schools. The length of the school day and year will be most effective if made in consideration with the nature of the community. Extending the school year to include the summer months may, for some schools, mean the development of a school camp; for others, the provision of the same type of activities as those included in the regular school year.

Moral Education

Morality must be implanted in children from their earliest years, from the time when they begin to understand that they must obey the commands of their parents.

Morality is the very essence of education. The whole purpose of teaching is interwined with it like a golden thread. Every institution must take part in this effort. Beside the school, this task requires a reformed theatre and proper censorship of television programs, films, and children's magazines and published books. There must be embodied theoretically the ideas of morality in the minds of the children.

Moral education, in the usual sense of the word, indicates instruction on the theme of morality. Such instruction can never rest on coercion, for this does more harm than good. Moral education lies in the ability to make the student capable of approaching life as realistically as his natural disposition permits. This naturally moral approach to life, in a way, creates a new world, and the student must learn to understand it, not as a whim which demands obedience and self-conservation, but as that which marks his life and makes him happy. To achieve this higher aim, instruction and education must work together, for studies are linked closely with the life and conduct of a man.

Society must also have in mind that moral youth will be the creators of a moral society.

With a moral society, we will not be building bouses of correction and prisons for adolescents, but for the same money we will build schools and libraries.

Parents must realize that the family has an enormous influence on the moral education of children.

Wise parents know that they must adopt definite times for feeding the children, that they must dress the children in good taste, and maintain ritualistic and national traditions. The parents must guard traditions, and then the children themselves will certainly value them.

Moral education also includes the training of a healthy patriotism, love for one's country. This patriotism must be devoid of any chauvinism, which only deforms a person. Patriotism is healthy when it is founded on principles of morality.

Much help in instilling in patriotism is given by national festivals, songs and historical tales. The chief basis for training in patriotism is the development of an elemental love for the native country, which usually, in the first years of childhood, is based on instinct and custom. Love for various places, neighborhoods and, also, one's native land, is based on deep psychological experiences. Children receive external impressions differently, and accept them without the slightest hesitation.

Ethics in Education

Ethics in education must rest upon the natural inclinations of an individual, that is, on his psychic disposition.

It is the task of every educator first to recognize the natural inclinations in individuals. Teachers must carry on their educational work in such a manner that the good tendencies in the students could bring some profit to all students as well as to society in the future.

In guiding the natural tendencies of students, the teacher simultaneously builds an urge in the students for self-education and improves the character of the students, while his activity arouses their interest.

Esthetic Education

The school must be the basis of esthetic education.

The school is the most authoritative in the question of esthetic education. The strength of the school lies in the fact that the ideal center of every pedagogical problem always is relative to the final goal of every pedagogical activity and to the formation of personality. The true pedagogical ideal is by nature active and at the same time responsible, and this responsiblity lies not only in individual pedagogues but also in the whole school.

All education, especially esthetic education, must come out of life; it must perfect the methods with the aid of which the needs of life may be satisfied.

Esthetic education has as its main task the making of assimilation of knowledge pleasant for children, not difficult or unpleasant.

Esthetic education is the most important element in the development of the modern cultured person.

Esthetic education develops esthetic feeling for the world and includes all artistic forms and colors. Esthetic education is also the center from which comes the planning of the thought and imagination of artists who see the world more clearly in its esthetic character. The problem of esthetic education also is very important, because the development of human solidarity is a necessary condition of social life which can be observed everywhere. The task of esthetic education joins that of ethical education, for ethical education polishes a person and helps religious education; it makes a person able to accept mystical, unattainable and mathematically unproved truths.

Esthetic education cannot rest exclusively on the natural inclinations of an individual; for a child can acquire esthetic taste through good education. To evaluate esthetic education properly, one must understand its psychophysical aspect, which produces an entire complex of psychic experiences. It is correct to evaluate esthetic education not so much from the esthetic side as from the pedagogical. To properly carry on esthetic education, a highly qualified person must be assigned to this very important work.

The sources of esthetic expression and satisfaction must be found in the normal experiences of everyday living.

Many resources for esthetic expression are available in school. The room is equipped with a small piano, two easels, a linoleum floor pad where children can paint, a clay table, a workbench, and the usual supply of paper, crayons, wool, scraps of cloth, beads and the like. The children are encouraged to explore these media, given instruction on how to use them, and provided ample time to work with them. When the playhouse is being furnished, many of the creative efforts are produced for that purpose.

Another resource is musical experience, as the children sing favorite songs, and experiment with rhythmic activities.

The activities in writing and telling stories continue to be rich experiences through the year, and are supplemented by the stories read to the children.

SUMMARY

The basic principles which can serve as guides to judging grammar and secondary schools have been presented in this chapter. They represent some guideposts for thinking through the problems and practices in schools. The most important outcome of the study of this book should be the information of a set of values or principles which students of education will use when they serve as teachers.

These principles are more extensively discussed in the following chapters of the book. Each chapter dealing with practices lists further specific principles that apply particularly to subject discussed.

FOR FURTHER STUDY

Alexander, W.M. and J.G. Saylor, *Secondary Education,* New York: Holt, Rinehart and Winston, Inc., 1950.

Bossing, N.L., *Principles of Secondary Education.* Englewood Cliffs, N.J.: Prentice-Hall, Inc., 1955.
—————————, *Teaching in Secondary Schools.* Boston: Houghton Mifflin Company, 1952.

Belth, Marc, *Education as a Discipline.* Boston: Allyn & Bacon, Inc., 1965.

Brameld, T.B.H., *Education as Power.* New York: Holt, Rinehart & Winston, Inc., 1965.

Childs, J.L., *Education and Morals.* New York: John Wiley & Sons, Inc., 1967.

Douglass, H.R., *Secondary Education.* New York: The Ronald Press Company, 1952.

Downey, L.W., *The Secondary Phase of Education.* New York: Blaisdell Pub. Co., 1965

Eby, Frederick, *The Development of Modern Education*. Englewood Cliffs, N.J.: Prentice-Hall, 1952.

Frandsen, A.N., *Educational Psychology*. New York: McGraw-Hill Book Co., 1967.

French, Will, *Behavioral Goals of General Education in High School*. New York: Russell Sage Foundation, 1957.

Full, Harold, *Controversy in American Education*. New York: The Macmillan Company, 1967.

Hahn, R.O., D.B. Bidna, *Secondary Education*. New York: The Macmillan Company, 1965.

Jones, R.M., *Contemporary Educational Psychology*. New York: Harper and Row, Publishers, 1967.

Krug, E.A., *The Secondary School Curriculum*. New York: Harper and Brothers, 1960.

Lee, F.H., *Principles and Practices of Teaching in Secondary Schools*. New York: David McKay Co., Inc., 1965.

McConnell, T.R., and others, "General Education", *Encyclopedia of Educational Research*. New York: Macmillan Co., 1950.

Morris, Van Cleve, *Existentialism in Education*. New York: Harper and Row, Publishers, 1966.

Pai, Yound, *Philosophic Problems on Education*. Philadelphia: J.B. Lippincott Co., 1967.

Smith, B.O., and others, *Fundamentals of Curriculum Development*. Yonkers-on-Hudson N.Y.: World Book Company, 1957.

Smolensky, Jack, L.R. Bonvechio, *Principles of School Health*. Boston: D.C. Heath & Company, 1966.

Stratemeyer, F.B., H.L. Forkner, M.G. McKim and A.H. Passow, *Developing a Curriculum for Modern Living*. New York: Bureau of Publications, Teachers College, Columbia University, 1957.

The Shape of Education for 1967-1968. Washington, D.C.: National-Sch. Public Relations Assn., 1967.

Vaizey, J.E., *Education for Tomorrow*. Baltimore: Penguin Books, Inc., 1966.

Wesley, E.B., *Teaching the Social Studies*. Boston: D.C. Heath and Company, 1950.

CHAPTER II

GENERAL EDUCATION

The Purpose of General Education

The purpose of general education is based upon the proposition that the various capabilities of young people should be developed as fully as possible so that they will be able to utilize them.

Learning consists in the modification of behavior through experience. The changing of behavior is the test of learning. If no change occurs, no learning has taken place. The experiences of others — past, present, or future — assume significance only as an individual learner is able to build them into his own experience. First of all, learning is an individual experience.

All learning consists in the fulfillment of purposes. The teacher sets out to discover the learner's purposes, and gears the situation in the classroom to them, or establishes new purposes. When a serious gap develops between the purposes of the teacher and those of the learner, certain kinds of negative learning occur. If we wish to avoid negative learning, we must seek to discover and capitalize on the genuine purposes of the learner himself. The learner cannot prepare himself for future action without completing his learning by present action.

Learning is no longer considered a mechanical process of developing a predictable response to selected or arranged stimuli. Learning consists in the application of intelligence to the solution of problems.

General education undertakes to redefine liberal education in terms of life's problems as men face them, to give it human orientation and social direction. Although general education seeks to discover and nurture individual talent, it emphasizes preparation for activities in which men engage in common as workers, and as citizens. Knowledge of our culture, evolving and developing ideals, standards, and values is not enough. General education must transform these abstract intangibles into the concrete realities of behavior. The goals of general education must focus clearly upon the attitudes, capacities, abilities, and values which are expected to be built into the lives of the students.

General education's task is to seek the growth and development needed by all youth. General education is largely dependent upon schools for attaining basic common aspects of the objectives of self-realization, and human relationship. A program of general education concerned chiefly with behavioral outcomes is bound to influence a staff to recognize content and method. They are impelled toward observing the effects of their teaching, and to know more about the aptitudes and interests of their students.

Behavior-Centered General Education

The behavior-centered general education programs have as their goals building in students the kinds of competence they need to meet life's demands.

This is an idea that is generally accepted by high schools. The graduates of their specialized vocational programs are required to show initial levels of competence in their chosen vocations. The graduates of elective science courses are expected to begin to exhibit relevant habits of thought.

General education must include both the help we give pupils in discovering and developing special abilities, and the provision of learning experiences.

It should be pointed out that much improvement in general education goals could be achieved by closer, more systematic planning on the part of teachers of the separate subjects. Even in schools where a core program has been developed, grade-level curriculum planning is still imperative.

The experiences through which individuals are introduced to rich possibilities.

The purpose is to deal with the experiences through which individuals are introduced to rich possibilities. These fields may be classified as pre-vocational (homemaking, industrial arts, business); cultural or vocational (art, music); or pre-professional (specialized mathematics, foreign language). A particular experience may (operationally) pass over to the "exploratory" realm when: 1. specialized facilities such as laboratories are required for its pursuit; 2. a special teacher is needed because of the depth of specialization pursued; or 3. special grouping is needed to facilitate certain specialized experiences.

These criteria should be interpreted only as convenient means of looking at school programs. There is no intention here of separating children into groups composed of explorers and non-explorers. All learning may validly be regarded as exploratory. The distinction between these two functions is simply operational.

The four areas most frequently scheduled as exploratory are music (vocal and instrumental), art, homemaking, and industrial arts. These courses appear under various names in different schools. Some schools report such specializations as sewing and foods in homemaking, or shop and drafting in industrial arts. In general, however, the four areas of music, art, homemaking, and industrial arts are still the most typical offerings in grades seven and eight.

In some schools these exploratory courses are alternated two and three periods per week, for a full semester or a year. Small groups might seek the help of the art teacher in developing a mural, or of the music teacher in preparing a song. A unit on personal grooming might call for a period of several days, working in the homemaking laboratory with the teacher. Plans for the use of these facilities would be developed in regular planning sessions of the grade-level faculties.

Special groups should also be organized to offer those with special talents a real chance to perform.

The goal of industrial arts is not vocational. It is possible that exploratory experiences here, as in any area, may arouse interest or uncover aptitudes that will suggest a later vocational choice.

Homemaking offers exploratory opportunities in the realm of home and family living. It provides an obvious application of principles of art, science, consumer economics, and personal budgeting, which other subject fields seek to teach.

A wide range of interests and abilities characterizes the high school pupil. Many of these interests turn out to be short in duration, but no less lively. The junior high school exploratory program faces an interesting problem of continuous adaptation to constantly changing interests. Perhaps the ideal plan might permit adaptation at any time and on short notice to new interests and needs. This dynamic kind of schedule has actually been used for school clubs and other student organizations.[1]

The Development of Effective Relationships

The process of learning through group experience calls for cooperation with others, working together on common tasks.

Successful relationship demand actual experience in order to be achieved. Our culture is a social one, in which we are faced continuously with the challenges of effective group living. Thus the development of effective group relationships becomes a prime goal of a life-centered classroom.

Relationships within a class are revealed to any teacher who takes the trouble to observe them systematically, and who listens to children. Teachers who are concerned about group relationships employ a number of devices to learn more about each pupil. A special technique for this purpose is the sociogram, in which the relationships are plotted on a bar-graph or a scattergram. On such a graph are plotted the answers to such a question as, "Who are your three best friends in our class?" The teacher will discover certain challenges and needs from his study of a class group. Teachers who make frequent use of sociograms have discovered that the patterns of relationships revealed by them shift frequently from day to day. Parents, too, can help in such record-keeping by observing changes in behavior that are related to the class goal.

1. Faunce, Roland C., and Clute, M.C., *teaching and learning in the junior high school* (San Francisco: Wadsworth Pub. Company, Inc., 1961), pp. 105-117.

There are many ways of organizing a conventional class for promoting various levels of relationship. The most fruitful tasks are those that involve choices, discussion, evaluation, planning, and student leadership. By class discussion the students have identified what they know, and have specified the kinds of things they would like to find out.

The evaluation of experience becomes an exploration. As we evaluate openly we can help students discover what they think, feel, and value.

It is not always possible to determine the results of learning experiences immediately; sometimes they show up long after the experience. Skillful evaluation should help every student to improve his own self-image. It can become the means by which students make realistic appraisals of his own strengths and weaknesses; it is a necessary base for self-direction.

> The evaluative process gives us the opportunity to get students to take school work seriously. As we provide them a share in deciding what is best and through that participation assuming responsibility for the success of the decision, we increase the probability that judgments concerning their growth will be meaningful to them; we increase the efficiency of the learning process.[1]

Understanding on the part of the public is extremely important in the program of the high school.

The public relations services of a high school may contribute publicity releases and use various outside-of-class activities to keep the name of the school before the public. Lay participation in the school is one of the better ways of promoting greater understanding.

The relationships, and the leadership within the class will have an effect on how ably the students select the problems for study. Some problems selected by students will lead to other related problems. Teachers confronted with related problems will have little difficulty in selecting a problem area for a resource unit. If teacher and class are together for a long enough period, and if the planning process is reasonably well mastered, all the really important problems will be attacked.

The teacher faces the task of helping each group to organize

1. Wiles, Kimball, *Teaching for Better Schools* (Englewood Cliffs, N.J.: Prentice Hall, Inc., 1953), p. 198.

itself fruitfully, to develop questions that have depth and value. The teacher must help find materials, often on a wide variety of problems or questions. He must help each group to develop a lively, interesting report employing a variety of communication techniques.

Organization of the class itself is a kind of group experience. The student council may be based on the core classes, in which case a regular session of reporting is needed.

School-Parent Relationships

In elementary schools, attempts should be made to draw parents into the instructional process, to get them to visit the school, confer with their child's teacher and to support the school.

But such relationship has great difficulty in continuing its success in secondary schools. There are a number of reasons for this decline in parent involvement.

The curriculum becomes more complex, less easy for parents to understand, and to assist their children to understand. They may feel that their younger children need their help more than their teenagers. Indeed, they may get the idea from remarks made by their older children that teenagers do not want their parents coming to school.

School marks are assumed to be a means of reporting achievement to pupils and parents, and are also considered a device for stimulating effort.

School marks are assumed to be a means of reporting achievement to pupils and parents. Such symbols as "A,B,C," etc. are often supplemented by parent-teacher conferences, letters from the teacher, and exhibits of the students' work which parents can examine during visits to school.

In recent years, the use of symbol marks has been somewhat reinforced by a wave of attacks on modern education. Research studies revealed that marks are not good enough for that purpose. Better methods are the parent-teacher conferences — a minimum of two conferences per year with each parent — supplemented by other means of reporting. It gives teachers new light on home backgrounds and relationships. At the same time they are the most useful means yet discovered of reporting the child's progress to his parents.

Following is a summary of values to the parents of the conference plan:

1. It helped the parent to become clear in his own mind as to what he wanted his child to gain from his school experiences.
2. The parent was given an opportunity to explain any pertinent facts about the child that would enable the teacher to work with him more effectively as an individual and as a group member.
3. Any maladjustment of the child at school was pointed out. If there was a difficulty at home, the parent and teacher were often able to find tentative means of solution for this mutual problem.
   The parent was assured of the fact that he was welcome at school at all times.[1]

Here, caution is expressed regarding the conference plan:

> We should strive to meet the following prerequisites to successful teacher-parent interviews. *First,* the teacher needs to be a relatively mature person psychologically; *second,* the teacher needs to feel secure professionally; *third,* the teacher needs to believe that parent conferences have value; and *fourth,* the teacher needs either in-service training or previous study in understanding the process of interviewing.[2]

Letters might entirely replace the conventional marking system, especially if used in combination with the conference plan. Much helpful information about a child can be obtained from parents' letters. Every effort should be made to provide time for writing such letters.

The *checklist* is another alternative to the symbol marking system — checklist containing a breakdown of such objectives

1. Cunningham, Ruth, and others, *Understanding Group Behavior of Boys and Girls* (New York: Bureau of Publications, Teachers College, Columbia University, 1951), p. 331.
2. Johnston, Edgar G. and others, *The Role of the Teacher in Guidance* (Englewood Cliffs, N.J.: Prentice-Hall, Inc., 1959), pp. 213-214.

as oral and silent reading, spelling, creative writing, class discussion, group leadership, etc. There may be space provided
for comments by the teacher and the parent. The checklist is
descriptive of the pupil's progress.

Beyond individual contacts, there are also values in *group
contacts* with parents. These can be provided informally by social
functions such as teas or classroom open-houses or exhibitions
of student work followed by refreshments. These parents'
meetings have a tendency to develop into a type of *parents'
club.* Following are activities of the parents' club:

1. *Social functions,* such as teas, suppers, mixers, picnics,
    and parties.
2. *Interpretation functions,* through which a clearer under-
    standing can be achieved, both of the aims of the school
    and of the progress their own children are making.
3. *Service and welfare functions,* such as improving the room,
    helping with lunches, raising money for such projects as
    going to camp.
4. *Resource functions,* in the regular instructional program
    of the classroom, enriching it by the many and varied ex-
    periences which parents have had.
5. *Planning functions,* through which the parents offer direct
    help to the teacher in making plans for the future and
    current units of work.
6. *Evaluative functions,* wherein parents help to appraise
    the progress of instruction and identify the significant
    successes and failures of the program which they have
    helped to plan. Through this evaluative role parents of
    a given room can themselves become competent interpret-
    ers of the instructional program to other parents in the
    school and to others in the community.[1]

It is a more common practice for the club to take part in the
first three of these functions.

*One important task of general education is to study man's re-
lationships and institutions as they appear in every community.*

Service projects that provide direct contacts with these insti-

---

1. Menge, J.W. and Faunce, Roland C., *Working Together for the Better Schools*
(New York: American Book Co., 1953), p. 102.

tutions are ideal means of learning about the community. Thus, many bridges have to be built from school to community:

1. Classroom groups in almost every subject field have made trips to various places to study every aspect of community life.
2. Classes have left the school to interview persons who have made trips to various places to study every aspect of community life.
3. Classes have made actual surveys of trends or conditions in their community.
4. Classes and other student groups have performed important services for community improvement.
5. Resource persons from the community have been brought into the school to aid in the study of problems.
6. Resource materials from the community have been brought into the school to aid in the study of problems.
7. The school has brought large and small groups of lay citizens into the planning of the educational program.
8. The school has utilized such agencies as the Boy Scouts, Girl Scouts, and may others in the enrichment of the educational program.
9. The school has drawn upon the resources of such community groups as churches and service clubs in programs designed to enrich the education of youth.
10. The school has reached out to serve youth not enrolled in school through recreational and vocational services.
11. The school has enriched community life by offering a vigorous program of adult education.
12. The school has provided physical facilities and leadership as a center for community action.[1]

In practice, many high school teachers have had trouble discovering a real need in the formal curriculum to induce students to make the required effort. There is need for civic awareness and responsibility, without which no community can come alive. The service needs of the community are practical, real, lifelike situations that challenge people to act. The challenges for service to the community, on the other hand, are ready-made for group activity. At every stage of the process, cooperation with groups

1. Johnston, Edgar G., and Faunce, Roland C., *Student Activities in Secondary Schools* (New York: The Ronald Press Company, 1952), pp. 291-292.

of adults in the community is very important.

Here, a word of warning may be needed. Students should not be exploited as free labor on behalf of some adult enterprise that they shared in planning. Teachers must look carefully at such projects, and ask themselves whether they are sound educational goals in which to participate.

Clearer understanding of the purposes and program of the school calls for full information about the school.

Parents need facts about the school. The community newspaper is interested in school news, and should be:

1. Written in clear, effective language.
2. The words used should be generally understandable.
3. The topics should be varied from day to day.
4. There should be a universal appeal in the topics reported.
5. It should avoid personal attacks or boasting.
6. It should answer the questions the reader may have about the topic covered.
7. It should feature some one aspect which has dramatic appeal.
8. It should be written attractively.
9. It should give supporting evidence.
10. It should mention and identify individuals.[1]

The school handbook and magazine, too, are helpful instruments for school publicity. Other useful and effective devices for school publicity are films, filmstrips, educational radio and television stations. But the best medium of all for effective school publicity are the students as interpreters of the program.

Student Activities

The progressive growth of learning in the lively classroom can be the source of new stimuli in the activity program.

Student voluntary activities—the older phrase "extracurricular" "extra-class" or "nonclass" activities—others call them "co-

1. Menge and Faunce, *op. cit.,* p. 72.

curricular,"—signify an equal, but separate status in relation to classroom instruction. In an effort to make available to all students the accepted values of student activities, the "activity period" was developed. This is a scheduled period for most student activities, varying in length from thirty to sixty minutes, and occurring every day.

Opportunities for social experiences exist everywhere and should be capitalized upon.

Preparation for social affairs may involve the class or club in discussions about manners and courtesy, in practicing introductions and invitations, and in developing many other skills. New schools are now recognizing this fact and are providing social living space in widened corridors, furnishing recreation rooms with equipment for games, using the library for quiet social experiences, and building an effective game period at noon around the lunch period.

There are certain objectives that the social program should achieve:

1. The social program should provide a wide variety of activities, appropriate to various stages of maturity.
2. Help should be given new students in orienting them to their new school, and to all students to help overcome their timidity and self-consciousness.
3. Students should participate in planning, carrying out, and evaluating social experiences.
4. Adults should guide, but not dominate.
5. There should be many opportunities to help less fortunate individuals.
6. Relationships between and among peers should be strengthened and extended.
7. Teachers should seek to promote wholesome social relationships, not only in student activities, but also in the classrooms.[1]

School clubs promote personal-social adjustment, and enrich the

1. Faunce, R.C. and M.J.C., *Teaching and Learning in the Junior High School*, pp. 129-130.

school program by providing exploratory experiences.

A good club program offers an opportunity for students to pursue a wide variety of interests. The rapid changing of interests dictates a rich and flexible program. In the good school, club members can more readily attain objectives of learning through actual practice of the skills. School clubs must also reflect a variety of maturity levels.

An Assembly Committee should set up the criteria for good programs and build the schedule for the year by securing cooperation from all groups within the school.

The Assembly Committee should report to the student council, and should include both students and teachers. Not only in the planning process but also in the staging of programs should there be roles for old and young. There should be a creative approach to program planning; students should plan assemblies, participate in the programs, and evaluate the outcomes.

Regularly scheduled assemblies are most often weekly, conducted during the activity period. There are a variety of purposes assigned by school principals to the assembly:

1. To unify the school.
2. To interpret the work of the school.
3. To strengthen existing interest and to broaden horizons.
4. To develop desirable attitudes and appreciations.
5. To assist in the selection of a vocation.
6. To develop a better understanding of critical issues and problems of our contemporary culture.
7. To furnish opportunities to appear before an audience.
8. To learn more about the community and how it functions.
9. To recognize superior achievement.
10. To encourage the development of good audience behavior.
11. To furnish wholesome entertainment as well as to educate.
12. To provide an opportunity to present certain administrative problems and to seek solutions of them.[1]

To the degree that learners are involved in the planning and evaluation of their activities, they will assume responsibility for their

1. Miller, Franklin A.; Moyer, J.H.; Patrick, R.B., *Planning Student Activities* (Englewood Cliffs, N.J.: Prentice-Hall, Inc., 1956), pp. 499-504.

own activities.

Learning activities based upon the goals and purposes of teachers and learners, arrived at cooperatively, develop self-respect in the learner and motivate him to do his best. The learner sees himself as moving toward goals which seem important to him.

It is necessary that the entire school participate in the publication of the school paper.

The *newspaper* becomes a project, carried on by a sponsor, with the aid of a small editorial staff. The few who participate may learn to write and to edit, to acquire the skills of leadership, and to evaluate journalism. The editorial staff may be organized like a club. A system must be developed for obtaining news stories, editorials, and features from the entire school.

There are a few suggested methods: 1. to elect a reporter from each core English class, or homeroom; 2. the publication of a brief class newspaper in each core or English section and to draw material for the school newspaper from these; and 3. to divide the school's classes among the various members of the newspaper staff, and give them one day each week to make contact with their classes and collect stories.

The other kinds of school publications seem to be worthwhile— the *magazine* and the *school handbook.* The magazine should be edited by a separate staff. A creative outlet for the literary or artwork of students is more appropriate to the school magazine. Poems, essays, plays, humor, sport analyses should be attractive. Anual revision or inserting a supplement each year seems important.

We learn how to relate to others as we relate to them, and then engage in reflective evaluation of our successes or failures.

The most fruitful tasks are those that involve choice, discussion, student leadership, evaluation and planning. Some student activities are organized for reading and speech purposes. The objectivities of speech are to improve informal communication, and to report effectively to a group.

Students must come face to face with problems of behavior that interfere with class progress. Self control and self-direction are worthy goals.

The satisfactions of participating in music should be available to all students.

All can play in the band or orchestra on very short acquaintance with musical instruments. Specialization can prevent the achievement of broad music objectives. The total music program should offer a wide variety of activities on various levels of interest and ability. It should be an integral part of the general education program in core, English, and social study classes. It should strengthen friendship, and provide opportunities for student leadership.

Games within the school's walls have numerous advantages over the interscholastic program.

The program of sports activities is another example of student experience would include varsity sports as a relatively minor part of a broad program for all students. At the base of such a total program would be the physical education classes, which have a much fuller objective than team games. The basic plan for sports activities would also include a school-wide intramural program. The games scheduled between schools would offer an extra opportunity for more able students. The program can be diversified to reach all students. With emphasis on participation for all, the disappointment of defeat is offset by the pleasure of taking part.

The objective of athletics is friendship.

The program should be considered an integral part of school hours. An intramural committee of the school council should be responsible for planning.

The school camping movement offers an opportunity to teach responsibility and citizenship.

There is a real chance for students to plan and carry on their own activities. The emphasis in modern school camping programs is an involvement of students in planning, in assuming responsibilities while in camp, and relating the learning experiences of the camp to the on-going classroom curriculum. These are not synthetic or verbal adult-asigned tasks, but responsibilities that youngsters can readily assume. The pattern has usually been for two sections to go to camp for one school week, which is built into the classroom curriculum by intensive pre-planning.

Each student in the class should be eligible to join any activity in which he is interested.

Planning a student's participation in activities is student business. The story of a student's experience in an activity or organization should be communicated to his home room or core teacher by the sponsor of the activity. The principal is responsible for the program. Every student, and also every teacher should be involved in the activities program. A systematic appraisal of student activities should be provided. It calls for continuous study of the program by all persons concerned. Parents should be actively involved in such efforts.

The primary function of educational leadership is the improvement of the learning process.

The modern secondary school puts its main effort into giving leadership toward improving the instructional program. The modern theory of leadership is oriented toward the service function.

Leadership based upon delegated legal authority is called "status leadership." The status leader serves as a member of the group to define what the group goals should be. This concept can be applied especially to the field of instruction and curriculum, but it functions as well in the area of administrative policies. A status leader can improve human relations among teachers and pupils, provide certain types of expertise, and promote and coordinate leadership within the faculty. While he cannot legally delegate his basic responsibility for administering a school, he may in practice permit his many leadership functions to be shared.

Shared leadership also provides for the development of leadership skills within a group. Curriculum change is carefully planned by teachers, administrators, and others concerned. Once a policy has been determined cooperatively, the status leader is the one to administer the policy to the best of his ability.

The most effective kind of supervision is that which serves to help the teachers achieve mutual goals that have been arrived at by the supervisor and the teacher. This principle applies to teacher-pupil relationships also.

Leadership that focuses on mutual growth, concerned with human relations and the way people interact with each other, is at the very heart of responsibility in school and classroom.[1]

In early studies of leadership, personal qualities or characteristics were stressed. However, research that was conducted did not adequately describe leadership behavior. This approach to analysis of what constitutes leadership is static rather than dynamic, since it describes an individual at any one time. It does not indicate how he would function under different conditions. Leadership is actually derived from the group and depends upon the group's perception of the leader. In other words, leadership is not a product of status but is a matter of how a person behaves when confronted with a particular situation. A leader in one instance will not necessarily be a leader when placed with a different group demanding solutions of different kinds of goals. Thus, the supervisor or teacher must be perceived as a leader in order to be most helpful to the group with which he works in promoting improvement of instruction or learning.

Pupil participation in leadership activities in secondary schools should give them authority for managing the affairs or developing the policies that are entrusted to them.[2]

Individual Exploration

The teacher's basic task is to build self-confidence by constant

---

1. Anderson, Vernon E., and Gruhn, W.T., *Principles and Practices of Secondary Education* (New York: The Ronald Press Company, 1962), pp. 333-334.
2. *Ibid.*, pp. 334-335.

encouragement, and through successful experiences.

The core teacher is responsible for a number of students; he has them for a larger daily block of time, and for two semesters or more.   He provides opportunities for the recognition and expression of individual differences.

Group members learn to lead and to participate in discussions, to speak freely, to clarify meanings, to formulate questions and answers, and to listen to others.

One of the most obvious outcomes of the small group method is increased command of the skills of oral discussion.   There may be regular programs on designated days, in which there are songs, recitations, plays, story-telling, reading of poems, etc.   During a semester, every student in a core class may have several opportunities to practice various skills of oral expression. Students with speech handicaps must be given intelligent help— above all, the courage to try.

The development of taste in reading is a recognized task of general education.

The classroom library should contain many good books; the reading corner should feature attractive exhibits of good literature; reports of reading should be a part of class procedure. If the teacher is not the best reader in the class, certain students should occasionally play this role.   Discussion of what is read orally or silently should be directed at developing criteria for judging effective writing, but the whole class should rarely, if ever, be expected to read the same book at the same time.

The classroom library should contain books representing many different areas of interest, as well as a variety of reading levels. Whatever the reading levels represented in the class, there are some common needs facing the core teacher.

The main purpose should be to help pupils develop interest in writing and a belief that they can write.

It is possible to build better writing habits by correcting a few faults each time, and by reading samples of the written work. A particular challenge to writing is presented when a class publishes a weekly magazine. An editorial board collects and edits the contributions and puts them into shape for publication. Short stories, editorials, and poetry predominate, but there is also a place for sports commentary, a humor column, and even continued stories that are too long for inclusion in a single issue. Selected poems and stories from the class magazine may be published in the school paper.

In schools where a separate science program is offered, it is still possible to build science experiences into general education by systematic planning among teachers.

The science consultant will find himself talking frequently to classes about science concepts, demonstrating various principles of science, and counceling individuals about science vocations. The science teacher might serve as a consultant to the core class, whenever a resource unit involves science experiences. Core groups studying such problems as health, community services, and natural resources will naturally become involved in science concepts.

A functional science program relates to the problems of living, deals with the effects of the environment on life, and the use of scientific thinking in the solution of problems.

The imperatives offer many directions for classroom explorations:

1. They need to gather facts and to think clearly about their meaning and their relationships.
2. They need to differentiate between facts and opinions, between truth and fiction.
3. They need to develop a wholesome curiosity about the nature of the earth and living things.
4. They need to understand the importance of natural resources and their conservation.
5. They need to grow in their understanding of biological structures and functional processes of growth.
6. They need to practice healthful and safe habits of living.
7. They need to adjust their ways of living to world of applied

science and invention.

8. They need to understand that cooperative living is imperative in a scientific world.[1]

The imperatives may build ways to mathematics, physics, biology, industrial arts, and to many other content areas of the high school.

Individual exploration may be conducted apart from the activities of a group or class, or as a planned part of the group project.

A more common interpretation of the term "individual exploration" has to do with exploratory courses, whether elective or required of all pupils. Exploratory experiences can occur in courses not so labeled, or even outside any courses. Following is a list of exploratory experiences:

art	science
choral music	creative writing
homemaking	general language
manual arts	typing
creative dramatics	folk dancing
public speaking	poetry writing
music appreciation	crafts
general business	hobbies
photography	literature
journalism	choral speaking

These experiences can be applied in core classes, in elective courses, and in other required courses.[2]

Provision for individual exploration, whether in courses or in student activities, calls for certain deviations from conventional procedures:

1. Individual differences in ability or capacity must be discovered and shared with other teachers.
2. Individual interests, hobbies, and vocational goals thus far developed must also be known to the teacher.
3. Learning materials must be varied.
4. Assignments must be differentiated.

---

1. Herriot, M.E.; Sands, Elizabeth and Stauffacher, H.W., "History and Objectives of Junior High School Education in California," *The Bulletin of the National Association of Secondary School Principals,* xxxv (Dec. 1951), p. 17.
2. *The Junior High School Program* (Atlanta: The Southern Association of Colleges and Secondary Schools, 1958), p. 59.

5. Time for individual and small-group research must be allowed.
6. Rich library and laboratory facilities are needed.
7. Evaluation must be an individual matter.
8. The school must offer as rich and stimulating an environment, and many avenues for individual exploration, as it can.
9. The schedule itself should be flexible.
10. The rules for the use of the building and for pupil movement within it should encourage individual exploration.

The relationship of student activities to the curriculum for individual exploration will come about only as there are systematic efforts to build it.[1]

SUMMARY

The purpose of general education is based upon the proposition that the various common capabilities of young peole should be developed as fully as possible.

General education is largely dependent on schools for attaining basic common aspects of the objectives of self-realization, and human relationship. A program of general education concerned chiefly with behavioral outcomes is bound to influence a staff to recognize content and method. They are impelled toward observing the effects of their teaching, and to know more about the aptitudes and interests of their students.

1. Faunce, *teaching and learning...*, *op. cit.*, pp. 212-213.

FOR FURTHER STUDY

Anderson, V.E. and W.T. Gruhn, *Principles and Practices of Secondary Education.* New York: The Ronald Press Company, 1962.

Cunningham, Ruth and others, *Understanding Group Behavior of Boys and Girls.* New York: Bureau of Publications, Teachers College, Columbia University, 1951.

Faunce, R.C. and M.J. Clute, *Teaching and Learning in the Junior High School.* San Francisco: Wadsworth Pub. Company, Inc., 1961.

Frederick, Robert, *The Third Curriculum.* New York: Appleton-Century Crafts, Inc., 1959.

French, Will and Associates, *Behavioral Goals of General Education in High School.* New York: Russell Sage Foundation, 1957.

Fretwell, E.K., *Extra-Curricular Activities in Secondary Schools.* Boston: Houghton Mifflin Co., 1931.

Gruber, F.C. and T.B. Beatty, *Secondary School Activities.* New York: McGraw-Hill Book Co., 1954.

Herriot, M.E. and others, "History and Objectives of Junior High School Education in California", *The Bulletin of the National Association of Secondary School Principals,* xxxv (Dec. 1951).

Johnston, E.G. and others, *The Role of the Teacher in Guidance.* Englewood Cliffs, N.J.: Prentice-Hall, Inc. 1959.

Johnston, E.G. and R.C. Faunce, *Student Activities in Secondary Schools.* New York: The Ronald Press Company, 1952.

Kilzer, L.R., H.H. Stephenson, and H.O. Nordberg, *Allied Activities in the Secondary School.* New York: Harper & Brothers, 1956.

McKown, H.C., *Extra-Curricular Activities.* New York: The Macmillan Co., 1952.

——————, *Home-Room Guidance.* Second Edition. New York: McGraw-Hill Book Co., 1946.

Menge, J.W. and R.C. Faunce, *Working Together for the Better Schools.* New York: Am. Book Co., 1953.

Miller, F.A., J.H. Moyer, and R.B. Patrick, *Planning Student Activities* Englewood Cliffs, N.J.: Prentice-Hall, Inc., 1956.

Thompson, N.Z., *Vitalized Assemblies.* New York: E.P. Dutton & Co., Inc., 1953.

Wiles, Kimbal, *Teaching for Better Schools.* Englewood Cliffs, N.J.: Prentice-Hall, Inc., 1953.

The Junior High School Program. Atlanta: The Southern Association of Colleges and Secondary Schools, 1958.

CHAPTER III

TEACHING AS A PROFESSION

The Role of the Teacher

The role of the teacher is not confined to that of instructor in classroom subjects. Individual students bring to the teacher many problems for which they themselves are unable to find workable answers. These problems are concerned with a variety of situations; they include vocational, educational, personal, social, moral, and religious matters. Thus, the teacher occupies the role of counselor as well as instructor.

The teacher not only attempts to answer questions raised by individual students but tries to develop in them the right approach to, and the effective skills for, the solving of problems of any type.

The role of the teacher also involves setting up and managing situations that will provide opportunities for developing skills and habits in group planning.

Teachers must be provided with sufficient background in the subjects that they will teach to give them an adequate reservoir of information, understanding, and intellectual skills upon which to draw in their planning and managing of students' learning activities.

The subject-matter education of teachers needs to be thought through quite clearly and not formulated merely in terms of so many hours of credit in designated fields. Formulation of the program must consider which of the subject matter courses prospective teachers should be urged or required to pursue because of the contributions of the courses to professional effectiveness.

Today, teachers are expected to share the task of designing the curriculum and developing courses for a particular school system.

The teacher of today is expected to know how to evaluate textbooks, to develop resource and teaching units, to select appropriate instructional materials, to choose and adapt content suitable to the age level and range of abilities, and to design evaluative instruments to measure the effectiveness of the course in terms of the objectives of the school.

These expanded responsibilities of the teacher for curriculum planning and course development heavily influence the programs of teacher education in both the pedagogical phases and in the subject fields of the prospective teacher.

This is an age of intelligence. Survival of national ideals and the preservation of individual freedom, as well as continued progress in all fields, depends upon the development of the mental capacities of the people. To accomplish this objective, the nation looks to its schools and teachers.

Teacher Education

Teaching itself must be pitched at an intellectual level comparable to that of the other professions. Too much of the teaching today is performed at the technician level. Many teachers follow hand-me-down precepts. This will doubtless change as teachers are better trained. The training and certification standards of teaching must be comparable to those of other professions.

Teacher education devolves principally upon the following group:

1. Administrators and instructors in schools and departments of education.
2. Instructors in courses which contribute to the general education of teachers.
3. Instructors in departments which give instruction in the subjects which teachers will teach in schools.
4. Supervisors who are concerned with in-service improvement through education of teachers.

Unusual effort must be expended to bring into the profession young people with desirable personalities and potentialities for profiting from instruction and learning experiences. Identification of such persons may be made at the first stages in the teacher-education program and continued through student-teaching.

An effective teacher must possess the type of personality, temperament, and disposition that will enable him to gain the rapport of students, to inspire students to put forth the effort to engage in learning activities that will result in the greatest possible development of the learner.

The nature of the teaching function necessitates development of many teacher competencies, which in turn determine imperatives for teacher education.

A teacher must be able to recognize the consequences of his goal - centered teaching behavior, and be a versatile and effective master of the means at his disposal.

Teaching, viewed from the point of view of the nature of knowledge to be imparted and skills to be taught, suggests teaching competencies. The wider, deeper, and more current the knowledge of a teacher, the greater his ability to make curricular choices; to enrich his teaching by appropriate references to adjacent disciplines; to keep the motivational level of his class high; to differentiate his technique according to the varying talents and interests of his students.

Teacher education has the inescapable responsibility of providing leadership in education at the school level, not just as research centers operating outside and above, but within and in cooperation with the schools themselves.

This function requires thorough familiarity with the schools and their constantly-changing environment, character, and responsibilities. This function requires a cooperative working relationship between school and university personnel, a relationship which receives its most efficacious stimulation through experimentally-oriented graduate university programs for higher teacher and school specialist training.

Individual review, extension, and correspondence courses provide excellent preparation for graduate courses.

Many students who have taken the required prerequisite courses for graduate work find that their scholarship has suffered in the interval between graduation and entry into graduate school. Individual review, extension, and correspondence courses provide excellent preparation for graduate courses. Graduate study differs from undergraduate study in both content and approach. Graduate through emphasis on research and systematic scholarship, may elevate the teacher to a level of a prominent teacher. Graduate programs for the professions have been centered upon the problems of the use of knowledge. Internship of postgraduate teacher education, and scholarly and research aspects commonly characterize graduate study.

New media may contribute to teacher education.

If it is deemed necessary to acquaint large numbers of teachers with the latest developments in teaching science, and if sufficient facilities are not available within commuting distance of the clientele for face-to-face workshops with the expert and for opportunities to handle new material, then television courses may be considered.

As to possible contributions to teachers education of the new media—radio and television, sound, film, video recording, and auto-instructional programs—at the outset, it is obvious that the teacher must know about them and their use in the schools, and recognize their best time and place of application.

In teacher education, productive media research must go further than a rudimentary study of the single medium as a separate instructional entity.

Media research must focus not only upon teaching methods and procedures but also upon the subject matter and skills to be learned. Media research has responded to the inherent complexity of phenomena being studied in much the same manner as has past research on complex social and educational problems. Issues become divided for detailed analysis into small segments extracted from the general problems. The studies of small components can wander in many directions, with the emphasis at any moment determined by scientific influences.

To offset limitations of time and control, recorded media provide interesting possibilities.

Recordings can be made at the convenience of subjects involved, and they can be used at the convenience of viewers. Recordings can be made of many versions of the same lesson, using different classes and different teachers. They can be cut, edited, spliced, or combined for specific instructional purposes. Recorded media seem to be most promising in assisting the observation and demonstration function of teacher education programs.

Professional Programs

Programs of the first type usually emphasize only such courses as educational, psychological method, and practice-teaching.

The latter patterns include in various ways the traditional subjects of the history and philosophy of education and the psychology of learning, as well as the study of such fields as human development, mental hygiene, school and society, and the organization and function of the different levels of the school program. Depending on the institution, courses in guidance, audio-visual instruction, or school administration may be required.

Educational programs must be sufficiently diversified in nature to provide learnings for the present and future needs of people, and must use learning and instructional materials and activities adapted and adjusted to the abilities of young people. The program of education must be of excellent quality. The quality in education must mean programs adapted to many types of individuals and consequently include provisions for the most academically capable, the less capable, and groups varying significantly in interests and backgrounds.

The educational program must provide for the development of those skills, attitudes, interests, and ideals that will insure cooperation and adjustment of individuals to one another, and of individuals to groups. At the same time it must develop ideals, habits, initiative, individual thinking and creative interests.

The effective program of teacher education must provide some understanding of the principles of mental health and mental hygiene.

Teachers should know enough about mental health to enable them to provide learning and social situations that would not endanger or impair but actually promote mental and emotional health.

Effective professional preparation of teachers involves, of course, backgrounds in the philosophy of education, in sociology of education, educational psychology, course-of-study construction, counseling and guidance, evaluation (including tests and measurements), management of extracurricular activities, community relations, methods of teaching the subjects in which the teacher will give instruction. Both methods and subject matter are tremendously important and absolutely necessary, but training in professional courses should consist largely of materials and learnings that go beyond the techniques of classroom methods.

The educational program for teachers should lead to continuous learning.

Under any conditions, as new knowledge becomes available and life changes, continued learning is a necessity for the teacher. The necessity for continuous learning is apparent in the subject taught by the teacher, and knowledge in general.

The professional program is the process of professionalization of the teacher.

Its purpose may be summarized as follows: a) to help the

prospective teacher gain essential knowledge about the processes of learning and education, the nature of learners at various stages of maturity, the functions and organization of education; and b) provide for the development of professional skills that permit the integration and translation of the total preparation for teaching liberal education, scholarship in subject fields, and professional knowledge into the successful practice of teaching.

Patterns of the professional program that are in operation today may be classified in terms of their placement and sequence in the college program, the organization of courses, and the curriculum emphasis. Because no standard plan has been generally adopted, many of the programs represent composite mixtures of various arrangements.

The professional teacher is usually the product of many forces:

First, a deep commitment, persistent interest, and intense effort on the part of persons who want to be teachers must exist. *Second,* the availability of teacher education programs that rise above the commonplace and ordinary, sense the need for both understanding and skill, and have an abiding interest in teaching both as a science and as an art, must be open to interested persons. *Third,* interested persons (parents, supervisors, administrators, professors, and other teachers) who provide moral support and encouragement for those who wish to dedicate their lives to providing improved educational facilities for the young must be present.[1]

The matter of general education of teachers began to share the focus of attention as important aspects of the program for the education of teachers.

It has been increasingly evident, not only that teachers should have a good margin of education and scholarship in the subject they undertake to teach and in professional theory and practice, but also that teachers should, both for personal and professional reasons, have a rich background in general or liberal education. In other words, the teacher should be not only a specialist, but also a person broadly educated in the various areas of con-

---

1. Stiles, Lindley J.; Barr, A.S.; Douglass, H.R.; Mills, H.H., *Teacher Education in the United States* (New York: The Ronald Press Company, 1960), p. 130.

temporary knowledge and culture.

The broad background that comes from general education supplies its possessor with insight into all types of social change and the significance of development in all fields of science. Although general education seeks to discover and nurture individual talent, it emphasizes preparation for activities in which men engage in common as citizens, workers, and members of family and community groups. General education undertakes to redefine liberal education in terms of life's problems as men face them, to give it human orientation and social direction. General education refers to those phases of nonspecialized, nonvocational education that should be the common possession of educated persons as individuals and citizens.

The professional program can be classified according to the manner in which the courses in education are organized.

In many cases this type of classification can refer to the organization of only certain aspects of the program, such as practice teaching.

Traditional course pattern. Courses in education are organized in a manner similar to other college courses, the content of which is too narrow to include some special division or topic within the general framework of the area of study (the oldest type of organization)—for example: "Teaching Arithmetic in the Upper Elementary Grades."

Correlated programs. The content of various education courses into longer blocks of study time under one or more instructors may be called correlated programs. Some institutions have used the term "core" to designate their attempt to achieve this objective. Such arrangements may be provided in only fused courses in such fields as human development, school and society, student teaching, and related methods and materials of instruction. Therefore, the organizational context of these correlated programs integrates content pertaining to society, the individual, and the learning-teaching process.

The block plan. Essentially, the block plan for student-teaching provides that the student engage in student-teaching and related study of educational principles, methods, curriculum, and materials for a block of time amounting to one quarter or one semester of the college year. During this block of time, the student usually devotes from six to ten weeks to full-time work in an offcampus school as an apprentice teacher.[1]

Two types of curriculum patterns can be identified in the professional program:

Multiple-track curriculums. Multiple-track curriculums range from providing distinctly different curriculum tracks for various levels of the school system (kindergarten, lower elementary, upper elementary, and subject fields such as English, speech, chemistry, industrial arts, or home economics), to the practice of differentiating only between programs for elementary and secondary-school teaching.

The chief virtue of the multiple-track curriculum is claimed to be the degree of specialization provided for different levels and fields of teaching. With a highly homogeneous group, it is possible to stress in a more detailed manner the professional knowledge and skills required for particular types of teaching assignments.

The single curriculum. The philosophy supporting the development of the single curriculum holds that teachers, like doctors and lawyers, should be given common certification to practice. It is argued that the same knowledge about organization and function of schools, learning, human development, and methods of instruction should be acquired by all teachers, regardless of their intended level or field of teaching. It is claimed that the specialized application of professional knowledge can be learned during student-teaching as well as on the job, or, in cases where intensive knowledge is required, through additional formal study at the graduate level.

The professional phase of teacher education may be said to differ from one institution to another in terms of its emphasis.

Two phases — one, the theoretical, the other, the practical — are becoming clearly defined.

Programs committed to theoretical emphasis tend to stress

1. Stiles, Lindley J.; Barr, A.S.; Douglass, H.R.; Mills, H.H., *Teacher Education in the United States* (New York: The Ronald Press Company, 1960), pp. 218-220.

the academic study of educational theory, history, and principles. Courses in methods of teaching may be scheduled apart, often in a separate semester from student teaching, on the assumption that the student himself will be able to integrate the practical application of theory and principles.

The practical pattern, which provides for substantial practice as the central emphasis in the professional requirements, is contrasted to the theoretical approach.

Proponents of the practical-emphasis curriculum argue that the first phase of the professionalization of the teacher must be to prepare for successful classroom teaching.

Essential characteristics of a program of professional experiences.

1. The program should be of sufficient scope and variety to afford responsible participation in all the major phases of the teacher's work.
2. The program should grow out of the regular teacher education curriculum and return to it to enrich and vitalize it.
3. The program should be sufficiently flexible to provide for individual differences in the abilities, needs, previous experiences, and professional goals of prospective teachers.
4. The program should be planned cooperatively by the student and members of the laboratory and college staffs in terms of the situation and the needs of the student involved.
5. The program should provide for student involvement in challenging and meaningful situations in an atmosphere of freedom which encourages him to test his ability to translate his ideas into action.
6. The program should enable the prospective teacher to engage in activities which will contribute to his competence in performing the following responsibilities of the teacher.
7. The program should be planned and conducted with a view to the benefits to be derived by the school and community.[1]

1. *Ibid,* pp. 220-237.

Programs of teacher preparation, even those of four years' dura-
tion, are too short to permit sufficient time to develop a sound
general education, scholarship in the subject field to be taught,
and skill in the art of teaching.

The school system must help teachers to learn the duties related
to such problems as administering discipline, organization of
courses, counseling students, supervising pupil activities, testing and evaluation, and working with parents and other teachers.
Even if more time were available at the preservice level, it would
be impossible to develop fully competent teachers in many institutions because of limited laboratory facilities for observation
and practice-teaching available to prospective teachers. Negative
attitudes toward programs of in-service education have often
prevailed and communities have objected to the cost of these
services.[1]

Perhaps the most potent force in support of programs of continu-
ing professional development for teachers has been the standards
maintained for certification.[2]

Certification standards prescribe the length of the period of
college preparation, the personal fitness for teaching, the emphasis in the program of preparation, and the quality of scholarship maintained. Such requirements have influenced local school
systems to organize programs of in-service education for teachers; they have also encouraged teachers to strive for higher
levels of professional preparation.

An essential aspect of each program for the preparation of teach-
ers is the attention given to evaluation.

Individually and collectively, plans, procedures, staff, facilities,
and graduates of programs of teacher education may be evaluated. The quality of the teacher education program is determined
by the professional competence of its graduates. Programs must
be studied carefully under the actual conditions that prevail
in order to evaluate teaching personnel accurately. The curriculum, instructional procedures, organization, facilities, and
personnel — all aspects of the program may thus be evaluated.

1. Laing, J.M., "Search of Reputability for Disreputable Supervision," *National
Association of Secondary School Principals Bulletin,* 42 (March, 1958).
2. Stiles, L.J., "Maintaining High Certification Standards," *Virginia Journal of
Education,* 50 (April, 1957), p. 16.

Standards and guides provide one approach to the appraisal of teacher education programs. Evaluation is made by teams of evaluators working with data supplied by the institutions about the various aspects of the program.

The evaluation of teacher-education programs can be thought of as an aspect of good teaching.

Testing as a part of teaching should not be done sporadically; it should be done continuously as a part of the teaching itself. The standardized achievement tests to certify teachers in lieu of certification by course credit are a new development on the administrative side.

One of the best ways to evaluate the teacher education programs is to follow the prospective teacher into service and see how he performs. The large class with more than one section and instructor offers a particularly interesting opportunity to appraise certain portions of the teacher-education program.

The educators of teachers should be able to demonstrate, as well as verbalize about teaching.

Every teacher educator should have daily contact with a group of elementary, and secondary-school youngsters with whom he can preserve and improve his skill in dealing with the young. It is not too much to expect that all educators of teachers show satisfactory skill in teaching.

The educator of teachers must have a deep desire to know and possess skill in research as a means of producing new insight; active research work is a helpful means of keeping the minds of teachers sensitive to the discoveries of others. The educative process has to be structured in such a manner as to make the whole operation a socially productive experience, as well as an effective learning process.

Research and experimentation, to be most fruitful, should enlist the support of the total faculty. Such participation will improve research design and cooperation to facilitate the study. It will also help to promote greater respect toward and acceptance of the validated results achieved.

Supervision

Alert and creative supervision can help the new teacher bring a professional approach to the problems of teaching.

By proving to new teachers that their services are valuable, supervisors will establish professional relationships. The supervisor assumes the role of the sponsor during the internship of the beginning teacher; serves as consultant, demonstrator, as well as subject specialist in the field of teaching.

Supervisors can guide the development of research competence and continuing scholarships, and help provide teachers with equipment and financial support for research projects.

The general supervisor who works out of a central office may need to be replaced by a person of greater specialized competence who works more closely with teachers in particular schools.

Helping the teacher adapt and extend his professional knowledge and skill to problems of a local school situation is a natural and necessary obligation of the employing system.

The in-service development of teachers — state departments influence by assigning supervisors to encourage school systems to assist teachers to improve their competence.

State departments may sponsor conferences, encourage research, and disseminate the results of research as a direct means of fostering the continuing development of school personnel.

Collecting and reporting information, promoting research, sponsoring conferences, and formulating statements of advocated policy are the major methods by which national groups have sought to influence teacher education.

This practice has been employed in the United States, by the federal govenment, by certain philanthropic foundations, and by business as well as industrial organizations. The objective of such efforts is the establishment of particular policies and practices for teacher education in selected institutions to serve as examples for other institutions to follow.

Characteristics of the Effective Teacher

The teacher, in the modern sense of the word, must also be an educator.

The educator must have, among other things, all those qualities possessed by all the best leaders of groups, or nations.

The concept of the teacher as a resource person recognizes him as a person with certain facts, skills, insights, and understandings.

The skill of the teacher in the problem-solving approach to learning lies in his ability to function as a resource person when the class lacks certain skills, facts, insights, understandings, and at the same time to utilize students when they have the required attributes for a specific situation.

Most students need the security of adult direction, at least at some point. Constant attention must be given by the teacher to his role in this regard. The teacher's responsibility is to provide a setting where pupils look directly at the course of events and are forced to reconcile differences in purposes, plans, and activities. The teacher may have to exert more direct influence than guidance.

Teachers must have high intelligence.

One of the indispensable qualities which teachers must have is high intelligence. This is the first mark of a properly qualified teacher. Knowledge and the use of good forms show that the calling of a teacher has fallen into the hands of the proper person. Intelligence gives the teacher a strong base on which he will rest not only the deep value of his calling but also the means of passing his hours of teaching, his approach to the children, and his common life with the teaching staff; but first of all it gives the teacher real authority. An intelligent teacher has developed his so-called professional spirit to a high degree, thanks to which he has his own individual approach to the children.

The teacher must, of necessity, be optimistic, for the pupils will then share conviviality; the school will be the second home, and learning will be a pleasure.

In every healthy body there is a healthy soul that incorporates joy and eagerness to work.   This natural optimism comes primarily from good health and, therefore, the teacher must be physically strong.

The teacher must be inspired by his work.

It must keep him spiritually fresh, for it is the first cause of his uninterrupted intellectual and spiritual growth.

A teacher must dedicate himself fully to his calling of teaching and educating.

A true teacher is one who has an inborn tendency toward the calling to be a teacher.   He has a ceaseless desire to continue training himself, for he constantly feels the need for progress in carrying out the mission of a teacher.

The teacher must stand on a high moral level.

When it is a question of psychic values, the teacher must stand on a high moral level, for he is a builder of character.

The teacher must first of all draw knowledge from his philosophy of life.

For his work to have proper success, it is not enough to draw knowledge from books, but the teacher must first of all draw it from his philosophy of life, and through knowledge, to a certain degree, the teacher can know the child better.

The educator must himself, first of all, know life; must first know how to adapt himself to its various manifestations; must know how to conduct himself, and must influence life.

To know life, to love life, and to know how to manage it are the chief qualities of a teacher. The educator who buries himself in one field, loses sight of life and so cannot prepare others for it. By this burial, teacher shows interest only in the subject which he constantly expounds in school. The teacher must take part in the most diverse manifestations of life.

The teacher should be permeated with the life of the modern school.

Present social development is proceeding along the line of the greatest democratization of culture and is breaking all the barriers between the school and life. In crossing the threshold of the school, the pedagogue introduces into the life of the school a certain degree of the life which is beyond its walls.

Teachers should be thoroughly trained and disciplined in at least one subject.

Teachers should possess mastery of at least one field of knowledge. They should also have adequate training in educational methods, peculiarly suited to the presentation of this field. The history teacher will know history and will know how to teach it, so that children will learn and remember the facts and understandings comprising the goals of instruction.

The teacher should know the difference between descriptive and normative generalizations, as well as the difference between the methods of verification and justification appropriate to them.

The teacher should be able to explain a statement by showing its derivation from other statements. In order to acquire logical knowledge of his subject, the teacher will need to study logic, philosophy of science, theory of knowledge, and analytic philosophy. Usually some formal work in these studies will be necessary. Courses in pedagogical method and curriculum development should emphasize the uses of such knowledge.

Teachers in an activity curriculum should have specialized train-
ing in child and adolescent developments, guidance, and project
methods of teaching.

A teacher in an activity curriculum may well have deeper interest and more specialization in one field of knowledge than
others. Much more vital is broad training in a number of general
areas. To work in close cooperation with children in problems
arising from their interests, and to do this in such a manner
that maximum growth will ensue, will require thorough understanding of child growth and development.

Securing the right teaching position is not ordinarily a matter
of chance or good luck.

Once the teacher begins to consider this important step seriously, he will find the task more complicated than he had
thought it to be. In some colleges there is a definite program
designed to inform prospective teachers about professional opportunities. In many colleges, those who are responsible for
teacher placement will be ready to help him at this point. Many
of the problems involve professional ethics about which the teacher may find himself uncertain. As a beginning teacher in the
secondary school, he is probably aware that his primary objective
is to insure the continued intellectual and personal growth
of the learners assigned to his classes. He also has another important objective, that of continuing his own professional growth.
His years in college have, no doubt, been profitable and satisfying. He has chosen a profession demanding breadth and depth
of academic background, sensitive understanding of human
behavior, and a high level of technical competence in guiding
the learning experiences. All this, of course, cannot be completely mastered in a few years of college work. More and more
school systems, therefore, are sponsoring in-service programs
which offer a variety of possibilities to teachers for continued
professional and personal growth.

The teachers who achieve the most growth on the job are those who engage in continuous self-evaluation.

They study objectively the success of their efforts in the classroom as evidenced by the growth of their learners. They utilize the help of persons in administrative and supervisory positions in analyzing their work. It is essential to their continued growth that they maintain a desire to learn how to do a better job; that they analyze their own teaching critically, that they expect and welcome help freely from those in supervisory positions. Certainly those persons who have supervisory responsibilities in their school system will be anxious to be of assistance, but most of the decisions on what went well or what went badly today and how best to proceed tomorrow will have to be their own.

The teachers must establish standards as a basis for appraising learner growth by using the scores of standardized tests, studying the recommendations in the state or local course of study, examining learners' textbooks, consulting with supervisors. In the light of these standards, the teachers will collect and analyze evidence of their learners' achievement — by observing them in a variety of classroom activities, collecting samples of their work, giving classroom tests, listening to what they say in discussions.

The teachers should analyze with other teachers numerous situations similar to those which concern them. They can do much to help themselves grow if they conscientiously reappraise and apply all they have learned about educational procedures to the particular classroom situation they face.

The teacher should expect help in evaluating his teaching procedures, his classroom organization, his use of materials, his plans for meeting individual needs. The persons responsible for his supervision will be available to give assistance when he needs them. He should expect such persons to visit his classroom, and should be willing to let them view the situation. His own insights as he evaluates his success in the classroom from day to day, and the insights of those who work with him in supervisory relationship will increase his understanding of his own capacities and needs as a teacher. A helpful approach to systematic self-appraisal is to evaluate himself in the light of the statements desribing the characteristics of an effective teacher.

The teacher must learn to understand children and their developmental needs.

Much that is needed to be learned about children can be gained from psychologists. More can be learned after receiving diplomas, degrees, and contracts. Education will be improved when things are put together that should be learned together. A child should not be expected to approach learning from the standpoint of the adult. The teacher should encourage the native capacity of the child to learn from experience, instead of letting it languish by giving him lessons.

The most important step the beginning teacher can take is to work cooperatively with pupils in all classes, and in extra-class activities.

He should participate in as many community activities as possible, which will give him valuable experience in working with others on projects of common concern. The beginning teacher may joint with one or two experienced teachers in taking suggestions directly to the principal.

Teacher-training programs need to sharpen their focus on those aspects of the science of instruction which can be improved.

The need for specialization exists is the teaching profession, as that the teacher can concentrate on those parts of the teaching process in which he is most highly skilled and best trained. Specialists need to be developed in curriculum planning, content presentation, learning experience selection, and other phases of instruction. The purpose of specialization is to increase the quality of the contacts students have in the teaching-learning process.

The college work that the teacher undertakes should be more than merely an accumulation of courses.

College work should be part of a carefully planned program for strengthening his teaching fields and for furthering his professional growth. Scientific discoveries, followed by technological adaptations, have affected the life of every person. An expanding economy and an increasing population have introduced many problem into our economic thinking. New research techniques and new applications of statistical procedures are being developed in many of the social science fields. Many graduate faculties in institutions that prepare high school teachers recognize this and urge that some of the work for an advanced degree be taken in broad fields: the humanities, sciences and social sciences. It may be that his own self-evaluation has helped him to identify areas in which his teaching skills are not as strong as he would like them to be. When this is the case, he might wish to plan early in his undergraduate program to take some work that bears directly upon his immediate teaching problems. Selecting the appropriate courses to improve his effectiveness as a teacher is a matter which he should weigh thoughtfully.

One of his most profitable avenues will be further professional reading. Professional periodicals should be a part of his reading program, but he should also endeavor to read significant new professional books. Many educational insights have been significantly influenced by findings from philosophy, psychology, anthropology, and sociology. Daily newspapers and magazines will add greatly to his understanding of what is going on in the world. Many household and popular magazines contain articles of professional interest.

Research indicates that there is great inequality and lack of uniformity in the types and amounts of scientific training that teachers have had.

The success of any science program depends on the teacher, and, of course, the work of the teacher to a large extent depends on her status and training. Most beginning teachers start their work in small schools where they usually teach generalized courses, or a number of different specialized courses. Yet, their college training in science is not designed for such teaching.

It is obvious that the colleges need to investigate the amount of science background that is desirable in the preparation of science teachers at both the elementary and secondary levels.

The teachers must work together toward the development of consistent balanced growth in meeting life situations.

There must be essential agreement as to objectives and values sought so that each teacher has a clear understanding of the world into which the young adult is going. Each teacher must be thoroughly familiar with the general characteristics of learners, and their development tendencies. If the new problem represents a significant demand for new knowledge or skills, time is to be taken for as extensive a study as is required to fill the gap.

The general skill in getting along with people and in adjusting to the flexible programs should result in ability to analyze the new situations and to adjust to it.

Teachers must take care that praise is not so excessive as to demoralize the student.

Praise should only confirm his higher status and must never lead to the student regarding himself as perfect. The chief object of praise is to encourage the child to better achievements. Praise must also compare the child's present status with the past. Furthermore, in censuring, the teacher must take care that the student does not lose confidence in his own powers, but to correct his own mistakes.

The teacher must always have good relations with the children.

The teacher as well as the parents, through using force, undermine their authority in the eyes of children. The teacher must always have good relations with the children. When he must to punish a student, it is enough that he change the tone of his voice or add some cautioning word; that is already punishment. It is to the interest of the teacher to treat the children as delicately as possible for, if a teacher talks for hours in a raised voice that is unpleasant, or even constantly scolds, that teacher has no resource left except to strike the children.

Teachers must not forget that the method of education of child-

ren is different from that used for older youth.

When a teacher wishes to win his pupils through friendly conversations, he must, first of all, consider with whom he is talking, whether with pupils of higher or of lower intelligence. It is not good to joke too often with students for, even if a joke has a good effect, this effect is very slight. A teacher does not win his students by joking, for his authority gradually will descend to the same level as that of his students. It is even less wise to joke with students of the lower grades, whose intellectual criteria are not yet properly developed.

In helping students study more effectively, the classroom teacher's role is obviously far different from the too prevalent practice of making a page assignment in a single text.

Such an assignment makes no provision for the wide range of reading ability in every grade and gives pupils no practice in setting their own goals.

Ideally, teacher guidance in study involves understanding the individual students — their stage of development and their readiness for a certain kind of learning; providing concrete challenging materials and suggesting timely topics; encouraging student initiative in setting meaningful goals.

The teacher must take into consideration that one discipline interests a child the most, and the others somewhat less.

Even if a given discipline interests a child the least, he must not ignore it and must try to master it to some extent. Thus, the child will be developed on all sides of his nature. The subject which is most interesting to the students must be considered as dominant in a given school, and, therefore, must be placed on the highest plane, but the teachers cannot neglect other subjects.

The teacher should give the students freedom of choice.

Teachers should permit children the privilege of choosing their goal, for this increases faith in their own powers and their awareness of dignity. Sometimes the teacher, by his orders, will quench the most joyful self-confidence. Then discernment fully disappears in the children, and work or even amusement assume the aspect of slavish fulfillment of obligations.

Teachers and parents must remember that children are gifted with a great capacity of observation, so that they cannot pretend before them.

A great wrong is done to children, their parents, and society, when a government entrusts the education of the young generation chiefly to those who have appropriate qualifications based only on diplomas. A diploma is not enough; seniority is not enough; for the teacher must have qualities which make him above the average person and worthy of being followed.

The educator must have those requisite qualities which are possessed by excellent leaders of groups or nations.

The expressions of a teacher should be saturated with moderate humor, for humor attracts the young, while a dry and formal mode of teaching repels them. The teacher's authority cannot rest only on the dignity of his office, but also on his spiritual qualities.

The teacher should dress attractively, but conservatively, until there is an opportunity to ascertain the customs in the school.

For women, this means hosiery, and for man a coat and tie, even in warm weather. Bright colors, attractive styles, and costume jewelry have a place in today's classroom, but they should be carefully chosen. Good judgement should be used. A good criterion to follow is to observe the more experienced fellow-teachers and follow their pattern.

The quality of voice can have a definite effect upon pupil behavior.

The way a voice is used will have far-reaching effects on classroom results. If one speaks in a monotone, annoyance is created.

If the teacher sounds competent, assured, and secure, the class is more likely to recognize and accept his leadership; if he sounds uncertain, dubious, and hesitant, they are apt to feel doubtful. Many a teacher has discovered that, with a little determined and well-directed practice, he can make a decided improvement in his ability to use his voice effectively.

One cannot teach effectively in today's secondary schools by specializing in only one major area.

Pupils will sometimes ask questions that explore the most minute details of the topic being discussed. They will push logical discussions to conclusions and generalizations. Their zeal for information and knowledge will not be confined to the textbook, the reference book, or the course of study. They will bring to school knowledge of events in the outside world.

The teacher's most effective role may be that of guide — one who comments on interesting and import contributions, and keeps the lesson and discussion directed toward worthwhile results.

The teacher will be entering into many new kinds of relationships with people — pupils, colleagues, supervisors, and parents. They will have several classes a day, each making its peculiar demands. There will be days when everything goes smoothly, and days when one emergency arises after another. The teacher's attitude toward his competence as a person will make a difference in the way in which he approaches his responsibilities. In spite of the most thorough preparation, some days will go wrong. There will inevitably be situations in which it is necessary to revise carefully laid plans.

Each teacher brings into the classroom his own expectations regarding the role he will play.

He may see himself as the subject specialist, or a person whose major responsibility is to inspire his learners to use his subject as a means of improving and enriching their lives. He may serve as a counselor and guide. The role he assumes depends upon his previous experience with teachers, and the satisfaction he has found in his relationships with people. Whether or not he is concious of the role he is playing, they will have a decided effect upon the way he works with his learners.

The teacher's authority rests upon the consensus of opinion in the local community in which he teaches.

The wise educator will never ignore the viewpoints and opinions held by the people of the locality which he serves. The authority of the educator ultimately rests upon two distinct but related bases. As an expert, his authority rests on verified and tested knowledge in those areas in which his services are needed both by society and by students. This expertise is derived from two sources: 1. his knowledge of the needs and interests of children; and 2. his knowledge of the materials and techniques required by the students in their growth and development. In both cases, it is important to note that expert authority is limited by the extent to which the teacher possesses verified knowledge, and by the extent to which this knowledge coincides with the needs and purposes of society and of the learner. But the final authority of the educator rests with the enlightened judgment of the whole society.

The teacher must place the goals before the eyes of the individual.

Education, considered from the perspective of the present day, can be regarded as a social activity, the value of which must be measured not only by the needs of the present but by those of the future. This goal of teaching and education must not be either the over-intellectualizing of the school youth or the overloading of them with a mass of knowledge, but it should be the awakening, with the help of educational processes, of their spiritual forces and the desire to be active and valuable citizens.

The educator must turn his attention to the physical dexterity of the students, and point out to the parents the way for physical development of their children.

The first of the main obligations of a teacher is to know in what conditions every child lives. The teacher must take part in the physical activities of the students.

Knowledge of sports gives the teacher the opportunity to observe the conduct of the young on the playing fields with respect to their attitude to the rules of game, to the umpire, to the opponents, to the environment, and to the objective. Through all the reflexes of the students, the teacher can analyze their temperaments, their will power, and even their intelligence. The knowledgeable cooperation of the teacher with the students in sports raises the authority of the teacher and educator, and will gain the sympathy of the young people. If the teacher does not make these necessary observations and conclusions, he will soon have no ground on which to base his pedagogical activities.

The teachers must be guided by the child's inherited natural traits in order to develop them.

The inherited effect in the formation of an individual is so deep that we cannot immediately fathom it. Nevertheless, the teacher must make every effort to learn of its extent and simultaneously seek practical means to direct the course of possible negative inherited traits toward a positive goal. The responsibility for negative traits in children lies with the parents or even with more remote antecedants whose physical or psychical lives were faulty. The teacher should investigate the quality of these traits in order to find the proper means of leading the negative traits onto a desired path.

Educators must take account of, and concern themselves with the educative effects of social conditions, institutional structures, and group atmospheres as these infringe upon the character and personality of students.

Educators must relate the work of the school to the society of which it is a part. They must aid students to comprehend and analyze the major forces operating in society, and the major problems which confront it. They must assist students to master the techniques and acquire the attitudes appropriate to participation in society. Intellectual analysis and comprehension play a significant role in shaping personality and character.

The teacher must live in sympathy with his students.

He must rejoice together with them, and in case of a misfortune befalling one of the students, the teacher must show that he also is sharing his sorrow.

The teacher must not overstep "the golden mean" in his relations with his pupils, otherwise he will not be a pedagogue in the eyes of students but will be considered artificial and unnatural.

The attitude of the teacher must be serious. The serious teacher must not understand as a pattern; he must not inflate himself and act like a walking encyclopedia, but he must maintain a serious attitude toward his students.

The educator must become acquainted with the lives of his students in all their nuances.

He must know the special ethos common to young people and even know the manner of speaking of his students, which is very little like the literary language. This does not mean that the teacher must cultivate all the customs of his students, but in beginning his work with the young, he thus acquires a point of contact. He must understand the reason for their joy, sorrow, good and bad efforts.

The teacher who wishes to gauge out-of-school influences on learners must have first-hand contacts with the home and the community.

Teachers should visit homes to sense family activities and relationships in each individual's home surroundings, and have some contact with the clubs and groups to which learners belong.

Identifying needs and concerns in the community setting involves the teacher being alert to social trends, even prior to the recognition of them by learners. Social trends touch on the lives of children not only through daily papers and magazines but through changing local circumstances.

Effective teachers try to have as much information as possible before questions arise.

The teacher's study and analysis of the pupil's characteristics must take into consideration personal traits and interpersonal relations.

Experienced teachers find that the pupil's home background is important in explaining many factors they need to know about him: the relations with parents, the social and economic status of the family, the interest of the parents in their child's schooling, and many other facts. The teacher can determine the real interests of a particular pupil and is able to devise worthwhile learning experiences which build upon these interests, but he needs a maximum amount of information from records, observations, and interviews.

Observation may reveal significant needs for improvement. The teacher-pupil conference is potentially of great value to teachers in understanding their students. Parent-teacher interviews are primarily for the purpose of the teacher's coming to understand particular pupils.

The teacher should make every effort to arrange a college schedule that will allow ample time if not a full-time teaching assignment to meet his student-teaching responsibilities.

Student-teaching is the culmination of pre-service preparation. Often one extra class or the chairmanship of one more committee makes the difference between being able to take full advantage of professional opportunities.

Genuine cooperation is not possible unless the individuals who are working together feel quite free to express their points of view.

Better ways of working are eventually developed in schools where individuals' concern and differences of opinion are expressed freely. In dealing with critical comments, each teacher has to remember that there are many effective ways of teaching, that different persons can have different values and standards and yet achieve effective results. Every profession grows through research and the testing of new ideas. Every profession revises its basic theories in the light of new evidence. And every profession has its critics — just and helpful, or unjust and destructive. The quality of education reflects the ideals, motives, preparation, and conduct of the members of the teaching profession.

Beginning teachers do not always realize what kinds of information about their pupils are likely to be of value until they actually begin to work with them.

No matter how well informed the teacher is in academic fields, or how good his theoretical command of psychological and sociological principles, his classroom efforts are not likely to be completely successful if he is insensitive to the needs, strength, weaknesses, and experience of his learners. It is natural for teachers to be concerned about the learning ability of the students in their classes. The teachers should also be concerned about the significant behavior that reveals how each learner's intelligence is functioning and how to adjust their teaching methods to give each one the help he needs.

Through their observations early in the year, the teachers may identify some individuals who seem to learn easily, and some who seem to have more than ordinary difficulty when faced with intellectual tasks. These early observations can show them how they might go about adjusting teaching procedures to individual needs.

The greater the disparity in social class backgrounds, the more important it will be for the teacher to set for himself the task knowing his students, their homes, and their community.

To understand, the teacher must see the circumstances, the homes and parents, listen to the aspirations expressed by parents, face the realities of the home that leaves the adolescent without adequate adult guidance. Each teacher should carefully adjust the general requirements in the course of study to the maturity, needs, and experience backgrounds of the learners. Not many teachers will be able to instill considerable understanding of a subject field without knowing much about learners as individuals. The teacher can help them to recognize that what they are learning does make a contribution to the effectiveness of their daily lives.

In summary of the theory of methodology are presented the following as characteristics of good teaching:

1. The maintenance of an atmosphere, social and physical, in the classroom which stimulates and encourages problem-solving activity.
2. The functioning of the teacher as a guide and helper rather than as a taskmaster and dictator.
3. The encouragement of friendly and efficient sharing and cooperation in all phases of classroom activity.
4. The use, so far as feasible, of pupils' own motives as guides in the selection of learning goals and experiences.
5. Careful understanding of and attention to the needs of individual learners.
6. Patterns of group organization which utilize fully group influences on learning.
7. The use of evaluative processes and devices to help learners make optimum progress.
8. Emphasis on and respect for accomplishment in the acquisition of understandings and skills needed by learners in solving problems attacked in learning situations.
9. Adequate and definite plans and resources for instruction which insure desirable learning experiences and permit flexibility in the classroom development of plans.
10. Use of an experimental approach that continually seeks better procedures and also evidence regarding the effectiveness of procedures tried.[1]

The teacher must serve the interests of the whole society.

He must not occupy himself with any policy other than that which aims to unite all the citizens under the banner of his state. Teachers also must refrain from cultivating political views or movements which they believe will not rebound in the future to the advantage of society.

---

1. Alexander, William M. and Halverson, P.M., *Effective Teaching in Secondary Schools* (New York: Rinehart & Company, Inc., 1956), p. 63.

The Effective Teacher Plays Many Roles

The most significant role of the teacher lies in the realm of establishing purposes of learning. He announces the lesson to be studies, assigns the tasks, and determines the resources. He is the only evaluator in the class. He sets the goals for the class, usually limited to mastery of materials or skills within his subject. The teacher is completely responsible for the discipline or control of the class. A good classroom climate is the product of clear purposes and meaningful learning. The ideal climate is one in which pupils and teacher are seeking to achieve the same purposes.

The teacher is the most influential factor in school. Curriculum, organization, and equipment, important as they are vitalized by the living personality of the teacher. Modern pedagogy recognizes more clearly than ever that, in learning situations, the personal influence of the teacher is more significant than subject matter achievement alone.

The teacher has a primary responsibility to have an awareness of contemporary change and to understand its significance, at least, in its major outlines.

The culture of the ages should find interpretation and appeal through the teacher. Schools depend upon teachers who can do more than teach in the traditional subject fields. They want student leadership in other forms of educational activity, extracurricular. The ability to direct recreational activities has become a very important requirement. Activity periods are part of the regular daily schedules of many schools.

The teacher who looks upon teaching as a profession will do well to consider a more thorough preparation than the minimum courses provide. The present educational practice is the result of many forces that the teacher should understand. The need should be emphasized for a good course in the Philosophy of Education. A course in the History of Education should be closely related to Philosophy of Education. A course in Educational Tests and Measurements is almost a necessity for the efficient teacher. Many training schools provide courses in Genetic and Adolescent Psychology. Wide reading and varied experience through rich experimental living must supplement the formal classroom work.

Every teacher should consider the way to attain the confidence of the student.

A teacher who acts calmly and judiciously in trying situations, is clean in personal habits, plays no favorites, and dresses neatly and appropriately, will tend to encourage these modes of reaction on the part of students, and at the same time keep their respect for himself and his position. The teacher whose genuine interest in the student has been demonstrated will find that interest repaid in student loyalty and esteem.

The attitude of the teacher should be complete loyalty to the leader of the school.

The work of the school is closely interrelated. The teachers must necessarily work together. The attitude of the teacher should be complete loyalty to the leader of the school. Administrator and teacher work together to determine large areas of school policy. The teacher should give full loyalty to the administration, and wherever it is possible for him to give assistance he should do so freely.

The teachers should participate in social life.

The teachers should participate in the social life of the community during the nine or ten months of the year that the schools are in session. Many of the social or extra-curricular activities of the school take place in the evening. Each community desires to have the teacher participate in its social life. The teacher should keep this broad picture of the function of the school clearly in mind as he approaches the problem of responsibility as teacher and citizen in the community. While the teacher is an influence on the life of the community, there are reciprocal benefits which enrich the life of the teacher and lessen a tendency to narrowness in outlook. It is highly desirable that the community have the benefit of trained leadership for its young people. Our educational endeavor will be seriously handicapped if the environment of our youth differs radically from the societal level maintained by the school.

Every teacher must in his own way be a psychologist.

The teacher is the central figure in countless situations which can help the learner to accept himself. Everything he does, says, or teaches could have a psychological impact. The teacher's expertise in these matters rests upon the fact that he is the bearer of knowledge and skills established either by scientific investigations or by the refinement of professional activities through the application of psychological and educational theory to the practical problems of the school. Teachers — as professionally trained persons — possess knowledge of educational processes and procedures over and beyond those possessed by the laymen.

The school is more than classrooms, corridors, and playing fields. It is a fabric of human lives, sometimes colorful and pleasant, sometimes rough. Depending upon the people, the organization of the school could be rich, varied, and stimulating, or it could be the inflexible, impersonal, routine.

In becoming a good teacher, there are at least three areas of development:

1. To gain a broad acquaintance with our culture and its problems.
2. Subject matter specialization is essential.
3. To be able to apply general and special education to effective teaching.

For the effective teacher, method and content are two aspects of an indivisible process. The knowledge he possesses and the practices he adopts are not separated in the classroom. He must help youth develop and understand their own values and emotional needs. The teacher must work effectively with groups as well as with individual students, using instructional materials and aids creatively.

Teaching is a demanding profession, in which each teacher must remain a learner, because the task is as infinitely complex as the people it involves. The truly competent teacher has a healthy, lasting respect and eagerness for "know-how", the more practical the better.

Working closely with an experienced teacher on the job is one of the most important aspects of the education of the teacher-to-be.

The education of teachers today is truly a cooperative enterprise — school administrators, classroom teachers, college faculty members and students, all share in the process. Students of education may be assigned to cooperating teachers in a number of ways. Of course, teachers are consulted before the responsibility for a student is assigned to them. Students may even be assigned for less than a half day — a period or two — for two or three half days a week, or perhaps for one or two full days a week. Observing adolescents in the classroom and relating theory to practice are obvious accompaniments of a well-rounded program of teacher education.

To the possibilities of differences in professional competence must be added personal differences in academic accomplishment, in talents, in insights, and in ability to adjust to new situations. Establishing good work habits is only part of the problem of developing effective human relationships. Every teacher is likely to have in his class one or more individuals whose inner tensions make it difficult for them to adjust to the patterns of behavior expected of the group. It is essential that the teacher have experience in helping to guide these learners, in being responsible for studying them, and in deciding what to do in group situations in which such individuals find it difficult to operate.

Responsibility for the intellectual growth of learners means guiding their learning experiences in the development of skills, in the acquisition of information, the formation of concepts and generalizations, and in creative expression. Every teacher must be able to translate what he knows about individuals into symbols or words that will convey accurate meaning to the learner, his parents, and the other teachers who work with him. How to conduct a conference with parents, how to interpret the school program to parents during a school open house — these are problems a first-year teacher must face. Many first-year teachers are overwhelmed by the multitude of minor details that must be taken care of in the course of a normal day. Perhaps most important, they must learn, through ample first-hand experience, how to manage their class work so that it proceeds smoothly while administrative responsibilities are being met.

The teaching experience should provide some experiences that prepare for operating as an effective faculty member. Much depends upon the feelings of security developed when the first contacts are made. There will be situations in which the student arrives after school has begun, and there is very little opportunity for any preliminary contacts. In such cases, care must be wisely exercised to insure that the student is accepted by the group as rapidly and easily as possible.

The students comment with appreciation on many specific steps taken to help them feel at home. On the first day of school this may involve helping learners to fill in registration forms, assisting with the distribution of books, and passing out lesson materials for the next day. Establishing effective interpersonal relationships is a time-consuming process. There should be joint planning sessions which will enable the student-teacher to grow through solving classroom problems under the guidance of an experienced teacher. These sessions should help to forestall at least some types of problems.

The key area of the preparation of the teacher is the subject field or fields to be taught.

For the elementary-school teacher, specialization is centered in the subjects common to the grade level at which teaching is anticipated. As knowledge is expanded, it becomes necessary to reorganize some subjects extensively. The new mathematics of the space age is far different from the mathematics most teachers have learned.[1]

Specially prepared teachers are needed, particularly for the general education program.

The evidence is clear that *core programs* make special demands on teaching competencies that are not developed through conventional programs of teacher education. Teachers trained in traditional programs had serious problems in adjusting to newer

---

1. Rourke, Robert E.K., "Some Implications of Twentieth Century Mathematics for High Schools," *The Mathematics Teacher,* 51 (February, 1958), pp. 74-86, No. 2.

curriculum practices and classroom procedures, particularly core programs. Problems in the areas of content, classroom procedures, and evaluation, which these teachers found most difficult, are not only those that core teachers must be prepared to deal with, but also those for which present programs of teacher education provide inadequate help. In the content area there are following in-service needs:

1. Broader training in more subject fields.
2. To become familiar with and learn how to use a wide variety of materials.
3. To learn how to organize activities around problems or centers of interest, as well as according to logic inherent within subject fields.
4. For understanding the relationship which various subjects bear to each other.
5. For better understanding of the community and ways in which the school and community can help each other.
6. For wide reading and experience programs.
7. For increased understanding of child growth and development.

Teachers' needs in the field of evaluation:

1. Help in learning how to observe, record, and understand the significant behavior of children.
2. Help in using new evaluative instruments to broaden the basis of the evaluation program.
3. Learning how to help students evaluate their own progress as a part of their work.
4. Better means of reporting to parents.
5. Continuous evaluation of the program by the total faculty.

The problems of classroom procedure are grouped into five areas:

1. Problems encountered in utilizing the needs and interests of children as a basis for curriculum development.
2. Problems encountered in attempting to use informal procedures in overcrowded classrooms.
3. Problems of organization of group activities which will

have a maximum developmental value for students.
4. Problems which stem from uncertainty as to the role of the teacher in teacher-pupil planning.
5. Problems of counseling and guidance.[1]

When teachers move away from a fixed course of study, a course outline, or a single textbook as the basic guide toward the use of problem-solving methods of instruction, additional understandings and skills are needed. These are fundamental to the processes of problem-solving, the understanding of growth and development, and the meaning of total learning. The phrase "of total learning" refers to the findings in psychology that show that the whole child is involved in his learning. His attitudes, feelings, health, and total personality structure are interdependent factors that condition and control the quality and quantity of learning. It is this concept of learning that makes group and individual guidance a vital function of core teaching. Problem solving methods require a wide background of understanding of many fields of knowledge; therefore, teachers must be familiar with the many subject disciplines. More specifically, the use of problem-solving methods requires skill in:

(a) teacher-pupil planning; (b) identifying problems of interest and concern to students; (c) organizing the problems for study; (d) determining goals and selecting criteria; (e) carrying on satisfying group work; (f) providing for individual differences through varied activities; (g) developing more effective communicative skill.[2]

The principles of learning that underlie effective teaching are the same for all ages and levels of learning. The application of these principles, however, must be adapted to the distinctive characteristics and varying needs of different age groups. Curriculum organization and classroom method can facilitate learning, but neither of these is the most important factor. The teacher is the key figure in the process of guiding children in their experiences. The quality of these experiences rests largely on the kind of person the teacher is. His background, his insights,

---

1. Reid, Chandos, "A Study of Teachers' Problems Resulting from New Practices in Curriculum and Teaching Procedures in Selected Secondary Schools," Quoted in: Roland C. Faunce and Morrel J. Clute, teaching and learning in the junior high school (San Francisco: Wadsworth Publishing Company, Inc. 1961), pp. 321-323.

2. Faunce, op. cit., pp. 323-324.

sensitivity, and his effectiveness determine the caliber of work accomplished.

The high school science teacher must make his subject matter vital, meaningful, and of real use to his students.

Since each subject has a potential contribution to make to many life situations, the various subject areas must be seen in relationship to each other. At the present time, the wealth of informational material needed to work on situations of everyday living with learners is not available. Simpler materials related to present problems are required in every grade. A wide range of other than printed materials — pictures, documentary films, radio transcriptions— is important.

The Teacher's Role in the Guidance Program

The teacher has to be the key person in the guidance program.

Guidance is essentially a process of helping the individual find purposeful direction in his learning. A guidance program can be effective only to the extent that it has the enthusiastic and intelligent support of every teacher in the school. The teacher meets the pupils daily in home room and classes; he has them in clubs and other extra-class activities, and he has opportunities to meet their parents and to become acquainted with their home-life. The teacher, therefore, is in an excellent position to locate pupils who are in need of guidance services.

Extra-class activities serve exploratory purposes in some schools. Each of these activities may, under the supervision of an able sponsor, provide pupils with many experiences to help them explore their potentialities and interests, and to evaluate their abilities. The teacher with resourcefulness and imagination can make a truly significant contribution to the guidance program through his work with pupils in extra-class activities.

The teacher must have some preparation for guidance activities.

If the teacher is to participate in guidance activities, he must have some preparation for it. Study in such areas as the psychology of the adolescent, mental hygiene, the psychology of abnormality, tests and measurements, and counseling techniques are very helpful. His understanding of adolescent children must be broad, including knowledge about their emothional problems, their physiological development, and their social relationships.

Home visitations by the teachers is essential as a basis for effective guidance activities.

Home visitations by teachers gradually have decreased, particularly in the heavily populated centers. In rural communities, the homes may be so widely scattered that transportation problems would obviate extensive home visitation.

The cooperation of the parents is essential to any guidance program. The teacher, by talking with the parent, may help bridge the gap between adolescents and teachers. The parents and the teacher can plan a program to meet the students' needs. However, if teacher cooperation is secured, the responsibility for interviewing can easily be shared, and the information obtained can be exchanged among several teachers. The results of such conferences, if summarized and placed in the students' folders, are then available to all the other teachers.

Teachers with an adequate understanding of parents can learn to conduct parent conferences with ease and skill. The entire responsibility for such contact can rarely be left to counselors, but it is desirable that classroom teachers share in parent interviewing.

The teacher's effectiveness in guidance through the core program.

The core program is one of the most promising developments for improving the teacher's effectiveness in guidance. The core teacher serves as the key person in the guidance program, in which guidance activities can become well integrated with the rest of the school program.

Careful observation is made of each pupil by the teacher. A conference with a pupil about his conduct is considered preferable to keeping him after school. The conferences not only provide much information about the pupils, they also give the teacher an opportunity to establish an effective counseling relationship with them.

Teachers should study the schedule of the school to plan a definite time for guidance. They should improve their preparation for guidance, provide for a better understanding of adolescents, and develop skills in evaluation and measurements.

Every teacher has opportunities to study the ongoing activities of his group for clues to the next steps.

The teacher, as a guide, evaluates the problems faced, and, through questions and suggestions, helps the group to see deeper implications and possibilities. Opportunities to explore should extend to every part of the school. Cooperative relationships are needed in the halls, on the playground, and elsewhere, when space must be shared with others. The playground can be the place where interests and abilities are evident.

The teacher can also use various classroom procedures to examine pupil strengths and limitations. Statements should also be included indicating the learner's growth in sensitivity to the demands of situations.

The teacher must see the program of education in the perspective of the major purposes of education.

Modern education places the teacher at the very center of the educational program. The responsibility of the teacher for this program today is far greater than it was yesterday. The teacher must see the program of education in the perspective of the major purposes of education. The teacher, for example, who is immediately responsible for the preparation of youths for certain vocations, needs to see the relationship of that preparation to the broad purposes as well as the more specific goals of that vocational education.

Modern curriculum building programs are generally organized on the assumption that the teacher cannot execute a program intelligently unless he has participated in its development.

Although the school personnel and the community together will plan the major outline of the educational program, the details must be the responsibility of the teacher. Modern courses of study, formulated as they are principally by teachers, are given over largely to suggestions for content and procedures. Responsibility for the development of an educational program can be made effective. The very nature of the teacher's place in modern education makes him an important agent of the school in establishing school-community relationships.

The ultimate goals should underlie all teacher's plans for learner activities.

The activities that will develop from his joint planning sessions with the learners will be simple or complex, depending upon the decisions he has made regarding the educative possibilities of the problem. The aim of the teacher should be to help his learners achieve clear and accurate understandings, which his learners must be able to apply intelligently in new situations. To achieve these goals, the teacher must provide experiences in clarifying and solving problems. Achieving these goals is an individual problem. The learners have to be placed in situations in which they are challenged by their classmates as well as by their teacher, if their findings are inaccurate or incomplete. As the teacher guides his students' learning, there will be times when he will be playing many different roles — telling, demonstrating, and explaining, or leading discussions.

The skill which the teacher displays will be a determining factor in the quality of his learners' understanding and growth. The details of the lesson will depend on the stage in the course which his learners have reached, and the specific help they need in order to develop accurate understandings.

If the teacher wants his learners to understand the topic under consideration, he will not always put top priority on securing information from books. Since understanding grows from experience, the possiblities for providing learners with concrete experiences are almost unlimited. The value of an excursion to develop experience is very important; and the teacher should explore the possibility of using materials from the audio-visual aids; he will have many offers of materials which can be helpful to teachers in developing experimental background. Before the unit is completed, the teacher may wish for some learners to set up exhibits, others to do a piece of creative writing, or still others to put on a demonstration, or a play. These may be valuable means of discovering what his students have learned.

The teacher should use concrete aids in a variety of ways in the development of an extensive study. He cannot tell his learners the concepts and generalizations he expects them to derive from their experiences, and expect that these understandings will actually be attained. As the teacher plans for the experiences, he hopes to develop more concrete concepts; he must consider how to stimulate his learners to think.

Working in a classroom with some type of audio-visual aid does not necessarily lead to more accurate concepts unless the learners are helped to react thoughtfully to what they have seen. The children have to know *precisely* what they are looking for. This means that they should have some rather definite questions in mind. Such background is very important. Without it, the teacher will have much more difficulty preparing his pupils for the coming experience. Even when the teacher is leading a discussion in an area where his learners have considerable reading background, it is important to challenge them to think about what they are saying. The teacher should not accept an answer phrased in the words of the text without making sure that his learners have drawn the correct conclusions. Learners often use words glibly, even when they do not know exactly what they mean. A word mispronounced, a word misused should clue the teacher to ask more questions.

One of the most important values of a discussion technique is that it enables the teacher to find where ideas are not clear. The teacher will use a variety of techniques to help his learners to arrive at more accurate understandings. If the teacher wants to be sure that his efforts to help learners develop accurate understandings have been effective, he will provide opportunities for the new information to be used. In a sense, the teacher is doing this every time he asks the question that requires a learner to apply his knowledge accurately in order to arrive at a correct answer.

The teacher must be careful, however, to assure that the summarizing process actually requires his learners to apply their new information, not merely to give back the words in the book or the words they have heard.

There are many types of recording devices that require the learners to think carefully in order to organize what they have learned.

If the learners have a series of specific questions in mind, they observe, listen, and study more intelligently.

It is very difficult to ask intelligent questions if one has had little or no previous experience in the area under consideration. The procedures the teacher uses to provide class experiences will vary with the problem and the opportunities at hand. It is wise to give an assignment on a topic and to make a general observation, then to use class time to summarize the findings. If the learners have sufficient background to raise intelligent questions, the teacher faces an important task — that of helping them identify specific problems as focal points for further study. The teacher can give his learners some effective experiences in outlining if he will let them help him decide how their questions can be grouped.

It is a good idea to make a permanent record both of the major and of the specific topics to be studied. This serves as a point of reference as work proceeds.

The teacher should determine just what the policies are in his school.

The principal will want to be consulted before the teacher and his class make plans for an activity not usually considered part of the regular classroom routine. Field trips, activities involving special use of the gymnasium or playfields, lunchroom or auditorium facilities, parties and programs to which parents are invited, are types of experiences about which the principal should be informed. It can be embarrassing to him and disturbing to his learners if he makes promises which he later discovers he cannot fulfill.

The teacher will need to know how much help on problems related to his regular classroom program can be expected from special teachers: reading specialists, speech correctionists, visiting teachers.

If the help of specialists is not readily available, the teacher will want to find out whether and when such assistance might be given. The specialist, will of course, need similar information from the point of view of his own teaching assignment.

Nonprofessional personnel can make many positive contributions to the lives of learners.

Nonprofessional personnel — the school secretary, the engineer, the custodian, the lunchroom helpers — are persons who can make many positive contributions to the lives of learners. They can also be very helpful to the teacher in locating needed materials or in providing special services. The teacher will need to ascertain just what help he can request of them and under what circumstances.

In most schools, every effort is made to develop an organization and policies that facilitate the work of teachers.

Efficient classroom management will depend upon the teacher's familiarity with the over-all policies of the system of which his school is a part, the general organization of the school building, and specific regulations. Some of these may be aspects of policy over which a principal has little, if any, control. In some cases, considerable flexibility within the general framework of the over-all policy is possible.

Among the policies usually established on a system-wide basis are those in the general curriculum design and the over-all organization for instruction, the teacher staying within the general framework of the course of study, but making whatever adjustments are necessary to meet the needs of learners effectively.

Some safety regulations should be established for the legal protection of teachers.

Accidents should be reported on special forms. There should be definite restrictions on how much first aid can be offered. The details of any corporeal punishment may need to be witnessed and reported.

Each school has special regulations and unwritten agreements. The regulations are stated in a building handbook, but others can be discovered only by listening and by being sensitive enough to know when to ask questions. In every school there should be some device for keeping teachers informed. It may be through the office bulletin board, through announcements over the school's intercom system, a mimeographed flyer that is in the teacher's mailbox every morning, sending a pupil messenger with a note, etc.

The success of a teacher will depend on how well he can work with others.

Those who employ the teacher want to know how effective he is likely to be as a member of a school faculty. He will need to understand the personal structure in his school, the responsibilities carried by his colleagues and the cooperative relationships. Frequently, during the meetings, special discussion sections are planned for beginning teachers. These afford opportunities to meet his supervisors, and to learn about the general organization of the school system. It will be the responsibility of his principal to make special plans to help him get acquainted. A variety of publications available in the school help teachers to become acquainted with the over-all organization of the district. There may also be a personnel handbook which desribes the administrative and supervisory structure of the school system. When he is a student-teacher, his cooperating teacher will undoubtedly take responsibility for orienting him to the school.

In most schools, the principal is the person with delegated legal responsibility for the welfare of the pupils and the staff.

The principal is responsible to the central administration

in his system or to the state department of education for accurate records. He is the first person parents consult when problems arise involving home-school relationships, and he is expected to give supervisory assistance to his teachers. The principal in many ways must count upon the good judgement, promtness, and concientiousness of his faculty. Situations in which a teacher senses abnormal emotional disturbance on the part of a pupil or a parent should likewise be brought to the principal's attention. Typically, also, permission for a pupil to leave school during school hours is given by the principal.

The Teacher's Role in Planning Instruction

Successful pupil-teacher planning must be based on careful teacher preparation.

The nature of the planning depends somewhat on the philosophy and practice of curriculum organization in the school.

The teacher should think of planning for the day's lesson as one phase of the larger problem of instructional planning which requires complete coordination and integration with the planning of the course. The teacher should possess a broad understanding of the subject matter, materials, and activities. This understanding will enable the teacher to anticipate probable difficulties inherent in the materials. The teacher must know teaching techniques to meet not only the general but the specific needs of a learning situation.

Materials of some form are necessary for every lesson or unit phase. These may involve subject matter as found in textbooks, library references, or apparatus and equipment of various sorts. These materials require very careful consideration by the teacher if the most appropriate are to be selected.

The teacher must not only be prepared to follow up effectively the answer to a question he has asked; he must also be able to analyze quickly an unexpected response, and see its implications. If a teacher's questions are poor, it means that his knowledge is weak.

The Teacher's Role in the Teaching Process

Every instructor should feel responsible for developing the best study procedures in connection with the subject taught.

Many teachers carry on their daily activities without having any idea of the changes which they seek to bring about in the behavior of their students.

The failure of many teachers to define their objectives clearly is the second weakness. If an objective is clearly understood, the teacher should be able to describe the kind of behavior which is expected of the student. To make really important changes in behavior requires time and many learning experiences.

Each subject has its own major values in relation to the big areas or needs of life. It is the duty of each teacher to know the significant contributions his subject can make in meeting the needs of youth. The maturity level is an important consideration in the selection and placement of content. Interest, also, must be generated, otherwise learning will be partial. With most objectives, however, learning does not stop with words—genuine attainment must be judged in terms of the degree to which a person is able to use, apply, and live out what the words signify.[1]

Real objectives must be first in the teacher's mind. When they are there, some possibility for pupil development exists; when not there, no amount of pedagogy can compensate for the deficiency.[2]

The teacher gives general direction to learning by keeping the principle of self-activity as a guide. But the activity cannot be considered abstractly or separately in determining its soundness; it must always be considered in connection with aims.[3]

In teaching, the activity of pupils should be the kind that produces results; it must be sound and psychologically reliable. If teachers use inefficient procedures in learning, there can be no high hopes for their teaching. Teachers should constantly experiment upon themselves to acquire a deeper understanding of how learning takes place. Every instructor should feel responsible for developing the best study procedures in connection with the subject taught.

Evidence is also available when planning next steps. In plan-

1. Butler, Frank A. *The Improvement of Teaching in Secondary Schools* (Chicago: The University of Chicago Press, 1954), p. 45.
2. *Ibid.,* p. 51.
3. *Ibid.,* pp. 57-58.

ning with learners, the teacher appraises the proposals coming from the groups, and decides whether it is appropriate to suggest related problems. A record of systematic observation of children may be made, and the accumulated evidence analyzed. Conferences with pupils and parents are another means of systematically collecting evidence.

Better understanding between home and school, and effective encouragement of learners can come through informal evaluative statements which can be written and shared at any time that the teacher feels it would be of interest to the parent.

Some educators have been responsible for educational progress and community understanding.

In some areas, contact between the school and the community consists largely of attendance reports, athletic events, and commencement ceremonies. Only through enlightened public support won by widespread public participation can the school find the strength to prosper. Most teachers today realize that lay people are extremely valuable and helpful to the educational program as resource persons.

The Position of the Learner

The students must believe that their learning is in their direct interest.

The school does not compel them to study, for they are studying not for the sake of the school, but for their own future.

The first and chief task of the school is to inform the students of what will be most useful to them in their lives; the second is to prepare them for life.

The student must participate actively in the learning situation.

The task of education is to give new sensations to experience which are connected with a subject. The fuller the circle of impressions, the clearer, stronger, and more durable are the observations.

When we speak of experience which goes hand-in-hand with activity and the evocation of various changes in the real world, then, on the other hand, intellectual recognition is joined into a whole with practical actions.

The application of practical activity in the school is not a whimsical expression of some trite pedagogical convictions; it is an inescapable need of the present and still more of the future years.

In pleading for practical activity in the schools, it should not be understood by this that the school must be overly concerned with material benefits. Rather, it should be concerned with striving to make a child capable of facing life.

The individual has a desire for and an interest in gaining new ideas, developing new interests, acquiring new skills, and gaining knowledge that is new to him.

The difficulty is that the teachers may have failed to devlop the interests or to stimulate the learning of new interests. Pupils are not easily interested if school work is repetitious and boring, or has little meaning and relation to their past or present experiences or to anticipated future needs.

Young people must learn to overcome various obstacles.

This must be done through an intense interest in a chosen goal. It is not good to focus attention on only one activity, for in a short time this activity becomes boring. One-sided teaching is also boring, for the mind then works in only one direction. The teacher should instruct in such a manner that the mind can work simultaneously in various ways, so that the student will not only remember but try to investigate, so that he may translate his newly acquired knowledge into activity.

The education of the student must not end with the completion of school.

The student should continue working independently and voluntarily, but he must also have obtained the basis for and the method of this further self-education during his study in school. Self-education is the only guarantee for a good future for every person. The educator must, therefore, indicate to the students the way to achieve their goals. The teacher must awaken in the students strong faith in the possibility of fulfilling plans through self-education.

Individuals learn most effectively when, by reason of their stage of development and previous experiences, they are mature enough to profit by the new experiences.

Maturation of the individual has a great deal to do with readiness to learn, not only physical skills but also skills and understandings in other areas. Young children who are forced to learn something before they are ready may develop maladjustments.

Trying to force pupils to learn beyond their capabilities produces abnormal behavior, frustration, and tensions, instead of producing early learning. In other words, the learning outcomes may be quite different from those desired.

Educational experiences should give the adolescent a sense of security and satisfaction with his own development as a person.

The adolescent should feel that there are some things which he can do better than others. Satisfaction with one's own development and one's relationship to others helps to build the right kinds of attitudes toward life.

Every adolescent behavior problem has a cause that the school may be helping to alleviate or to aggravate.

Each case is a problem in itself into which the teacher must probe to find the cause. Behavior problems of pupils have a relationship to every phase of school life. The class as a social group may hinder as well as facilitate and support learnings considered desirable by the school.

SUMMARY

In this chapter we are concerned primarily with how the teacher can work with the total class in developing personal understanding of the many aspects of adjustment faced by the adolescent.

The teacher, in the modern sense of the word, must also be the educator. He must have, among other things, those qualities which are possessed by all the best leaders of groups or nations. The teacher must have great intelligence. It gives the teacher a strong base on which he will rest not only the deep value of his calling, but also the means of passing his hours of teaching. When it is a question of psychic values, the teacher must stand on a high moral level, for he is a builder of characters.

The teacher who sees his role as one providing guidance for the student will find that there are many ways in which these guidance activities are performed. A teacher who considers the needs of young people will seek to work closely with their parents.

The student must believe that his learning lies in his direct interest. He must learn to overcome various obstacles. His education must not end with the completion of school. He must continue working independently and voluntarily, but he must have obtained the basis for and the method of this further self-education during his study in the school.

FOR FURTHER STUDY

Alexander, W.M., and P.M. Halverson, *Effective Teaching in Secondary Schools.* New York: Rinehart & Company, Inc., 1956.

American Association of Colleges for Teacher Education, *Evaluative Criteria for Accrediting Teacher Education.* Washington, D.C.: Amer. Assn. of Colleges for Teacher Education, 1967.

Baxter, Bernice, *Teacher-Pupil Relationships.* New York: The

Macmillan Company, 1941.

Bigelow, K.W., ' *Teachers of Our Times.* Washington, D.C.: American Council on Education, 1944.

Bossing, N.L., *Teaching in Secondary Schools.* Boston: Houghton Mifflin Company, 1952.

Butler, F.A., *The Improvement of Teaching in Secondary Schools.* Chicago: University of Chicago Press, 1954.

Combs, A.W., *The Professional Education of Teachers.* Boston: Allyn & Bacon, Inc., 1965.

Cosper, Cecil, *Student-Teaching Theory and Practices.* New York; Greenwinch Bk. Pubs., 1965.

Faunce, R.C. and M.J. Clute, *teaching and learning in the junior high school.* San Francisco; Wadswoth Publishing Company, Inc., 1961.

Gelinas, P.J., *So You Want to Be A Teacher.* New York: Harper & Row, Publishers, 1965.

Grambs, J.D. and others, *Modern Method in Secondary Education.* New York: The Dryden Press, 1958.

Hunt, E.C., *Education of Teachers.* Columbia, S.C.: University of South Carolina Press, 1944.

Jersild, A.T., *In Search of Self.* New York: Bureau of Publications, Teachers College, Columbia University, 1952.

Larson, K.G., *Guide to Personal Advancement in the Teaching Profession.* Englewood Cliffs, N.J.: Prentice-Hall, Inc., 1966.

Melby, E.O., *The Education of Free Men.* Pittsburgh: University of Pittsburgh, 1955.

Schueler, Herbert, *Teacher Education and the New Media.* Washington: Amer. Assn. of Colls. for Teacher Educ., 1967.

Simpson, R.H., *Teacher Self-Evaluation.* New York: The Macmillan Company, 1966.

Risk, T.M., *Principles and Practices of Teaching in Secondary Schools.* New York: American Book Company, 1947.

Rivlin, H.N., *Teaching Adolescents in Secondary Schools.* New York: Appleton-Century-Crofts, Inc., 1948.

Wahlquist, J.T., *An Introduction to American Education.* New York: The Ronald Press Company, 1947.

CHAPTER IV

EFFECTIVE TEACHING

Ten Basic General Principles

Ten basic general principles which operate in every good teaching-learning situation:

1. *Education is guided and directed growth.*

The assignment must provide for direction and guidance in accord with the other principles of learning.

2. *The pupil's activities are given direction only by some goal which he seeks to attain.*

The assignment should obviously create situations in which pupils will find goals.

3. *Problem-solving is the way of learning.*

Whether the assignment is planned to contribute to a concept or to a skill, it should constantly challenge and not merely inform the pupil. Standards of achievement of any sort are goals which the pupil approaches effectively only in the problem-solving way.

4. *Learning is most effective when optimally emotionalized.*

This principle is inseparable from interest, and interest is assured if principles 1 to 3 are functioning.

5. *Persistence in problem-solving behavior varies with the explicitness of the directions which the pupils receive.*

The assignment must avoid the one extreme of being a mere recipe for motions which pupils are to make, and the other extreme of giving such inadequate guidance that the situations created are so vague and indefinite as to fail to challenge.

6. *Knowledge of progress is a powerful incentive to effort.*

The assignment must enable the pupil to make progress and to know that he is making progress.

7. *All learning involves integration.*

The assignment must not be a nondescript collection of miscellany. It must be unified by an integrating principle.

8. *Application of the learning product is essential if transfer is to take place.*

The assignment should reveal: (1) opportunities to employ learning products developed in previous assignment; (2) opportunities to apply the meanings, insights, and skills acquired while working with the assignment to the pupil's work in other classes, in his extracurricular activities, and in his out-of-school environment.

9. *Independence in learning is encouraged if the pupil has some choice in what he is to do, how he is to do it, and when he is to do it.*

The assignment should show evidence that all pupils, not merely the bright ones, enjoy as much freedom of action as is consistent with direction and guidance of learning in groups.

10. *Because of individual differences, pupils should not begin necessarily at the same place, nor proceed necessarily at the same rate, in the same direction, and in the same way.*

The assignment must be flexible. It must be subject to change on the spur of the moment for individual pupils, without handicap to the remainder of the class. It must provide an abundance of related optional situations allowing for both quantitative and qualitative differentiation. It should allow for the incorporation of the pupil's own suggestions as the work with the assignment proceeds.[1]

The learner must be active in some way with respect to what is to be learned, whether it is information, a skill, an understanding, a habit, an ideal, an attitude or an interest. The activity must be repeated if the desired learning is to be achieved. For some reason *repetition*, if it takes place under favorable conditions, tends to result in more permanent learning in the fields of skills and habits than in the fields of information and memory in general. The immediate effect of any activity is conditioned by the richness of the experience. One remembers best those experiences which were particularly painful or particularly pleasurable. Perhaps one of the most desirable and powerful types of pleasurable effects is the knowledge of progress or achievement. Ideas which have been in the mind of the learner, associated as to their place in space, develop the property of association so that the recall of one tends to bring recall of the other. Special and important is the *principle of sequence*. When one idea,

---

1. Billett, Roy O., *Fundamentals of Secondary-School Teaching* (Cambridge: The Riverside Press, 1940), pp. 174-175.

feeling, or act has occured in the experience of an individual immediately preceding another idea, feeling, or act, the recurrence of the former tends to cause the recurrence of the other. The applications of this principle are widespread, especially in learning which involves sequence in the formation of habits, the development of skills, and memorizing.

Modern education has as its purpose the gaining of abilities by the exercise of independent and self-directed study activities.

Studying independently is one form of self-activity which is predominant in modern schools. The responsibility of a teacher is making supervised or directed study periods fruitful. Growth through directed study comes about by real mental effort. The observation of pupils at work, the examination of their written exercises, the analysis of their methods of preparing the lesson, and the collection of information about pupils are the basis of remedial help. The teacher is best qualified to decide when independent study can be undertaken as the most effective activity. The teacher must keep the learning processes balanced, as determined by the nature of good learning, on the one hand, and the nature of the pupil's capacities, on the other. Group discussions after extended study provide an opportunity to determine the status of achievement.

Every important ability demands its proportionate amount of self-activity.

The concept of education supported by self-activity implies that pupils must earn their own living, that they must develop muscle and mind, that they must work to become strong, that they must think to become thinkers. The teacher gives general direction to learning by keeping the principle of self-activity as the guide.

Improving the ability to study should be the concern of teachers in all subjects.

Every instructor should feel responsible for developing the best study procedures in connection with the subject taught, and the most effective way to develop these procedures is to set the stage so that the teaching demands the use of them. Merely putting a set of study suggestions in the hands of a pupil will not suffice; ideal study habits are gained and lived out only through study which requires the use of correct procedures to attain designated objectives.[1]

Much teaching is poor because it lacks real objectives.

Understanding is derived through mental activity different from that which is involved in pure memorization. Rote memory is necessary when material demands it, but cruelly wasteful and educationally detrimental when used upon material that is logical.

Learning is a science governed by the laws of the mind, and any gross violation of these laws retards educational progress. Learning is reacting, but the kind of reacting always influences the kind of learning. Pupils cannot have knowledge pushed into them by teacher activity alone; they must work for it. The pupils learn by reacting, but they should also know the sound activities which constitute the general reaction.

As far as pupils are concerned, something of real value should emerge from method, otherwise the effects of instruction are flat and fleeting. Selection of the most worthwhile objectives is a principle of teaching, and it is one of the most important.[2]

Too often it is concluded that objectives are only those factual and informational materials found in books, generally textbooks, materials which are memorized, recited in class, and kept in storage for final examination. The first point under the "Nature of Objectives" is to realize that processes are quite as important as products — sometimes immeasurably more valuable. The processes in learning should not be overlooked; they are too valuable in facilitating the acquisition of the end products.

A teacher must watch the development of processes because they underlie and support the growth and attainment of products.

Teachers must be everlastingly on detective duty to find the

---

1. Butler, Frank A., *The Improvement of Teaching in Secondary Schools* (Chicago: The University of Chicago Press, 1954), p. 253.
2. Butler, *op. cit.*, p. 29.

processes behind the products.

Objectives should be set forth in completeness; the demands of living and enjoying and succeeding determine the nature of what should be taught; pupils must know, must be, must feel, and must do; merely knowing is not enough. Real objectives must first be in the teacher's mind; when they are there, some possibility for a pupil's development is near; when not there, no amount of pedagogy can compensate for the deficiency.[1]

Learning is a science governed by the laws of mind, and any gross violation of these laws retards educational progress.

If teachers themselves use inefficient procedures in learning, there can be no high hopes for their teaching until efficient methods have been incubated. Choosing the right activities in directing study can be done best by knowing the types of learning and the most effective activities included under each one. Both the types and the ingredients of each type need scrutiny to enable one to direct self-activity along psychologically sound lines. In very few instances is only one type of learning sufficient; there is generally a combination of several types.[2]

The teacher should work with individual learners in order to build positive self-concepts.

Each learner physically, socially, emotionally, and intellectually presents his own individual pattern of development. The teacher will understand him better as an individual if he studies carefully the school records that provide background information about each learner, and other sources that provide him with vital personal data. The teacher will not change a student's concept of himself merely by admonishing him that he can do better work. The learner will need many satisfying experiences before he begins to put himself on a right way.

It is helpful to check on an impression of a single individual by looking at others with the same trait in mind.

Experienced teachers do not try to collect all their data in the early moths of the school year. They do not rely on observation

1. Butler, *The Improvement of Teaching...*, *op. cit.,* pp. 46-48.
2. *Ibid.,* p. 73.

alone as a guide to knowing their learners. Records, written assignments, class discussions, and a variety of tests and inventories will all help to make a general appraisal of the strengths, weaknesses, and experience backgrounds of learners. Selecting topics for reports can give many insights into the interests of individual learners. Planning sessions or discussion, homeroom, and extracurricular activities often reveal the reasoning power of learners. It is helpful to insert questions into a demonstration or explanation to make sure that learners have understood. The independent work sessions afford an opportunity to judge how effectively learners are able to use the principles.

Tests have value at many points in the teaching process — for preliminary surveys for checks on progress — and should be carefully analyzed for evidence of progress and new needs. Many teachers use data collected in individual conferences. These conferences are used to go over the learner's work for the report period, and to talk to him about his progress. It is often possible to talk with pupils during laboratory periods. System-wide achievement tests are sometimes administered, and individual teachers encouraged to order tests to secure whatever additional information they want in their specific fields.

Any teacher who is sharing with youth his insights into an aspect of their cultural heritage should strive to develop awareness of the contributions of his field to daily living.

As the teacher becomes better acquainted with his learners, he will discover that the behavior patterns acquired by individuals in meeting new developmental tasks can be extremely varied. The teacher must use as much caution in catagorizing the motives for an individual's behavior as he would in classifying his intellectual ability. Insights into the developmental tasks his pupils are facing should also help to plan his teaching. Certainly the teacher will not choose to teach only those aspects of his subject field which have a practical application to the life of his learner.

Any teacher will help learners to achieve more mature ways in meeting developmental tasks.

The success of his lessons, as well as his relationships with learners, will depend on his growing sensitivity to the cause of behavior. Learners who are facing difficult adjustment patterns need consistent help. Life with his learners will be more satisfying if he senses the values of the peer group and view these manifestations objectively. Learners preoccupied with meeting needs for status, for security, and for independence from adults may not give full attention to legitimate classroom activities. Actually, there are many times when the effectiveness of students' learning depends upon the teacher's sensitivity to factors related to their physical and psychical needs. Therefore, the effectiveness of his help as his learners face problems of learning will often depend on how sensitive the teacher is.

The key to enrichment of the learner lies in shared evaluation and generalization, a natural outgrowth of cooperative approach to problem solving.

Such evaluative and generalizing activity should be continuous through an experience, but should be a culminating activity also to bring together in a more complete fashion the learnings of a group. Until teachers give the opportunity for something more than an individual test of an objective type, pupils can hardly supply the kind of evidence on the quality of a learning experience, helpful to the teacher in planning future experiences with learners, and helpful to pupils in seeing the whole range of educational outcomes which could exist for them.[1]

Every instructor should be skillful in securing information and in organizing, evaluating, and reporting results of study and research.

Illustrative behaviors: The teacher

1. Decides on his purpose before planning action.
2. Practices good study and other work habits when he has intricate thinking, reading, and planning to do.
3. Consults some good periodicals if seeking information

1. Alexander, & P.M.H., *Effective Teaching, op. cit.,* pp. 216-217.

on political developments, foreign affairs, homemaking, scientific matters, book reviews, etc.

4. Uses common sources of printed information efficiently, e.g., dictionary, encyclopedia, almanacs, and card catalog in a library.

5. Asks questions in such a way as to secure accurate information of public services, offices, or persons likely to have special information when in need of it.

6. Constructs line, bar, and circle graphs, diagrams, pictographs, and statistical tables to express quantitative relationships.

7. Uses the typewriter or writes well enough to meet his needs. Is able to draw relevant information from several sources, correlate it, make a defensible set of conclusions.

8. Manifests a fair knowledge of the relative reliability of various sources of information: two or more newspapers, radio and T.V. commentators, consumer guides, and government publications.

9. Develops skill in noting and recording information in outline, notes, and summary statements.

10. Uses a readily acceptable footnote and bibliographical form in identifying sources of information and ideas.[1]

General Procedures of Getting Acquainted with Students

The first prerequisite for individualizing instruction is for the classroom teacher to possess a broad and thorough knowledge of all factors which influence each student's classroom learning.

The records provide valuable insights in gaining an understanding of the students, but the teacher should supplement this information with the results of his day-to-day contacts with and observations of the pupils.

Teachers obtain information about their students through personal interviews, study of student autobiographies, keeping anecdotal records, and making case studies of students. The student's relationship with other members of the group and the role he plays in activities should be observed.

1. French, Will and Associates, *Behavioral Goals of General Education in High School* (New York: Russell Sage Foundation, 1957), pp. 92-93.

*The teacher may need to know the circumstances associated with
a particular past success or failure of the student.*

Important information concerning these matters may be obtained by means of personal interviews with the student. The interview may become an extension of classroom activities in which the student has already acquired feelings of security and a confidence in the teacher. The main purposes of interviews are: to get better acquainted with the student, to obtain insights into his needs and interests, and to assist him in meeting his needs. A knowledge of specific needs which students themselves recognize as important is useful to a teacher in the selection of learning experiences. Data concerning the student's home and family background are especially significant in understanding him. Children from homes of low economic levels may not have the experiences necessary to provide them with readiness for school activities. The human values are shaped by the nature of the community. An adolescent cannot be fully understood unless he is viewed against the background of his community life.

The teacher should be able to identify evidences of physical weaknesses or disease. Adequate health records should include information concerning illness or physical defects.

The results of a test of general mental ability is a sound basis for predicting success in many school subjects.

*Research studies reveal that the item of greatest importance
in teaching success is that of the nature of the pupil-teacher
relation.*

Studies show at least three critical factors in these relations which secondary school teachers should recognize: the *first*, the teacher's personality; *second*, the teacher's understanding of the general nature of effective learning in relation to teaching method; a *third* factor closely identified with the other two is that of the teacher's insight into the characteristics and problems of adolescent learners. Extended treatment of these factors is in EDUCATION, Vol. I (The Philosophy of Education).

Suggestions for Making Teaching Effective

Explanations must be made in the light of the background vocabulary and previous experience of the learner.

Care must be taken: (1) to fill in gaps with necessary background for understanding new materials, sometimes in the form of a review; and (2) to put learners in an **appropriate** frame of mind for many new ideas or learning activities — perhaps sometimes by developing interest or a desire to learn, sometimes by explaining the purpose of the learning activity.   At least three important general principles of teaching seem to grow obviously out of this principle of learning: (1) The approach to new learning activities should be made in such a manner as to utilize previous mind-sets; (2) quite frequently, time and care must be devoted to setting the stage for reviews, discussions, lectures, etc., to prepare the learner for coming learning experiences; (3) the probable effect of any learning stimulus, materials, methods, or activities upon the learner must be considered in the light of what he already knows, and of his interests, abilities, concepts, and tastes.

Certainly, more specific principles of teaching procedure have their source of validity, at least in part, in this principle of learning. Among them may be mentioned the following:

1. Proceed from the simple to the complex.
2. Proceed from the concrete to the abstract.
3. Proceed from the near to the remote.
4. Proceed from the psychological to the logical.[1]
5. Proceed from the general to the specific.[2]

The failure of many teachers to define their objectives clearly.

Each subject has its own major values in relation to the big areas or needs of life. It is the duty of each teacher to know the significant contributions his subject can make in meeting the needs of students. *Interest* must be present in the class, otherwise learning will be partial. Interest is the cause, when the educational process works smoothly. A knowledge of students' interests is significant as one basis for the selection of learning materials.

1. Mills, Hubert H., and Douglass, Harl R., *Teaching in High School* (New York: The Ronald Press Company, 1957), pp. 89-90.
2. Teaching should not be built on fragmentary facts and data. They could be, and often are, useful as illustrative material which deepens one's knowledge. At the outset students should be acquainted with problems in their full dimensions and only subsequently should this knowledge be perfected by fragmentary facts.

In utilizing the present interests of students, the teacher should recognize his responsibility to assist students in extending the scope and variety of their intellectual interests. To create interest is not so easy. A demonstration, a story, an illustration, or event may serve to give initial momentum to learning. Interests are of two kinds: *direct* and *indirect*.

Direct interests are those exhibited by adolescents in watching television, in hearing funny stories, etc.

Indirect interests are those that are studied because of the need to know something.

From studies, it is clear that adolescents take considerable interest in their social activities, in sports and games. These interest patterns broadly parallel at least some of the major elements in the curriculum.

Interests do have strong motivational force, however, and current interests of youth might be used as leads to more formal studies. Certain patterns of interests tend to appear at various ages; these patterns sometimes provide valuable clues to grade-level designation of certain subjects, topics, or literature selections. If interests did not provide the basis for the curriculum, some other approach to the question might. The term "needs" is welcomed by many as at least a partial solution.

Once identified, needs may serve as a basis for objectives, or may even replace objectives as usually stated, and serve as independent criteria for decisions on curricular organization, content, and teaching procedures.[1]

The *needs* and *interests* of the pupil constitute the criterion of curriculum content. The purpose espoused by the child-centered school is the maximum development of human personality. The felt needs and interests of the individual indicate the existing character of the personality.

Needs and interests are shaped by cultural forces and judged by socially derived standards. They define the present status of the learner's personality.

The needs and interests are a central factor in the determination of the standards by which the quality of education must be

1. Krug, Edward A., *The Secondary School Curriculum* (New York: Harper and Brothers, 1960), pp. 60-64.

judged.

The notion that education consists in the mastery of subjects is seriously defective even on the intellectual side, for the attitudes and methodology appropriate to the scientific enterprise are as important as the various sciences.

Motivation is the bringing together of many inclinations and drives possessed by pupils, and the utilization of these inclinations. The center of motivation in school is the teacher, who is a source of stimulation. Good teaching in itself motivates, because good teaching includes, among other things, good purposes and wise direction of learning. The pupil becomes tired of mechanical acquisition of facts and definitions. The students are not interested in school work that has little meaning and less relation to their past or present experiences. The problem for teachers is to find the kinds of experiences in which pupils will want to participate because they see a need for them. It is a teacher's job to guide pupils to select experiences that will broaden and expand interests.

It is well-known among teachers that some individuals learn more readily than others. Tests of intelligence and achievement have long indicated that individuals differ in rate and retention of learning. Standards should be individual standards, requiring a higher level of achievement from the most capable students.

The learner must be encouraged to engage in activity necessary for learning, not because of direct interest, but because by so doing he may gain something he wishes or avoid something he does not like. The student must wish for something and must feel that to engage in a given activity will enable him to attain the satisfaction of that desire.

One of the arts of teaching is that of capitalizing on the felt and expressed goals of learners, and of making these goals explicit and meaningful.

Fundamental is the feeling of worth attached to the goals of the learner and the problems he faces in achieving them.

Assuming that the teacher and the students have arrived at a set of goals and purposes of learning experience, we find that they are in a position to develop activities for their achievement.

Experiences are fruitful only when they have meaning for the learner.

An experience in apparently meaningless diagraming of sentences or the memorization of a grammatical rule may be confusing and irritating to a pupil who does not understand what he is doing nor see any reason for doing it. Forcing learning procedures cause abnormal behavior, frustration, and tensions instead of producing early learning. In other words, the learning products will be entirely different from those desired.

There are two important means of studying the adolescent to find out more about his nature, needs, growth, and development: (1) through the investigation of research findings in the areas of child development, adolescent psychology, and mental hygiene; and (2) through observation and study of individual youngsters and groups of adolescents.

Educational experiences should give the adolescent his development as a person.

The development of the adolescent must include opportunities for satisfaction and accomplishment. He should feel that there are some things which he can do better than others can. Satisfaction with one's own development helps to build the right kind of attitudes toward life.

Mental, social, emotional, and physical development must all be considered if we are to view an individual's growth process.

The process of growing up has unity.

The teacher should not apply repression and punishment to the critical attitude that usually accompanies this period of growing independence.

For adolescents, it is a period of conflict in more than one way, but this is a fortunate aspect of natural development.

School should help to alleviate every adolescent behavior problem.

In order to help youth with their daily problems, teachers of the secondary school must know youth. They must be familiar with the nature of adolescents' whims, fancies, worries, fears, and hopes. Behavior problems of pupils have a relationship to every phase of school life. Teaching that permits shy, quiet youngsters to isolate themselves from the rest of the group does them irreparable harm. Mental hygiene has such a direct bearing on progress that every undergraduate student ought to have a good understanding of this field before he goes out to teach.

The motor type of learning is initiated by some encouragement from the teacher.

Writing, singing, and dancing are typical examples of ability based on motor activity. The precept of the processes involved in this skill is developed by demonstrations, graphic productions on the blackboard, and verbal explanations. Some skills require little exertion and little attention during practice.

Memorizing should be the fixation of ideas after these ideas have been mastered.

Memorizing is an important form of learning used frequently in secondary schools. Before asking pupils to memorize, build up a background of meaning in which the materials to be memorized can take root, grow, and hold fast. The background, of course, cannot be developed to the same degree with all materials, because some materials admit strong associations and meanings, while others have feeble, background-producing possibilities.[1]

Many teachers seem to think that the recitation of word symbols is the real test of accomplishment, whereas this reiteration is usually an echo of sounds from hollow places. Reiteration is too often only veneer, deceiving the teacher and pupils alike as to the knotty, cross-grained, unseasoned, and cheap wood beneath. The shabby cloak of rote memory must not be worn and assumed to be a real garment. So many definitions, theories, and rules, reduced to prompt mental responses by hard and

---

1. Butler, Frank A., *The Improvements of Teaching in Secondary Schools* (Chicago: The University of Chicago Press, 1954), p. 92.

laborious memorizing, could be almost as well-worded by the pull of a meaningful background, to say nothing of the immeasurable better learning and retention.[1]   A *background, is an essential activity in memorizing materials.   The act of memorizing will be quite easy and permanent if the background preceding memorization has been developed.*

Learning should be unitary, not fragmentary.

Unitary learning implies that what is to be learned is larger and more involved than a few scattered fragments.   Unitary learning is the combining of one part with another part until a whole emerges.   It becomes purposeful in terms of cause and effect relationships, functions, and understandings.

Unity is dependent upon degree of understanding and proper guidance of learning.   Unity implies wider and deeper meanings, and includes broader interpretations and applications.   Unitary learning is relative; the dimensions of unity will vary with the learners involved and with the objectives under consideration.[2]

Good teaching, as contrasted with poor teaching, is not necessarily the doing of entirely different things, but the doing of the same things in fundamentally different ways.

Directing study is the giving the right kind and proper amount of assistance so that pupils can proceed effectively on their own powers.   It is necessary in creating a proper mental attitude to embark upon a radical change in teaching procedures.   Learning and teaching cannot be considered separately.

The kind of directing can be determined only by knowning the capacities of pupils and the activities needed in a particular learning situation.

The assignment affords a very opportune time to bring forward simultaneously the aims and the most appropriate types of learning.

In every assignment there is presented the possibility to organize and unify the learning from day-to-day, and to call attention to relationships that gradually culminate in a skill, idea,

1. *Ibid.,* p. 93.
2. *Ibid.,* pp. 94-105.

concept, attitude, or ideal.

The assignment, if properly developed, creates mind-set through a gripping approach, gives the objectives, suggests methods, and provides study and work materials.

The questioning procedure or some form of direct teaching develops viewpoints, ideas, and insights which are difficult or impossible for pupils to get without the teacher's guidance and direction.

The assignment, in summary, affords an excellent opportunity for the teacher to utilize a portion of her time to the best advantage. The setting forth of aims, arousing a desire to study, selecting the right processes and procedures to be used during study, and the promotion of unity while learning is in progress are significant possibilities. They can be incorporated into any assignement.[1]

Good teaching methods include provision of learning experiences especially measured to the individual students.

Homework — in the sense of uniform, regular (daily) assignments to do after school hours is generally of little value in high school. A much better provision is a broader type of assignment which provides a variety of activities suited to the needs of individual learners. Any homework is worth doing right, and the teacher is obliged to give directions that are clearly understood.

The kind of homework given, and the kind of studying done, are influenced by the kinds of examinations students are expected to pass.

If tests stress merely the recall of facts rather than the power to use information, students tend to focus their attention on details. If tests call for problem-solving and the ability to use facts, students are more likely to read, and to draw conclusions.

The kind of studying done also depends a great deal on the nature of the assignment.

Exercises that can be done mechanically encourage copying,

1. Butler, *The Improvement of Teaching..., op. cit.,* p. 189.

while an assignment that calls for initiative, imagination, and individual effort rules out copying, and challenges the student to work effectively.

Ideally, parents help the child by pointing out principles involved, giving illustrations of them, and making suggestions for the pupil's own study.

Any decision regarding homework should take into account many factors: home conditions, the amount of homework given, its relation to the time for study at school, and the stimulating quality of the curriculum which may lead to study activity at home.

The Elements of Effective Learning

Learning Situation. The learning situation is the environment in which learning occurs—the classroom, library, playground, auditorium, gymnasium, or other school facility. The situation includes the learner and other people as well as physical objects, also the intangible drives within the learner and his relations with others which stimulate learning.

Motives. All individuals have several basic drives, needs, and interests which constitute motives. Certain primary needs which individuals have in common, such as hunger, are modified by experience and social acceptance. Many secondary or acquired motives arise from an individual's experience.

Goals. Within the learning situation, there are incentives to seek goals related to the learner's basic motives or problems. Identification of the goal is the problem clarification step.

Goal-Seeking Activity. When the learner becomes aware of an incentive toward a goal he finds desirable, he may be considered to be stimulated to goal-seeking activity—that is, his awareness of the desirability of approval from other means. At first, his behavior may be irrelevant, confused, and inefficient.

Mental Processes. Experience which changes behavior, that is, results in learning, is characterized by certain mental processes we may further identify as *differentiation, efficiency, integration* and *generalization.* Behavior becomes differentiated when the learner is able to distinguish between the success of different activities in goal attainment; when he realizes that courtesy brings smiles and loud talk does not, he has attained a degree of differentiation. When he practices various courtesies until they become more typical of his behavior than discourtesies, he has acquired some efficiency in this particular learning. When he is able to attach particular relations between the responses of individuals to specific courtesies, he is developing some integration of the whole idea. His conclusions regarding when and with whom what courtesies to use represent his generalization of the learning. These mental processes represent ultimate goals of effective learning, and are important considerations in teaching methods.[1]

Resources for Teaching and Learning

Since textbooks constitute an important material resource in the curriculum, careful selection becomes vitally important.

There are many supplementary teaching tools which help determine the effectiveness of teaching. The most effective classroom instruction makes full use of all the teaching tools that can contribute to better learning. The skillful use of all materials in their rightful place leads to better learning.

It should be remembered that the textbook, important as it is, does not constitute all there is to schooling. The teacher is of far greater importance.

Studies of modern textbooks indicate that they are more profusely illustrated, have much more color, are built around problem areas to a much greater extent than the older ones. However, there is much room for improvement.

Textbooks have been called the child's other teacher. They should not be neglected by parents and workers for schools. Systems for selection of textbooks have changed considerably over the years. Some publishers have prepared science units in pamphlet form for use in the classroom, in addition to using magazines, commercial pamphlets, and government bulletins in science courses. All these have great value in motivating students and supplementing the textbook.

---

1. Alexander, William M., and Halverson, Paul M., *Effective Teaching in Secondary Schools* (New York: Rinehart & Company, Inc., 1956), pp. 46-47.

Knowledge of facts, skills, and understandings is important as they are combined into actual behavior.

The facts, skills, and understandings contribute the materials for clear thinking. The child must be able to distinguish between fact and opinion, between the important and the unimportant. Every child in good modern schools is working toward these goals. The modern teacher encourages children to use the meaning of connected discourse to recognize particular words. The modern teacher and the textbook writer have many types of information which enables them to be more effective in selecting and emphasizing the most useful, and avoiding futile instruction in less useful or misleading rules, conventions, and procedures.

A better learning situation is one in which information from various subjects is drawn as needed to solve problems.

The program of studies in a secondary school should provide both common learnings for all pupils as a part of their general education and varied experiences to develop special interests and activities. These experiences should be common to all pupils, those who go on to college and those who do not. These common experiences should be suited to the maturity of the pupils.

The school needs to consider the number of courses concerned with problems of home and family living. Uniformity of school teaching will not develop individuality. Any tasks pupils are asked to perform must be achievable in order to be integrating. Pupils in secondary schools ought to work on tasks in which they can succeed, the accomplishment of which will contribute to their security.

Where the student can make use of his talents and interests in contributing to the group, his experiences will strengthen his confidence in himself.

If students are to have the most effective learning experiences, they should be able to participate in setting their own goals, in planning with the teacher the activities to achieve those goals.

Cooperative study helps to solve the problem of motivation because pupils are working on their purposes.

The classroom in the secondary school will be more in the nature of a workshop in the broad sense, where the teacher and pupils work in at atmosphere of respect and understanding.

The secondary school should give many opportunites for investigation of different points of view; cooperative investigation will create opportunities for action.

The careful planning of a piece of work, carrying through the plan together, and stopping to see what progress is being made is the best practice.

Scientific inquiry promotes weighing of information, suspending judgment, using many sources of data, reasoning from facts, and arriving at sound conclusions. Experiences in satisfaction, security, and self-respect do not recognize any subject boundaries. In the classes of teachers who understand the learning process and have set up ability in scientific inquiry as a definite goal for their pupils, there are groups working on different aspects of problems. Pupils use library sources to gather data, interview people to get information, and read from a number of other sources to get further information. The common learnings in forward-looking secondary schools in the hands of sympathetic teachers include opportunities to be creative. A permissive atmosphere gives the pupil a sense of security and a desire to explore.

When teachers are conscious of the need for development of self on the part of each pupil, they use materials that are suited to varied abilities and interests. Teachers can follow the newspapers, magazines, movies, and radio for opportunities to bring the subjects up-to-date.

Work in specialized areas should give pupils a feeling that they are a definite part of the learning process.

Youth should have experiences with tasks in which they can succeed, experiences with challenging problems for investigation. During this period of formal education, youth should have an opportunity to discover their genuine interests. There should be no barriers to youth who have a keen desire to invent. Exploration of interests also lays the basis for the selection of an occupation.

Vocational education at the secondary school level should prepare for broad fields of occupations.

As a part of education in the secondary school, it is a responsibility to provide the necessary work experience. In developing vocational education, the school needs to survey community needs and employment conditions. Employment requires little pre-employment training of a specific nature. Some phases of industrial arts, home economics, and agriculture in junior high school years are commonly referred to as prevocational training, while the community provides the laboratory for actual work experience. A survey of the community, in which the school participates, can reveal how adequate is the education for vocations offered by the school.

Extra-class (Extra-curricular) Experiences

The major function of extra-class activities is to provide opportunities for students to learn and practice a variety of skills and personal-social understandings.

Extra-class activities are only part of the curriculum and should never be regarded as all, or even most of it. Excessive enthusiasm for extra-class activities sometimes leads to statements that every student should take part in them. The activity period should not be written off as a liability, for it serves in some cases as the only effective solution of still another problem, that of providing the time for activities to take place. The activitiy period is often combined with the home room and is used some days for home room business, other days for activities, with certain days designated for clubs, student council meetings, etc.

On club days, the students who do not belong to clubs stay in the home room to study or go to the library. The activities depend to a large extent on the spontaneity of student initiative and control, but there is still a need for faculty sponsorship. Faculty sponsorship, however, means faculty assignments. This becomes the third major administrative problem in extra-class activities, joining the first two in determining the limits of student participation and the finding of time in the daily schedule. Teachers who sponsor activities, then, will have more work than those who do not. There are three possible ways of resolving this awkward state of affairs: (1) to assign other extra duties of some kind to teachers who do not sponsor activities; (2) to provide extra pay for the activity sponsors; and (3) to reduce the classroom teaching loads of the activity sponsors.

While the major purpose of extra-class activities is to foster personal-social development, it is by no means the only purpose. Many activities contribute to the furthering of academic understandings and skills. Extra-class activities also offer another means of vocational exploration and guidance. Since lifelong interests may be formed in activities as well as in classroom studies, the area of leisure-time use is served as well. Extra-class activities, therefore, may have many purposes, some of which are also served by classroom studies.[1]

The program of extra-class activities should be broad and varied.

In extra-class activities, there is much more freedom for pupils to plan and carry on various projects. These activities provide desirable learning experiences for pupils. The pupil with poor speech habits or little musical talent should have the opportunity to achieve growth in the areas in which he is interested.

Extra-class activities help pupils acquire certain personal qualities, explore various interests, talents, and abilities. The principal and faculty should plan the entire program of extra-class activities for the school, having pupils participate insofar as their time and ability permit. All groups who are in any way concerned with extra-class activities should participate in evaluating them.

Extra-class activities provide just as important learning experiences as the classroom instructional program. They should be carried on largely during school hours. Pupils' clubs are a significant part of the extra-class program. One characteristic of

1. Krug, Edward A., *The Secondary School Curriculum*, (New York: Harper & Brothers, 1960), pp. 527-532.

club activities is the attempt to meet the interests of all students. The participation of pupils in the administration of the school is most commonly provided through the organization of a student council, which should be given considerable responsibility for school discipline.

The pupil publications in the secondary schools are the school paper, yearbook, magazine, and pupil handbook. The handbook is prepared by the faculty or principal to help orient new students to the school (as an administrative device).

The effectiveness of social activities depends to a large extent on the manner in which they are planned and carried on.

Music activities in some schools have been incorporated into the instructional program, but more often they are offered on an extra-class basis. Such instruction is essential if pupils are to have the help they need to develop their individual talents.

Dramatic activities in high school are too few to give more than a very limited group of pupils opportunities to participate.

Activities designed to prepare students for responsibilities of leadership.

Those activities include control of pupil elections, provide safety patrols on streets adjoining the school, control pupil conduct in the cafeteria, and make policies for extra-class activities. The council, which consists of twenty members representing various classes, determines policies in those activities of direct concern to pupils, plans and finances assembly programs; and sponsors annual, or semi-annual scholarships. The student court, whose sessions are open to the student body, is the only student group that imposes penalties. These include depriving the offender of school privileges; the pupil's parents are informed of any penalty imposed by the court; and placing him in the custody of a member of the advisory board. Usually the student council is the legislative body which formulates policies and makes regulations. The election is planned and conducted according to regulations prescribed by the council. Each pupil organization prepare a budget which is submitted to the council for approval. The council then prepares a composite budget for all activities.[1] The daily schedule of the school should be analyzed to see if additional time can be made available for pupil activities.

Study indicates that extra-curricular student activities most nearly related to civic, literary, religious, and political activities engaged in adult life have the greatest value.

The rapid shift in educational thinking was the major factor in accepting extra-curricular activities into the school. The *purposes* of student extra-curricular activities, in general, are now merged with the larger aims and processes of modern education.

The participation of immature students in the governmental activities of the school is utilized as an educative device.

The educational process assumes the gradual development of learning skills on the part of the pupil under the careful guidance of the teacher. Student government is to be thought of as student-participation in government. The student working together with the school staff develops his understanding and skills in setting up the rules that should govern the school community. The *student council*, as one of the forms of student activities, is usually thought of as the agency through which the student body participates in the government of the school.

Work experience for specific job training is a feature of high school vocational programs.

The general values of work experience are applicable to many students, but this does not justify required work experience, which is sometimes advocated by enthusiasts, although not practiced in the schools. Many high school students have paid part-time jobs. These do not become school-related work experience unless the school definitely relates the work to the attainment of instructional purposes. Such purposes include specific job training, vocational exploration, the development of personal qualities, and the application and further learning

1. National Association of Student Councils, *Student Councils Handbook* (Washington, D.C.: National Association of Secondary School Principals, 1949).

of the instructional fields. Those who are low or below average
in academic ability may also profit from the general vocational
values of work experience.[1]

Activity programs must supplement regular class programs.

Every subject field has implications for activity programs which
can supplement the classroom experience in these areas. Each
teacher can introduce elements of the activity program into the
classroom. The extra-class program must be well organized
and properly administered. In any phase of the curriculum, the
teacher is one of the major factors in the extra-class program.
Therefore, sponsorship of an activity should be considered in
the total work load of the teacher. Some activities can and should
be scheduled outside the regular school hours. One of the major
contributions of the extra-class program is the provision of opportunities for the child who can go far beyond the work that is
offered in the classroom.

School publications go far beyond classroom activities. They
offer a more specialized experience for students with ability and
interest in the journalistic phases.

*Classroom instruction should be enriched and extended by extra-
curricular (co-curricular) activities in which students extend and
test their experiences.*

"Extra-curriculum" or "co-curriculum" can be defined as that
part of the curriculum which is not included in pupils' regular
courses and which does not carry credit for graduation.

The *aims* of the extra-curricular program are the same as those
of the curriculum, and they contribute to these aims by (1) rein-
forcing classroom learning; (2) supplementing formal studies;
(3) aiding total life adjustment; (4) integrating learning; and
(5) democratizing school.[2]

Although the extra-curricular program does foster all the
educational goals, certain goals seem to be particularly congenial
to it:

1. To help pupils develop qualities of leadership, group cooperation, and other qualities essential to effective demo-

---

1. Krug, *op. cit.,* pp. 534-536.
2. Frederick, Robert W., *The Third Curriculum* (New York: Appleton-Century-
Crofts, Inc., 1959), p. 55.

cratic living.
2. To help pupils acquire certain personal and character qualities, such as self-confidence, poise, initiative, resourcefulness, courtesy, and self-control.
3. To help pupils explore various interests, talents, and abilities in a manner which would be difficult in the usual classroom program.
4. To assist pupils to be active and creative, and to gain the satisfaction that comes from accomplishing things that to them are interesting and worthwhile.
5. To give pupils an opportunity to apply many of the fundamental skills and much of the knowledge which they acquire in other ways in the classroom program.[1]

School service projects are obviously closely related to work experience as a general category in the curriculum.

Such projects may be legitimately included in the school program at all times. Among possible projects along these lines are school cleanup campaigns, paper and scrap drives, preparation of vacant and available land for playgrounds or athletic fields, community beautification, etc. Such projects are identified as distinctive features of a high school curriculum.

The in-service activities are among most important steps toward greater professional competence.

There will be some professional activities in which the teacher will be expected to engage—building meetings, departmental meetings, supervisory conferences, system-wide meetings to discuss matters of policy and curriculum.

The in-service activities are opportunities for the teacher to work with colleagues on problems of mutual concern, to learn about educational philosophies and special aspects of the program in his school.

Many school systems sponsor workshops and institutes in which teachers are given opportunities to work on specific instructional problems under expert leadership. The teacher should be involved in sufficient activities to feel part of his school system and to

1. Anderson, Vernon E., and Gruhn, W. T., *Principles and Practices of Secondary Education* (New York: The Ronald Press Company, 1962), p. 280.

become well acquainted with his colleagues. It will be important for him to come with problems and questions and with an alert interest in the topic being studied. The teacher will gain much more from meetings where he and his colleagues are working on problems of mutual concern. In most schools, changes are made only after thorough discussion and planning. The teacher must be willing and patient to work through the established channels for decision-making.

Professional organizations represent another important means of promoting professional growth. They provide an opportunity to work with colleagues on professional problems. They help to bring the teacher in contact with new developments in the profession through the research and the publications which they sponsor and with those persons giving significant professional leadership.

The extra-curricular program furnishes excellent opportunities for learning experiences to fit the needs of all individuals.

Extra-curricular activities help satisfy the need that students have for independent thinking, for independent action, for belonging, and for achieving. In the school they can provide encouragement and help to students interested in fields beyond the usual scope of the curriculum. They deserve the same careful planning and supervision as any other curricular activities. The following principles should be held paramount:

1. The co-curricular (extra-curricular) program should be planned so as to assure its fullest contribution to the educational aims of the school.
2. Each activity should be guided by a competent and sympathetic member of the faculty.
3. Every pupil should have ample opportunity to participate in the program. The school should support enough different activities to permit each pupil to participate in congenial activities.
4. Co-curricular activities should be recognized by inclusion in the school schedule. Each activity should be selected at a time that would allow each interested pupil to participate.

5. Participation in co-curricular activities should be based on democratic principles. No pupil should be barred from any activity or office because of financial or social consideration.
6. Pupils should be given adequate opportunity to develop leadership qualities. These can best be developed by allowing pupils to hold offices of responsibility and trust under guidance.
7. Co-curricular activities should reinforce and supplement curricular activities by utilizing approaches and materials not possible in regular classroom and furthering learnings additional to those fostered in regular curricular activities. They should not, however, repeat classroom activities.
8. The co-curricular activities should be so administered as to avoid the development of false ideas and attitudes and the setting up of false or inadequate value systems.
9. The activities should be pupil-centered and , as far as feasible, student-planned and directed. All activities included in the curriculum should reflect pupil interests, purposes, and needs.
10. The co-curriculum should be flexible. It should be easy to add new activities when desirable and to drop old activities when they have outlived their usefulness.
11. The co-curriculum should be adequately financed. Because it is a real part of the curriculum, funds should be provided by the School Board. No matter where the funds come from, however, measures for adequate fiscal supervision and control should be maintained.
12. The co-curricular activities should be subjected to continuous evaluation and revaluation. As a consequence of this evaluative process the best co-curricular programs will probably be in a continual state of revision.[1]

Many college-bound students are pointing toward professional schools in their higher education.

The vocational objectives, furthermore, need not necessarily be identified with specific vocational training and are never to be exclusively identified with preparation for the industrial trades. Both of these are essential parts of the curriculum for some students, but they do not even begin to define the range

1. Clark, Leonard H.; Klein, R.L.; and Burks, J.B.; *The American Secondary School Curriculum* (New York: The Macmillan Company, 1965), pp. 384-385.

of activities related to the occupational objective in the secondary school.

Occupational competence as an objective in the secondary school may be broken down into the following specific functions or objectives:

1. To provide vocational guidance for all students.
2. To help every student develop skills and understanding relevant to success in many occupational fields.
3. To help every student develop the personal qualities generally needed in work relationships.
4. To provide some students with essential preparation for advanced professional study.
5. To provide to some students under some circumstances specific training in the skills and techniques of particular occupations.

Group instruction in various classroom studies can provide accurate information about job trends and opportunities.[1]

SUMMARY

The chapter includes the principles—statements which may act as guides in organizing and in improving secondary schools. They are not rules or laws which must be rigidly followed, but since they represent the best educational thinking, based on facts and investigations, they should be followed as far as circumstances permit.

The fundamental consideration in the high school curriculum is to remember that high school exists both to transmit culture and to foster individual development in various aspects of living objectives. Some work in high school is directed toward specialized preparation for jobs, although highly specialized education for this purpose is primarily the responsibility of the college, university or vocational school.

In this chapter we have come to see that extra-class activities have a significant contribution to make in the educational growth of the child.

1. Krug, *op. cit.*, pp. 118-120.

FOR FURTHER STUDY

Alexander, W.M. and P.M. Halverson, *Effective Teaching in Secondary Schools.* New York: Rinehart & Company, Inc., 1956.

Anderson, V.E. and W.T. Gruhn, *Principles and Practices of Secondary Education.* New York: The Ronald Press Company, 1962.

Anderson, R.H. *Teaching in a World of Change.* New York: Harcourt, Brace and World, Inc., 1966.

Billett, R.O., *Fundamentals of Secondary—School Teaching.* Cambridge: The Riverside Press, 1940.

Bode, B.H., *How We Learn.* Boston: D.C. Heath and Co., 1940.

Bottrell, H.R. *Teaching Tools.* Pittsburgh: The Boxwood Press, 1957.

Burton, W.H., *The Guidance of Learning Activities.* New York: Appleton-Century-Crofts, Inc., 1944.

Butler, F.A., *The Improvement of Teaching in Secondary Schools.* Chicago: The University of Chicago Press, 1954.

Callahan, S.G., *Successful Teaching in Secondary Schools.* Chicago: Scott, Foresman & Company, 1966.

Clark, L.H., R.L. Klein, and J.B. Burks, *The American Secondary School Curriculum.* New York: The Macmillan Company, 1965.

Colman, J.E., *The Master Teachers and the Art of Teaching.* New York: Pitman Publishing Co., 1967.

Eye, G.G. and L.A. Netzer, *Supervision of Instruction.* New York: Harper and Row, Publishers, 1965.

Frederick, R.W., *The Third Curriculum.* New York: Appleton-Century Crofts, Inc., 1959.

French, Will and Associates, *Behavioral Goals of General Education in High School.* New York: Russell Sage Foundation, 1957.

Garrett, H.E., *The Art of Good Teaching.* New York: David McKay Co., Inc. 1964.

Krug, E.A., *The Secondary School Curriculum.* New York: Harper & Brothers, 1960.

Lueck, W.R., *Effective Secondary Education.* Minneapolis, Minn.: Burgess Publishing Co., 1966.

Maslow, A.H., *Motivation and Personality.* New York: Harper and Brothers, 1954.

Miller, Richard, *Perspectives on Educational Change.* New York: Appleton-Century-Crofts, Inc., 1967.

Mills, H.H., and H.R. Douglass, *Teaching in High School.* New York: The Ronald Press Company, 1957.

National Association of Student Councils, *Student Councils Handbook.* Washington, D.C.; National Association of Secondary School Principals, 1949.

Noar, Gertrude, *Freedom to Live and Learn.* Philadelphia: Franklin Publishing Co., 1948.

Oliva, P.F. and R.A. Scrafford, *Teaching in a Modern Secondary School.* Columbus, Ohio: Charles E. Merrill Books, Inc., 1965.

Plath, K.R., *Schools within Schools.* New York: Bureau of Pubns., Teachers College, Columbia University, 1965.

Rothney, John, *The High School Student: A Book of Cases.* New York: Dryden Press, 1953.

Stone, J.C. and F.W. Schneider, *Commitment to Teaching.* New York: Crowell Collier, Inc., 1965.

Strang, Ruth, *Reporting to Parents.* New York: Bureau of Publications, Teachers College, Columbia University, 1947.

——————, *Guided Study and Homework.* From the NEA Journal, October, 1955.

Tevens, A.C., *Techniques for Handling Problem Parents.* Englewood Cliffs, N.J.: Prentice-Hall, Inc., 1966.

Yaeger, W.A., *School Community Relations.* New York: Dryden Press, 1951.

Young, M.D., *Innovation and Research in Education.* London: Routledge & K. Paul, 1965.

CHAPTER V

THE GROUPING OF CHILDREN

The Term "Adjustment"

The term "adjustment" does not necessarily imply passive or blind conformity to the group. It means rather the achievement of satisfactory social relationships without abandoning individuality or personal standards.

Such adjustment is a necessity to everyone. Students who achieve such adjustment easily are able to devote more of their emotional and mental effort to intellectual achievement in school work.

The social characteristics of adolescence are of great importance to the educator. Even the most severe advocate of intellectual development realizes that the attainment of this goal by individual students is often fostered or hampered by degrees of social acceptance or adjustment.[1]

In individualizing instructional activities, it is particularly important that flexible methods of teaching be employed.

The means of achieving flexibility in teaching methods is to use a sufficient variety of instructional material to reach all students. The teacher should be well-informed concerning the various abilities, needs, and interests of pupils. He should explore every possible source of instructional materials in order to gather a variety which will provide something for every pupil's ability and interests. The examinations and tests should be studied for the unit in the light of the individual differences among the students.

Good teaching must consider the variations among students

1. Krug, Edward A., *The Secondary School Curriculum* (New York: Harper & Brothers, 1960), p. 49.

and provide for them in some manner.

The difference should be dealt with in such a way that students will progress in accordance with their capacities to learn. The work of a teacher must be so directed that the real purpose of the school will be realized. If the differences pertained only to the intellect, the problem would be difficult enough, but there are so many additional traits which enter into the problem that the solution becomes perplexing.

The progress of a pupil should be determined by his capacity to master the materials. He may finish a year's work in a few months, or in one, two or more years. When he has finished the unit or division of work under consideration, he moves on to the next unit or division. At the basis of such *individual instruction* is a standard that each pupil must reach; and, once a pupil reaches the standard, he proceeds to the next assignment. The essence of the plan is *acceleration.*

The other solution is to keep the class together, but to provide for the differences by enrichment, that is, to give more and more different materials so that the brighter or more able pupils learn more but do not separate from the class. The idea of providing projects so that each member can work up to his capacity doing more, or more difficult projects. If the general capacities of the pupils in a particular school, or of those pupils in a particular grade, are determined, and then the pupils are placed into groups so that each group has pupils of nearly the same capacities, such grouping is known as *ability* or *homogeneous grouping.*

The pupils are divided into three groups: the high, the average, and the low. In reality, there can never be a group in which every pupil has the same amount and kind of talent as every other member in the group, and the members in a group can never be equally endowed with the same capacities to learn.

If pupils are found to be slow in their learning, there must be causes for the slowness.

The causes must be a lack in those powers which produce rapidity and depth in learning; in other words, the powers of ready insight, abstract reasoning, strong retention, analytical adeptness, and quick recognition are not sufficiently developed. Under these circumstances the call into action must be employed. The teaching should be motivated. Backgrounds should be built up so that words connect with realities. Repetition will be necessary to instill many of the habits, skills, and ideas, and more physical activity should be woven into the classroom learning, because abstract book learning soon becomes monotonous to these pupils.

Difference in "Mental Age"

The average child reaches a "mental age" of twelve at the same time he reaches the chronological age of twelve. But intelligence tests show that a substantial number of children reach the mental age of twelve at the age of ten, or of fifteen. Any school system must be based on a regular progression of grades, from first grade right on up through high school and college. The school grades should be based on *mental* rather than chronological age. The extra-curricular activities should be carried on by groups of children of the same chronological age.

Grouping does not guarantee that all pupils in a certain group are equal in capacity to learn.

There are individuals who are good in one subject and relatively poor in another. Bright pupils are keen observers; they profit from experience. These pupils are quick in their thinking and analyzing; their learning is rapid and retention is strong. These pupils can study independently.

An *average-ability* group of pupils in one school is not exactly the same as an average group of pupils in another school.

Individual instruction should have for its main purpose the maximum development of each individual according to his capacities.

Development must be thought of in terms of broader growth of learning. Such kind of teaching aims to provide particular conditions so that pupils can progress at their own rate by following a definite set of activities leading to specified standards.

Probably the greatest contribution of the plan is the idea of planning exercises so that pupils can, by following directions, work at their own rate until certain prescribed standards have been reached. Independent study must include the ability to evaluate, to organize, to verify, and to come to some solid conclusions.

The essence of learning by projects should be found within the learner.

Such kind of learning can be called a project when a pupil considers an aim so vital and worthwhile that he is willing to work under his own power and under natural and free conditions.

Learning by project is just another way that might secure from pupils a better attitude, a kindlier feeling, a greater expediture of effort, all for the purpose of securing more efficient learning.

In mixed classes are found pupils who possess capacities ranging from the highest to the lowest.

In such classes the pupils will remain together, that is, they will begin the course together and complete it at the same time; there will be no acceleration; each pupil will be studying the same *unit* or *division* of subject matter, and will pass on to the next phase of the work with all the others in the class. *Unitary learning,* however, implies that what is to be learned is larger and more involved than a few scattered fragments. It means that a skill, concept, appreciation, understanding, or insight has been fully attained. The learning continues until the accomplishment has been realized. The learning is partial, incomplete, and fragmentary.

To reach the standard, with the capacities varying widely, some pupils must exert themselves fully. The quantity and quality of the work must be regulated so that the achievement of all pupils will be in keeping with their capacities to achieve.

The unit assignment covers a field of work requiring several weeks' study before it is completed. The exercises for more able pupils are themes, character sketches, dramatizations, oral reports, biographies, readings, or other suitable projects. These assignments should be constructed in accordance with fundamental principles of learning. The basic ideas should be included in the minimum requirement demand demonstration, experimentation, emotional learning, sensory-experience learning, and problem-solving. All of these should be found in the learning of pupils who can complete only the minumum. It is wise to make assignments that throw as much responsibility upon pupils as can be done. But, there should be enough direction so that pupils will study effectively. A careful introduction of the pupils to some of the elementary phases of the procedure would be desirable at first; and then, after the pupils learn to adjust themselves to the new learning situations and the teacher becomes more confident of the ability of groups, more involved parts of the procedure can be introduced gradually.

The educational program and activities for exceptional pupils should be a part of the high school program for the usual pupils.

The mentally retarded pupils should have the opportunity to share with the rest of the student body in recreational activities, physical education and the use of the lunchroom. For academic instruction, they will need special class instruction from an especially trained teacher.

To provide success experiences, the school must take the student where he is, and advance him at a speed which will insure optimal growth in keeping with his potentialities and interests.

A complete diagnostic, treatment, and education program for many handicapped pupils requires the services of personnel from a number of disciplines.[1]

Leader-Member Roles in Group Work

Leadership is a function earned by a person from a group which sees this person as possessing the kinds of skills, facts, attitudes, and understandings necessary to assist the group in achieving its purpose at the time.

This concept argues against a generalized kind of leadership for all times, places, and circumstances. It suggests the sharing

---

1. Dunn, Lloyd M., *Basic Principles of Special Education* "The Exceptional Pupil — A Challenge to Secondary Education," *Bulletin of the National Association of Secondary-School Principals,* vol. 39 (January, 1955), pp. 10-11.

of leadership depending on the situation which a group faces. Situational leadership gives greater recognition and acceptance to individual differences.

Any member of a classroom group should at times be in a position to give facts or opinions pertinent to the solution of the problem.

The fact-giver may draw upon generalizations from his own experience, or he may furnish findings which he has at his disposal from study in preparation for the solution of the problem. Pupils should be able to differentiate between *facts* and *opinions* and be urged to label their contributions as one or the other. This process will lead to greater importance attached by pupils to sources of facts and to the nature of reasons for opinions. Humor, summarization, restatement, and attempted reconciliation of opposing positions can be tried by leader-members interested in preserving the group.

Leadership must be shared for the full effectiveness of the group to develop.

The effectiveness of the group will depend on the degree to which all members are concious of these skills and are responsible for seeing that they are exploited to the fullest.[1]

Special Needs of Learners

Effective classroom organization is one important factor to be considered.

Established practices in providing for individual differences are already operative at two levels, the administrative and the instructional. Administrative procedures include the following: comprehensive programs of student activities, elective subjects, special and remedial classes, promotional policies (acceleration of brighter students), homogeneous grouping, and counselling on the basis of educational and vocational goals.

Experts disagree about grouping yougsters according to ability.

Opponents of "ability grouping" point out that it produces

1. Alexander and P.M.H., *Effective Teaching...*, *op. cit.*, pp. 190-198.

relatively small change in the range of individual differences, and that many differences in academic achievement continue. On the other hand, this method helps to the classroom teacher.

Subgrouping within a class provides flexibility and ease in making changes according to the purposes of the teacher and students. Some subgrouping plans are organized for direct instruction in a specific skill, such as reading. Others are organized on the basis of children's interest, such as committees in social studies, science or library activities. There are many opportunities for student grouping simply by organizing the curriculum in terms of vocational aims. The commercial students are separated from the college preparatory; the future industrial workers are separated from the general non-college academic students. And there are distinctions among the curriculums. Class organization should be flexible so that the teacher can modify the grouping to meet new needs or situations.

The social climate of the classroom is important in developing effective control. The teacher's personal attitudes influence the emotional and social climate of the classroom. The author-itarian methods of control induce pupils' attitudes of self-concern and of competition with others.

Subgroups of gifted children can do advance study, work on special projects, or explore common interests.

The teachers should be alerted to the desirability of special assignments for the gifted in their classes and that they should be instructed by school supervisors and principals in the kinds of enrichment that are possible. There are several ways of giving instruction and guidance to gifted pupils in regular classes. Such pupils are identified and taken out of their regular classes for special educational experiences, or the able learners spend half the day in regular classes with pupils of their own age, where they have an opportunity to work together in music, art, and physical education. During the rest of the day, the intellec-tually superior are grouped together in a workshop type program, where they not only work on problems and projects at their own pace but also get instruction in the school subjects.

The schools which are particularly geared for pupils with

special gifts or talents provide specially qualified teachers and conditions in which the pupils are highly stimulated. Under favorable conditions, a program that *partially* segregates the gifted seems most desirable. Under very poor conditions, special classes or even special schools may be necessary to help gifted children develop their potentialities.

Most educators stress the desirability of offering gifted pupils broad and diversified educational opportunities.

Some recommend widespread adoption of acceleration, and others endorse acceleration only as a temporary expedient and particular solution of the problem. An excellent summary of studies in this field has recently been written by D.A. Worcester who stresses these values of acceleration:

1. First of all, acceleration recognizes the facts of life. Children differ from each other markedly. Some develop much more rapidly that the others. Usually those of greater academic potentialities are also more mature socially and emotionally.

2. Failure to accelerate involves dangers. There is evidence to show that gifted children who are held back with those of their C.A. (chronological age) are more likely to develop behavior and personality problems than are those who are accelerated. There is danger, also, of promoting lazy and careless work habits among those who are educationally beyond their classmates but who are held back with them.[1]

This writer advocates early entrance, with a provision for later acceleration for those who were not identified for early entrance and for those whose capabilities have become so developed that they are no longer working efficiently in their present group. The senior high school freshman college years seem to offer one of the best possiblities for later acceleration.

Those in favor of making special provisions for the gifted point to the need of better programs for locating talented students. Such a program would make use of intelligence tests, academic and non-academic aptitude tests, and would,

---

1. Worcester, Dean A., *The Education of Children of Above-average Mentality* (Lincoln: University of Nebraska Press, 1956), pp. 33-34.

of course, take into account such factors as personality, interests, and motivation. If the school were large enough, sections of all classes in the fields of both general and special interest education could be set up. There is no reason why a capable student should not get as thorough an education. – We have to give the average student equal opportunities, but not by sacrificing the best minds. Intellectual ability can be detected by the age of eleven or twelve. We should keep the door open for a longer time. But we should not allow him to waste his time.[1]

The social and physical environment for learning should be ideal.

The social environment influences learning. The disturbance in a classroom is mainly caused by the misconduct of a few pupils which interferes with the work of others. This disturbance is commonly called poor discipline. From the teacher's standpoint, there are two aspects of discipline: 1. the preventive side, and 2. the corrective side. But it is impossible to treat these two aspects as distinct and separate from the complete act of good teaching. The suggestions listed under prevention and correction will be of great value in guiding pupils to gain better standards of conduct.

Suggestions for prevention.

1. Prevention should precede correction whenever possible.
2. The physical conditions of the room may operate to produce disciplinary situations. As far as possible, the teacher should try to make the ventilation, lighting, heating and seating ideal.
3. The lack of dispatch in beginning the class work may lead to disciplinary situations. The class period should begin with vigor and promptness; there should be no delay due to lack of preparation.
4. The lack of dispatch in the conduct of routine matters may lead to disciplinary situations. Supplies should be handled efficiently and in orderly fashion.
5. Idleness is a very common source of disorder. Pupils should be profitably employed during the period.

1. *Ibid,* p. 36.

6. The teacher's position in the room frequently influences her control. The teacher should, as a rule, stand before her class while teaching.
7. The teacher's alertness frequently influences her control. She should see and hear all that takes place; she should give constant attention to pupil responses.
8. Pupil's location frequently determines his chance for making disturbances. Disorderly pupils at the remote ends of the class should be moved closer to the teacher.
9. As a rule, disorder should never be suggested in advance by prescribing rules, punishments, and threats for misdemeanors that have not occurred.
10. Personal qualities, such as cheerfulness, courtesy, friendliness, sympathy, enthusiasm, and fair play, influence the teacher's control.
11. Mannerisms, peculiarities in voice and dress, and poor and careless English may influence the teacher's control. Slang, unpleasant voice, extreme style in dress, personal peculiarities should be remedied in order to increase the teacher's influence over pupils.
12. Lack of knowledge of subject matter on the part of the teacher may lead to the loss of respect for teacher and ultimately to loss of control of the class. There should be no lack of preparation, either daily or general on the part of the teacher, which might lead her pupils to question her knowledge of the subject taught.
13. The subject matter should be applied, connected with pupil's experiences, illustrated, made vital rather than treated as so much to be learned.[1]

Suggestions for correction.

1. The aim of correction should be constructive, not retributive. Correction should strengthen the pupil's self-control, self-direction and sense of responsibility.
2. The intensity of the correction should be suited to the individual. Pupil's motives differ, their temperaments differ, their sensitivities differ; discrimination is therefore required for each pupil.
3. There should be a definite relation between the mis-

---

1. Butler, Frank A., *The Improvement of Teaching in Secondary Schools* (Chicago: The University of Chicago Press, 1954), p. 327.

conduct and the correction. The correction should eliminate the inclination to repeat the act.

4. As a rule, the group should not be punished for the misconduct of the few. This implies that only the offenders should be corrected.

5. Where correction is necessary, it should be made judiciously, without excitement or undue emotions.

6. Private conferences should be usually preceded before major corrective measures. The teacher should talk over the matter with the pupil.

7. If possible, the teacher should administer her own correction. To send all cases to the principal or some other person lessens the effectiveness of the correction and weakens the pupils' regard for the teacher.

8. Correction should be consistent and certain. All pupils should be held to the same conduct.

9. Corporal punishment, if ever employed, should be used sparingly, and as a last resort. This correction should be used for younger children rather than for older pupils.[1]

Physical environment.

A list of physical conditions:

1. The temperature of the room should range from 68° to 70° Fahrenheit; 70° is the maximum.

2. The air should be in motion; drafts, however, should be avoided.

3. The air should be pure, fresh, and clean.

4. The air should be moderately moist rather than dry. A range of humidity from 40-60 per cent is considered the best.

5. The best light is unilateral and from the left.

6. The glass area of the windows should not be less than 15 per cent of the floor area.

7. Blackboards should be so situated that pupils are not required to face the light while looking at them. Boards should be located in walls with windows, especially in walls where boards would be immediately adjoining windows or placed between windows.

8. Window shades should be adjusted to secure the best

1. *Ibid.,* pp. 329-330.

lighting possible. Shades should be adjusted to protect
pupils from too intense brightness of the sun.

9. The teacher should occupy a position in the room such that
pupils are not required to face the light while looking at
her. Facing a light means facing the wall with windows.

10. The room should be neat, clean and attractive.[1]

Small and Large Group Instruction

*The most realistic approach to the initiation of cooperative
group work is devoted to a consideration of ways necessary to
achieve goals.*

Most teachers begin a school year by talking about the total
year's work in terms of goals, subject matter, materials, evaluation, and the like. Seldom, however, is there any attention paid
to ways of working. Any teacher falls short of the potentialities
of cooperative group work if he does not incorporate in his planning some provision for discussion. Sharing the learnings from
varied experiences may create acceptance of various methods.

*Opportunity should be provided for the maximum development
of individual capacities.*

It is necessary to have a clear picture of the differences among
individuals. Talent is wasted if a learner has neither opportunity
nor encouragement to pursue a special interest, whether this
interest is music, art, science, or any other socially valuable
area. No matter what the system of classifying learners, teachers
must be prepared to provide individual and small group experiences to meet individual needs. If all around development is
to result, a student must feel that he can contribute from an
intellectual as well as from a social point of view.

*The lack of opportunity for the individual to express himself
in his unique fashion results in lack of motivation and achievement level.*

Involving learners in setting the goals and objectives of a class

1. *Ibid.,* pp. 325-326.

and in developing the procedures and activities for achieving their purposes have become the basic element in the teaching-learning situation. If group education develops in individuals a lack of initiative, fear of making decisions, the thoughtful teacher should recognize these potential problems and be willing to attack them.

Flexibility in assignments and methods of reporting individual and group progress seems to be indicated.

The premium in the decision-making on sequence of learning activities should be placed on pupil needs and differences, rather than on arbitrary arrangements by the teacher. A group must mature in its ability to reconcile differences in values, opinions, judgements, and decisions. Group members, on seeing division of opinion, should delay voting by asking for more facts, by trying to persuade each other, or by attempting compromise. Out of such activity, mature groups arrive at the point where general agreement is reached. The assumption of responsibility for interim activity is even more a test of class morale. Most of the excuses are subterfuges for lack of interest, failure to understand the meaning and sequence of learning activities, and a general feeling of unrelatedness between pupil's goals and the activities of the class.

Grouping would tend to bring together learners of approximately the same chronological age.

Special talents and interests, and the judgement of teachers might play a part in deciding to which class a learner might be assigned. Students can be grouped for learning on many bases other than age. The drama group or the homeroom may cut across all age and grade levels. Student councils, social functions, athletic activities, and other such projects may well be the concern of all ages and levels of development. Grouping, whether within the class or the school, thus becomes an instrument used to foster learners' growth.

Grouping within the total class must be flexible if learners with similar needs are to be brought together. The flexibility in scheduling makes possible more efficient provision for a variety of activities.

Special groups can be organized on many bases and for many purposes.

Groups can also be organized with regard to need, with each student working in the area in which he realizes he knows the least. A combination of special talent and interest draws a group together. The major contribution of a group activity for some students may be the experience of learning to work cooperatively with others. The most valuable contribution that can be made to a gifted student is to teach him how to pursue his interests independently without direction.

The teachers often fail to use an important device of group generalization, that is, pooling the individual reactions to an educational experience.

The method is group discussion, but the nature of the discussion calls for special skills in weighing sources, in judging conflicting data, and in asking and answering questions. It is the most important skill for individuals and groups to develop, and requires patience and practice from teacher and learners alike. The teacher should prepare participants in the discussion by offering a structure for their remarks.

A small group is the learning group in which the individual interacts with others.[1]

An attempt must be made to establish a warm climate in which students are secure to ask, to propose, and to criticize. The small-group teacher can give students more individual attention. Small-group activities are characterized by a high degree of student participation. Discussion in a small group must be based on teacher-managed objectives. The most effective small group teachers are those who listen to a discussion and know when to straighten out ideas or to suggest different approaches to problem situations. The small group teacher can give students more individual attention.

1. Beggs, David W., *A Practical Application of the Trump Plan* (Englewood Cliffs, N.J.: Prentice-Hall, Inc., 1964), p. 99.

The small-group structure does not guarantee that everyone will be highly involved in group work, but it does provide the opportunity for more students to participate. Each day every student should be given some sense of pride in accomplishment. It has been generally concluded that students will do about what they are expected to do.

The great task of motivating students to want to learn become individualized in the small group.

Small groups allow for meeting differences in ability by grouping pupils according to their level of development into three or four subgroups.

The use of small groups for practice in skill development stems from the elementary school, particularly in the teaching of reading. In this situation, a class is divided into small groups, based on their stage of development. Varied materials are provided suited to varying levels of ability. A teacher must learn how best to share his time with groups, according to the needs of the groups.

In the experience of a class with the use of small groups, evaluation should be made of the activity.

The cumulative effect of evaluation of purposes and procedures is to build on strengths and gradually to eliminate weaknesses in small group procedures. — Small-group operation is only one method of organizing learning experiences. A class which operates on a small-group basis must provide for sharing experiences. The reporting and sharing phase is the culmination phase of small-group work.

The teacher's role in supervision of small-group work.

As the teacher moves among the groups, listening to their deliberations and plans, the teacher may urge on demand a certain procedure, decision, or action. The teacher can be a source of real help. Close contact by the teacher with all groups provides opportunities to observe these developments, to call attention to them, and to raise questions with the group of how to cope with these problems.

The skillful teacher can use class discussion of the report both to help the reporter identify his strengths and weaknesses and to help the other learners compare their own development with whatever standards are stated or implied in the discussion.

Throughout this discussion of learning we have been dealing with learning as an individual matter. The easiest way to teach might be the tutorial method, except for one very important factor in learning, that of group influence on the individual. Individuals can learn better in groups, provided the group is so organized and the teacher's guidance so used that each individual is helped to more effective learning than he could acquire on his own. Groups of learners may help individuals practice skills. Frequent use of such practice situations helps learners acquire a degree of efficiency in their learning. Evaluative procedures may be more adequately planned by several learners trying out their ideas and their conclusions on each other than by one learner.

The nature and purpose of the large-group instruction demands that it be combined with small-group activity and individual or independent study.[1]

The nature of the learning activity determines the group size in which each activity is appropriate. In large groups, content and background information which builds on the learner's previous experience is given. This is done by stimulating lectures, by the systematic use of film strips, recordings and overhead projector. In addition, it is appropriate to test, to give basic assignments, and to employ resource specialists. It saves time to perform these activities daily for one or two hundred students, rather than repeat them five or more times for traditional size groups.

The only defensible motive for large group instruction is that it makes increased learning possibilities available for students. Conferences with other large-group teachers and visits to other schools have some value.[2]

1. *Ibid.*, pp. 114-116.
2. *Ibid.*, pp. 122.

Independent study is distinguished from guided study in that it is done without direct supervision of a teacher.

The teacher is concerned with its motivation and evaluation, however. There are two broad levels of independent study, *teacher-assigned* and *student-assigned.*

Study assumed by the student is the higher level of independent study. Here again the measure must be the student's ability and personal mental characteristics.

Teacher-directed study is determined by the student's understanding of a particular subject. Student-assumed study, on the other hand, is the expression of a particular interest by an individual student. Both levels could not be expected of all students from every teacher. In some areas students want to do more independent study than in others. The quality of both kinds of study is different. Quality is bounded by the learner's ability, his motivation and his responsiveness. The rate of accomplishment is low for the student of low ability. To demand the same level of independent study from all students is to defeat the fundamental goal of individual development.[1]

More planning is necessary in the cooperative problem-solving approach.

There are practical limitations to the amount of time which can be used for this purpose. Too long periods of planning by teacher and group before actual study and activity begin will be frustrating to everyone.

The factor related to the planning and organizing of a group for a learning experience is the differences in quality and quantity of effort among learners and the varieties in kinds of activity.

A learner may not be content always to contribute in the same fashion to the group solution of a problem.

At this point guidance by the teacher and group is important so that *rotation of duties* and responsibilities is an accepted pattern of procedure.

1. *Ibid.,* p. 124.

The potentialities of competition and cooperation are always present and need constant consideration by teachers and learners.

Individual differences in any classroom — social, intellectual, physical, and moral — may be seen in a pupil. These differences are bound to raise acceptances and rejections among the members of the group. The problem for the teacher is to prevent these "rejections" from creating a school atmosphere which is not conductive to good teaching and learning. Cooperation is a basic motivational factor which can be emphasized. Classrooms which do not supply opportunities for youth to plan, act, and evaluate together are neglecting the preparation of pupils for adult activity. The school must supply opportunities for cooperation.

The *study report* is an example of material which in part may be helpful to a teacher in making judgements and adjustments in a pupil's group relations. The case conference is a more fruitful approach to the study of a pupil. The case conference provides the opportunity for sharing opinions and for consensus on constructive measures to help the pupil with his problems. The projective techniques are another cluster of information-gathering devices. The autobiography, the pupils' reactions to pictures, and unfinished stories can be employed by teachers if used with observation. The picture represents an experience which a pupil has had to the extent he may project his own feelings, attitudes, and understandings into the responses he makes to the questions. The sociogram is a technique for studying relations among individuals in groups. A teacher gets information from pupils on their attitudes toward and understandings of other pupils. These judgements may help a teacher understand the tensions which exist in the classroom. The best techniques for getting to know and understand pupils are observation, and extra-curricular participation.

The most frequent provision for individual differences is the grouping of pupils according to their differences within classes.

This grouping is usually on an informal basis, as contrasted with the formal homogeneous grouping between sections. That is, the class works together much of the time as a total group, but the students may be grouped for instruction in such basic skills as reading and spelling. For others, they may be kept in groups according to reading speed and comprehension, but with the pupils moved readily from group to group as their skills improve.

Homogeneous grouping means that pupils, on the basis of some criteria, are placed in different classes for instructional purposes.

The most common one is to group students according to their ability to do school work. Where this plan is employed, pupils are arranged into class groups on the basis of such measures as the intelligence quotient, mental age, and estimates of pupil abilities prepared by the teachers. This plan for homogeneous grouping is easily administered.

A *second* plan for homogeneous grouping is based on the *elective courses* or *curriculums* in which pupils are enrolled; and the *third* plan of homogeneous grouping is the grouping of pupils according to reading ability, quite prevalent in the elementary school. Most of the research on the subject of homogeneous grouping has been concerned with those plans for grouping which are based on measures of pupil ability.

Homogeneous grouping appears to be most effective with pupils who are below average, and least effective with those above average. The most important thing is what teachers do to individualize instruction within the various groups, once they are arranged according to pupil ability levels.[1]

Intellectually Gifted Children

The brilliance of the success possible with the very bright or gifted child has the greatest social importance.

Ordinarily, bright children demonstrate their ability early in their formal education. But sometimes the bright child is not suspected to be as capable as, in fact, he is.

One persistent educational problem with the bright child is that he is able to get by with little work and make acceptable or even above average grades with minimum effort and appli-

1. Gruhn, William T., and Douglass, H.R., *The Modern Junior High School* (New York: The Ronald Press Company, 1956), pp. 210-214.

cation. Escaping real effort may be momentarily satisfying, but it develops poor attitudes and habits.   Many bright students graduate from secondary schools never having learned how to study. As a result they may never get to universities, may apply themselves poorly, may miss out on opportunities for advanced or specialized work.

The schools need more educational discipline in dealing with gifted students, and need to size up superior students early so as not to lose their potential development.

The best studies show, however, that students with high ability are good in almost all subjects.

The terms "fast learners" or "slow learners" merely mean aptitude or lack of aptitude. One must admit, of course, that individuals have greater aptitudes for certain things than for others.

Aggressive Children

The classroom teacher has to bolster up the shy child and slow down the overconfident one.

The aggressive child is often selfish and domineering. He uses bragging and assumes confidence to cope with situations when he is uncertain.

There are also children who exhibit behavior in seemingly random ways. In one situation their lack of sureness may lead them to take one tack, whereas in another situation, they take a different tack. The problem is to reach a better balance. In coping with these children, the classroom teacher has to bolster up the shy child and slow down the overconfident one. This is not to say that all children should be the same, or adjust in the same way. But the overconfident child has to be taught to be more effective by other means than trying to force himself on people. He has to be taught to evaluate the situation better and only then act. The shy child has to learn to make an effort.

The overly confident child generalizes too freely from some

instances of achievement to all opportunities: "I can do it." A disciplined cutting-back is a remedial step in which the teacher can help the child to measure his efforts step-by-step.

Children with Orthopedic Handicaps

The handicapped child generally shows more genuine fear responses than does the normal child. All handicaps carry with them general tendencies toward certain psychological reactions. The teacher can usually find his way easier with this type of student, in the educational process, than he can with many others.

Retarded or Slow-Learning Children

The teacher has to set about exposing these children patiently and consistently to their learning tasks.

The teacher has to recognize that his results will be less, even though his efforts are greater than with other students.

The retarded or slow-learning children constitute probably the largest category of exceptional children.

There is a growing trend toward separating the most educationally disturbed children and putting them into specially created classes and schools. Compared with regular schools, such special classes handle the children in smaller groups, prepare particular educational materials for them, and provide teachers with more help in dealing with them. Very often these classes do not exceed ten to fifteen children.

The classroom teacher of exceptional children has a much harder job than other teachers. No educational objective can be realized; only a modicum of control of their overt behavior can possibly be accomplished.

Retarded or slow-learning children show many variations in their efforts and in their performance from day to day. A disciplined routine is needed, but the amount of discipline must be carefully regulated.

SUMMARY

In this chapter we have tried to develop practical ways to set up the learning situation so that the student will be active. Good teaching must consider the variations among students and provide for them in some manner. The work of a teacher must be so directed that the real purpose of the school will be realized. The progress of pupils should be determined by their capacity to master the materials. Development must be thought of in terms of broader growth of learning. This kind of teaching aims to provide particular conditions so that pupils can progress at their own rate by following a definite set of activities.

FOR FURTHER STUDY

Alexander, W.M. and P.M. Halverson, *Effective Teaching in Secondary Schools.* New York: Rinehart & Company, Inc., 1956.

Baumgartner, B.B. *Guiding the Retarded Child.* New York: John Day Company, Inc., 1965.

Beggs, D.W., *A Practical Application of the Trump Plan.* Englewood Cliffs, N.J.: Prentice-Hall, Inc., 1964.

Bent, R.K., and H.H. Kronenberg, *Principles of Secondary Education.* New York: McGraw-Hill Book Co., 1949.

Burton, W.H., *The Guidance of Learning Activities.* New York: Appleton-Century-Crofts, Inc., 1952.

Butler, F.A., *The Improvement of Teaching in Secondary Schools.* Chicago: The University of Chicago Press, 1954.

Crow, L.D., W.J. Murray, H.H. Smyth, *Educating the Culturally Disadvantaged Child.* New York: David McKay Co., Inc., 1966.

Dunn, L.M., *Basic Principles of Special Education* "The Exceptional Pupil — A Challenge to Secondary Education," *Bulletin of the National Association of Secondary - School Principals,* Vol. 39 (January, 1955).

Frankel, M.G., F.W. Happ and M.P. Smith, *Functional Teaching of the Mentally Retarded.* Springfield, Ill.: Charles C. Thomas, Publishers, 1966.

Goetting, M.L., *Teaching in the Secondary School.* New York: Prentice-Hall, Inc., 1942.

Gruhn, W.T. and H.R. Douglass, *The Modern Junior High School.* New York: The Ronald Press Company, 1956.

Krug, E.A., *The Secondary School Curriculum.* New York: Harper and Brothers, 1960.

Parrish, B.M., *Education of the Gifted.* New York: Twayne Publishers, Inc., 1965.

Riessman, Frank, *Helping the Disadvantaged Pupil to Learn More Easily.* Englewood Cliffs, N.J.: Prentice-Hall, Inc., 1966.

Rubin, E.Z., C.B. Simson, M.C. Betwee, *Emotionally Handicapped Children and the Elementary School.* Detroit: Wayne State Univ. Press, 1966.

Telford, C.W. and J.M. Sawrey, *The Exceptional Individual.* Englewood Cliffs, N.J.: Prentice-Hall, Inc., 1967.

Thomas, R.M., *Aiding the Maladjusted Pupil.* New York: David McKay Co., Inc., 1967.

Thomas, G.I. and Joseph Crescimboni, *Guiding the Gifted Child.* New York: Random House, Inc., 1966.

Terrance, E.P., R.D. Strom, *Mental Health and Achievement.* New York: John Wiley & Sons, Inc., 1965.

Westby-Gibson, Dorothy, *Grouping Students for Improved Instruction.* Englewood Cliffs, N.J.: Prentice-Hall, Inc., 1967.

Worcester, D.A., *The Education of Children of Above Average Mentality.* Lincoln: University of Nebraska Press, 1956.

CHAPTER VI

GUIDANCE — "A"

Goals of Guidance

The goals of helping pupils to understand their problems and to assist each other in solving them are guidance goals.

Guidance is essentially a process of helping the individual find purposeful direction in his learning.

Guidance involves both helping the child adjust to a required pattern and adjusting the pattern to fit the child. Guidance movement operates through classrooms and homerooms, counselors and teachers; and the basic agent of the process is the classroom teacher.

The teacher must know the pupils well. Some flexibility is needed in relating to pupils' needs, and the core teacher generally enjoys some freedom of adaptation. The very nature of the core curriculum, organized as it should be around the problems and needs of the pupils themselves, lends itself to group guidance.

The problems of human adjustment have more recently formed the central core of studies. Using sensible criteria for the selection of the problems, a teacher and a class can move directly toward clarification of the concerns of young adolescents, toward helping them to solve their problems of adjustment. Some homeroom teachers keep the same group for at least two years. The same possibility exists for the core teacher. Not only does the core teacher have fewer pupils for whose guidance he is primarily responsible; in some schools he remains responsible for the same group for two or even three years. Such continuity of relationships has a significant, positive effect on the quality of the guidance role of the teacher. He can learn a great deal about a group of youngsters in the longer period of time. The group itself develops a family feeling and learns better how to interrelate, and how to give its members support.

Teachers who use such techniques as the following are exemplifying good guidance methods in the regular classroom:

1. Studying the needs, interests, abilities, and problems of each individual in a class.
2. Analyzing the relationships that exist between individuals and sub-groups in a class.
3. Helping groups of students to discuss, analyze, and define problems of current interest that they need to solve for themselves.
4. Guiding students in working on the solution of real-life problems.
5. Deepening their insights and enriching their interest.
6. Helping students to evaluate their own growth.
7. Guiding students in the techniques of group self-control.
8. Giving students insight into their own behavior.
9. Helping them to make increasingly wise choices among alternates.
10. Helping them to learn from their own mistakes.
11. Helping them to respect themselves and others.
12. Helping them to get along well with others.[1]

Guidance is the emphasis of individualized aspects of teaching, plus all the technical aspects of counseling and psychotherapy.

Establishing a personal relationship, gaining understanding of the individual pupil and making available to him an experience which he needs for his best development, this is *guidance.*

Guidance services are indispensible in any high school program based on a recognition of and provision for differences among students.

The notion of guidance is made somewhat complicated by the existence of two kinds of guidance activities: *individual counseling* and *group guidance.* Guidance is whatever is done for the explicit purpose of helping individuals understand themselves

---

1. Faunce, Roland C., *Secondary School Administration* (New York: Harper and Brothers, 1955), pp. 135-136.

and develop the capacity to make intelligent decisions and plans.
The emphasis on the individual in most definitions, however,
is on what the individual learns, not how he learns it.   Group
guidance, therefore, should be used sparingly and should assume
a role distinctly subordinate to that of individual counseling.
Indeed, it seems likely that group guidance without individual
counseling should not be attempted.   The central concern of
guidance in schools, however, is with educational choices.   These
choices determine the curriculum of the individual student.
In making them, the student presumably develops increased
understanding of himself.   This kind of guidance is to a certain
extent directive, not in the sense of the counselor's making decisions for the student, but in his presenting information and
raising questions that the student should take into consideration.

*Educational guidance first of all deals with choices of subjects
for study.*

The effectiveness of this educational guidance depends on the
counselor.   He must, of course, know a great deal about adolescent development, college requirements, and tests.   In addition,
however, the counselor must know the classroom studies, the
nature of students, objectives, and content.

Although educational guidance is central to the responsibility
of the school, *vocational guidance* and *personal-social guidance*
follow as natural consequences.   Vocational guidance is the one
aspect of vocational education that the school cannot avoid.

Personal-social guidance suggests to many the invasion of the
private affairs and lives of individuals.   Counselors do not force
discussion on students and ought not to propose questions on
personal-social matters, with the single exception of those dealing with course selections in relation to personal interests.   What
personal-social guidance provides is the opportunity for students
to discuss.   Obviously, any counselor who deals with personal-
social matters should be a person of wisdom, understanding,
sensitivity, and judgement.   A part-time guidance specialist
or counselor is usually a part-time teacher.

The homeroom teacher can assume some guidance responsibilities, including those of individual counseling.[1]

1.   Krug, Edward A., *The Secondary School Curriculum* (New York: Harper
and Brothers, 1960), pp. 512-524.

Effective Guidance

Four major types of help for individual learners are presented: guiding the development of basic learning skills, providing special learning opportunities, using special services, and using administrative provisions. [1]

Teachers can give most effective help to individual goal-seeking activities through many of the special learning opportunities. In problem-solving situations there is some type of information to be secured. Reading of textbooks, periodicals, newspapers, and other printed materials is probably the most used of all skills for securing information. Teachers who find individuals experiencing difficulty in getting information from books should establish whether the pupil's difficulty is in basic reading skill, in lack of knowledge of how to use the book or other material. Pupils can be helped in these skills by general class sessions devoted to use of resources, but individual pupils still need special help. The most effective way of giving help to most pupils is to work with them in the library with the materials concerned. Difficulties occur most frequently when pupils do not have an understood motive for acquiring the skill or do not understand how to perform it. The learner must be helped to find specific ways of checking on the information contained in a book as well as that given by a person.

A skill that is learned by an individual always has meaning, for a skill is an act that is performed relatively identically in similar situations. But definitions, principles, and other types of understandings that do not operate identically because of the variables they involve are not skills; teachers may seek to have them memorized by the students.

The nature of the particular learning experiences under way in a good learning situation might demand an extended period for class discussion at one time, and continued extension of the period for small groups at another time.

Modern activity programs provide for experience with communi-

---

1. Alexander and others, *op. cit.*, p. 351.

cation forms more close to everyday interests and needs.

Radio, television, movies, newspapers and magazines are media of communication much more appropriate to present-day living. School activities should, therefore, be geared more realistically to the interests of students with a view to refining tastes, and developing skills. A more vital activity is the field trip which may be used to serve as an exploratory experience; it can also enrich classroom instruction, to verify previous information, class discussion, and conclusions. The trip from the destination can be altered so as to allow many observations to be made of points of interest. The learners should come to a field trip destination with questions, and equipped with notebooks. The field trip should require careful evaluation by pupils, teachers, and parents. For example, the following evaluation guide would assist teachers and pupils in assessing the quality of their field trip experience.

Was the trip a success?

1. Did the trip answer the pupils' questions?
2. Were the pupils enthusiastic and satisfied with the trip?
3. Were the pupils willing and eager to make assigned reports?
4. Did the pupils cooperate enthusiastically and well?
5. Did the pupils abide by majority rule?
6. Did pupils gain a greater respect for their property and the property of others?
7. Did pupils get a better understanding of the geography of Dearborn?
8. Did pupils gain appreciation of Dearborn's culture such as its schools, churches, libraries, pupilic buildings, parks and museums?
9. Did the trip develop in the pupils a sense of loyalty for and an appreciation of the many wonderful things in Dearborn?[1]

The field trips over a period of time can be an accumulation of information about field resources. Direct experiences provide real opportunities for learning which can be used in many ways.

---

1. Department of Audio-Visual Instruction, *Field Trip Handbook* (Dearborn, Mich.: The Schools, 1950), p. xviii. Quoted in: W. M. Alexander, *op. cit.,* p. 302.

The modern secondary school should be organized to provide adequately for many kinds of learning experiences.

The organization of the total school should be carefully planned so that all pupils may be able to participate in all aspects of programs of the school — extra-class as well as class activities. The total program of the school day needs to be so planned that all activities are programmed within the regular school day. Programs need to be developed whereby such large schools may be subdivided in order to help teachers know pupils individually and to help them. Staff, parents, and pupils jointly plan a program within the general curriculum framework, arrange their own assemblies, activities, parent meetings, and the like.

The library serves an important function in instructional programs of the modern high school.

It provides materials for laboratory work in classrooms, references, stimulation for recreational reading, and materials for various school-wide service programs. The central library must service classroom groups with books and learning materials of all kinds. All teachers must work closely with the librarian in order to plan the most effective use of materials.

In the high school, the superintendent or principal has the responsibility for setting up a planned program for the use of audio-visual aids.

The high schools should have an audio-visual center of at least one room for making repairs and keeping equipment, supplies, and catalogs. This center also serves as headquarters for audio-visual clubs, which provide recreation, hobby, and service functions for high school students.

The school lunch program helps develop good nutritional habits, cooperation, social graces, and responsibility.

A manager plans menus and sees that good food is secured, prepared and served. He also plans work schedules, prepares budgets, and keeps accounts. A manager works closely with the school lunch committee.

The Function of a Guidance Person

Almost every activity in the school program should serve as a path for guidance.

Guidance is a process of problem adjustment under the direction of a trained teacher or special guidance person who can help the individual find his own solution of his problem. In the extra-class program, the school provides opportunities for exploration and for helping pupils obtain information as a basis for guidance. In the guidance process, the individual must learn to examine the advice given, the experiences of others, the information which he has relative to his problem, and arrive at a conclusion. The function of a guidance person is to help the student develop a process of self-evaluation.

The school must plan an organization of services directed toward the fullest development of each student.

The *aim* of the school is to help the individual develop a happy and mature personality, to utilize his abilities and talents, and to help to adjust to environment and circumstances. The young person faces the need for constant re-evaluation of his behaviors. Each young person must learn to adjust himself emotionally and socially. There are also many human resources that may contribute to the guidance program.

The guidance program should extend into every classroom, and every student activity.

The guidance program in the secondary school should be concerned with any problem or adjustment which must be made by the students. The guidance specialists should understand the peculiar problems of youth; they should know the demands of youth, have a sincere interest in youth, and in the guidance activities of the school.

Every secondary school should organize guidance and counseling activities.

One of the most serious handicaps to guidance in educational planning is the lack of school time available for individual conferences with pupils concerning their educational problems. Such conferences can be exceedingly helpful. Every secondary school should organize guidance and counseling activities, and should have available a staff of competent specialists in such areas as psychology, psychiatry, health, evaluation and measurement. The selection of leadership for the guidance program should be given careful consideration.

In secondary education, which is officially considered as a college preparatory function, the guidance activities should be enlarged.

The professional guidance movement has set up rigid programs of training for those who are to do guidance work. Today the guidance function becomes identified with the total educative program of the school. Today the curriculum is not thought of in terms of concrete subject to be studied. It is thought of rather as consisting of those experiences which develop the individual socially, and vocational competencies necessary for effective living in society.[1]

There are some guidance activites recognized by authorities on guidance:
1. The analysis of the individual.
2. Information:
    a. Occupational
    b. Educational
    c. Referral
3. Counselling
4. Placement
5. Follow-up of the school-leaver.[2]

To provide a well-rounded educative experience requires that the school be concerned with the total living environment of

---

1. Bossing, Nelson L., *Principles of Secondary Education* (Englewood Cliffs: Prentice-Hall, Inc., 1955), p. 463.
2. *Ibid.,* p. 469.

the learner.

The school today must draw upon the wealth of community resources as a natural and effective basis of learning. The learner must become involved in those desirable forms of activities made available to the school in the extended resources of community life. Learning through experience goes on continually in whatever environment that learner finds himself. It is highly important that the quality level of the child's community living be kept as high as possible, and that all the rich resources of the community for worthwhile living be utilized. The school, therefore, becomes inextricably involved in the educational possibilities of the total community environment, and the community in turn becomes involved in the educative process.[1]

One of the most widely used guidance activities of the junior high school is the homeroom.

The organization of the teacher's activity is usually looked upon as a way of giving more individualized guidance in the departmentalized organization of secondary education. The change from the single teacher of the elementary school classroom to the many teachers of the departmentalized junior high school presents some problems. Some aspects of instruction can be presented in a much more efficient manner in the extra-class program.

Evaluation

Evaluation is a process of making value judgments.

The primary purpose of evaluation is to promote further growth. Involved in the continuous process of evaluation is periodic collection of tests or other data as a means of determining progress.

Parents and other laymen share in the evaluation process. They help teachers gain better understanding of students by providing significant information about learner's needs — the cooperative action in which the school, the home and other

1. *Ibid.,* pp. 478-479.

community agencies supplement each other in the guidance of students.

Community members can work with the school to help students see new possibilities and new needs, the community contributing to education in expert advice, in planning, in materials and in practical experience.

The primary means of evaluation are tests designed to check the pupil's acquisition of knowledge and skills.

Evaluation is an integral part of the learning process, with teacher and learners reflecting on work done and planning the next steps. Evaluation of the educational program is as basic to the work of the teacher as is self-evaluation to the learner. Teachers, too, are learners as they test the soundness of their decisions on curriculum issues and seek to find ways more fully to implement those decisions.

The basic step in evaluation is clarifying the goals and values to be reached.

Goals are set by the problems with which they are dealing — the knowledge, concepts, skills, and attitudes required to work, to judge, to discuss, etc. Stating goals in behavioral terms indicates the kind of evidence that will show whether the goals are being realized. There must be some that relate to the skills of living in a world of change, to life situations, to understanding the ideas of others. For teacher and for learner, goals stated in terms of behavior become tangible items toward which pupils can work.

The statement of goals prepared by curriculum committees includes specific objectives for varied maturity and capacities — for young children, for intermediate grades, for adolescents, and for adults. Even when behavioral goals are differentiated in terms of age levels, they should not represent the same standard for all members of a class. The behavioral goals are important for learners, but they are normally achieved with little help from the school.

Growth in one area must be evaluated in terms of total growth.

For example, Susan's general intellectual ability may suggest that she is capable of more advanced thinking in arithmetic. But she may be handling completely all the situations calling for arithmetic confronting her while, at the same time, she is struggling to overcome patterns of English usage learned at home. In planning experiences with Susan, the teacher would weigh her potential growth in mathematics against goals in language usage. Ability, mental and physical health, feelings, work habits, home backgrounds, standards and values held, human relations, problem-solving ability — these and many other factors affect the goals desirable for any one individual at a particular time.[1]

Evaluation of the educational program must be based on the goals and values sought.

Cooperative planning always involves evaluation of what is needed and how well it is being provided. Evaluation of the curriculum must include consideration of the experiences with which learners are being helped to deal, school organization, and administrative relationships which affect these experiences.

The school is concerned with guiding learners in the complex situations of home, school, and community, viewed in the light of life situations. Evaluation must be concerned with the experiences which children are having both in and out of school. Evaluation of educational programs, like the evaluation of pupil progress, is a continuous process and one which must be based on a clear evidence gathered as teacher, parents and administrators together consider educational programs.

When evaluation is an integral part of the teaching learning process, pupils are continually encouraged to take realistic looks at both their strenths and their weaknesses, and to participate in planning the next step.[2]

Learners are not protected from failure, and they must face the reality of not being chosen for a job because of inadequate skills. Also, teachers feel responsible for helping learners set

1. Stratemeyer, Florence B.; Forkner, H.L.; McKim, M.G. and Passow, A.H., *Developing a Curriculum for Modern Living* (New York: Columbia University, Teachers College, Bureau of Publications, 1957), p. 483.
2. *Ibid.,* p. 83.

higher standards.

Pupil progress should be evaluated and reported in terms of the total objectives of the school.

The teacher evaluates by comparing this measure with expected progress. The child should know day-by-day how well he is doing, with a formal report at the end of a marking period.

The main source of information about pupil progress resides in the records and transcripts of their academic grades. Formal evaluations are held when examinations are given, but informal evaluation is occurring as students and teachers ask themselves how they are doing. The function of evaluation is that of helping the learner achieve greater understanding of himself and thereby make fundamental improvements.

The teacher's evaluation of the child is better tested, too, when supported by the child's homework efforts.

There is an opinion that too little attention has been given to the matter of homework in the over-all program of education.

Much of the evaluation of a child's work by the teacher is of an informal nature.

Sometimes the teacher's informal evaluation takes the form of a comment, but at other times it may consist of a formal conference with a student. The teacher makes some type of note during or after each interview, and subsequent interviews bring conservation around to the points noted. Teachers often use observations of pupils to reach judgments about their progress. Therefore, teachers whose classes are in the areas in which observation can be most profitable, especially laboratories, may work out schemes of work that assure some deliberate observation of each pupil. Products in the laboratory give significant evidence of the pupil's progress.

Self-evaluation by the student should be employed whenever it may contribute to more effective learning.

Self-evaluation is particularly appropriate in core-classes, English, social studies, science, industrial arts, home economics, art, and physical education. Student progress is ultimately motivated by the pupil's own planning. Teachers should help students in self-evaluation through counseling techniques. Tests made by the teacher and by students may be of substantial help in self-evaluation. Students frequently have reason to drill themselves on formulas, meanings, spellings, and other learnings. If drill is carried on intelligently, there is an element of self-evaluation. Teachers need to give a great deal of attention to the thought processes indicated by students' analyses of their own work.

Group evaluation has possibilities for stimulating individual self-evaluation.

Review of what has been learned about a particular topic may stimulate individual pupils to ask themselves what is being said.

Learners need objective evidence if they are to grow in their ability to evaluate themselves.

Also, the teacher is going to have to summarize and interpret his evidence for parents, administrators, teachers, and others. The teacher will have to determine the types of evidence appropriate for evaluating growth toward a variety of goals, the amount of evidence needed, the means of making this evidence as accurate as possible, and the ways of using the data collecting process.

Objectives should determine the specific kinds of evidence to be collected. The broader the objective, the more difficult and complicated the evaluation process becomes.

A necessary step before beginning to collect evidence is to translate broad objectives into specific teaching goals. The most helpful procedure for defining goals precisely is to state them in terms of learner behavior.

The ultimate list of behaviors of the teacher should be his own, built in terms of the objectives of his courses and for the particular learners assigned to his classes. Behavioral goals should be meaningful if they are to indicate the types of evidence that can be observed or collected.

The teacher will need to employ everything he has learned about observing learners if he is to be successful. This does not necessarily mean that he must collect all types of evidence at once. He can make plans, however, for systematic sampling of behavior. The experiences of the teacher will help him to identify the aspects of daily work and also will help him develop some proficiency in concentrating on those learners for whom he needs more data.

Standardized tests are widely used in secondary schools.

The high school teacher tests periodically. He places the marks upon the report cards, and judges whether his pupils pass or fail. The mark, rather than progress toward important educational goals, is made the chief purpose of the pupil. When marks become an end of learning, permanent and significant learning suffers.

Standardized tests are available to help in diagnosis of pupil difficulties, evaluation of achievement.

These tests can be administered by teachers to the entire class or individually. It can be helpful to determine common needs of students relative to a particular subject.

The practice is generally to use diagnostic tests for students.

There are published diagnostic tests, but the teacher may also prepare his own diagnostic tests for some purposes. The tests may be used, both for screening purposes to determine what pupils have particular difficulties, and for identifying the specific difficulties, as a basis for individual help to these pupils.

Situational tests should be used and developed by teachers.

Systematic observation of children, a record of observations may be made, and the accumulated evidence analyzed. Conferences with pupils and parents are another means of systematically collecting evidence. There are many kinds of standardized measures (test, inventories, scales) of specific aptitudes, interests, attitudes, personal-social adjustment, problem-solving, and health and physical development.

It is important for the teachers to remember that, no matter how carefully the test is administered, the score may not represent the learner's true capacity.

Many factors may enter into a low score — lack of knowledge, emotional tensions, or gaps in special areas that invalidate a good performance. Evidence with regard to the achievement of many behavioral goals is secured through observation of pupils in day-to-day living. Situational tests should be used by teachers. For example:

An automobile is moving along an icy road when the rear wheels suddenly begin to skid toward the ditch at the side of the road. What should the driver do to keep the car on the road? Why?

Tests which provide opportunities to use ideas in concrete situations, or to show how concepts are implemented, are built on the theory that something can be said to be learned only when individuals can and do use it appropriately. This does not mean that standardized tests of skills or information have no value. Rather, it points to the importance of selecting tests which evaluate the goals toward which individuals and groups are working.[1]

To measure effectively and thoroughly all the outcomes of a program for any type of instruction is virtually an impossible task.

Yet, evaluation of some type is necessary. For that reason, investigators are constantly attempting to develop new methods of evaluation, trying to improve on the older methods. Studies indicate that one of the most widely used techniques of evaluation is the standardized achievement test. In addition to teacher-made tests and standardized tests, research shows that other

---

1. Stratemeyer, *op. cit.,* pp. 489-491.

evaluation techniques are sometimes used. In elementary school especially, observational techniques are often utilized; and in the secondary schools, projects, reports, and experimental work are often used in evaluating the outcomes of learning.

The program of evaluation in a modern school function derives its guidance from the statement of purpose which determines the curriculum of the school.

The curriculum should help pupils develop the kind of behavior which represents progress toward the desired goals. In other words, evaluation recognizes the concept of the *whole* child in a learning process. Any evaluation that merely seeks to determine how much a pupil has learned of the material covered in the book is *not* sound.

Evaluation is a continuous, culminative process which is rooted in the nature of the individual learner, and the goals of the school.

Evaluation attempts to secure as complete a picture of the individual as possible. The staff of the school cooperatively can state their goals clearly and define each in terms of student behavior. Each teacher can simply state what kinds of changes in pupil behavior he desires to bring about. Staff meetings should clarify the kind of student behavior desired, and the kinds of experiences needed to promote it. The learner helps define accepted goals in terms of his own behavior.

Evaluation must be necessarily operated through sampling different aspects of behavior at different times in a variety of learning situations. Effective evaluation requires the cooperation of pupils, teachers and parents. Pupils can help collect much valuable data regarding their own progress and problems. Each child should be evaluated in terms of his own abilities and interests, rather than be compared with others. Equal achievement does not necessarily indicate equal abilities. Tests are usually given after units or books have been completed, primarily for the purpose of reporting to parents. The "grades" serve primarily the function of recording student progress to the student himself, to parents, and to school. Tests used as diagnostic tools can help to reveal errors, problems, difficulties as well as satisfactory growth, learning, and achievement.

Cooperative evaluation of achievement.

The modern secondary school places emphasis upon the growth of the individual. These schools understand that learning is an active process and that the learner must recognize goals which are important to himself. Self-appraisal plays a vitally important part in good evaluation programs. In modern secondary schools, the pupil is an active participant in the program of evaluation. Under the teacher's guidance, the pupil discovers his strength, weaknesses, problems, and his special abilities.

The teacher collecting evidence is responsible for indicating the objectives to which it is related.

This procedure facilitates the task of the homeroom teacher by broadening the basis of interpretation. These data are carefully interpreted by the teacher in the light of what he knows about the pupil, and summarize coherent pictures of individual progress toward the objectives of the school. This summary is not made in marks, but in paragraphs immediately intelligible for professional use.

Many high school teachers keep an individual evaluation folder for each pupil for whom they are primarily responsible. In this folder, the teacher and pupil regularly collect and interpret evidence relating to the personal and social goals of the individual: written papers, objective and standardized test scores, samples of answers, etc.

Instead of narrowly measuring the command of specific areas of subject matter, teachers should be concerned with a broad view of the learner's total growth.

Many of our important goals do not lend themselves to objective testing. Test data can be helpful if they are used intelligently as partial indications of growth. Beside the achievement tests there are also intelligence, personality, and aptitude tests. Besides test scores, other data exist for evaluating pupil growth. The guidance-oriented teacher will collect and study evidence of growth from a considerable number of sources:

    health data
    school marks
    student activities — participation record
    work record — employer's appraisals
    anecdotal records
    work samples
    autobiographies
    self-analysis paragraphs
    wishing-well tests
    opinions of other teachers
    sociograms
    judgements of other (individual) pupils
    interview records
    interest inventories
    questionnaires about study habits, hobbies, jobs
    attendance record
    letters to and from parents
    group appraisals by peers
    statements of pupil regarding school or life plans
    results of parent conferences
    student self-appraisals
    student appraisals of others
    student appraisals of class progress
    data on family and home
    case studies by teachers
    court records
    reports from church or other community groups
    time budgets
    follow-up data[1]

The core teacher will make good use of data from these and other sources. He will learn all he can about the group's background in the elementary and secondary schools. He will note changes in students' atitudes toward each other and in their readiness to assume responsibilities. All these and similar factors affect the guidance of a class. They help the teacher determine

1. Faunce, *Secondary School Administration,* pp. 151-152.

his role, in terms of what help is needed.   They will help him to
plan class sessions in such a way as to promote interaction.

Remedial classes (in larger secondary schools) are provided,
especially in reading, speech, composition, and mathematics.

Remedial classes are staffed by teachers competent in the
skills concerned.   Are sections of a subject in which students
with low test scored are placed in remedial classes; this is especially of summer school classes.   An effective program of instruction should bring students to a standard of work that is
appropriate for their individual ability, rather than bringing
all of them to uniform grade standard.   Students who are above
average in abilities should be expected to achieve much better
than the accepted grade norms.

Cumulative Records as a Guidance Aid

Cumulative records assist in improving teacher relations with
students, and in creating a better understanding of the student
in his school activities.

The cumulative record is an organized, objective record of
information about the student.   It is developed by all staff members cooperatively and used by all staff members.

Cumulative records are necessary because they make available significant facts useful in guidance.   In some extreme cases
it may be advisable to record certain confidential materials on a
separate form so that it may be removed from general use.

The principal shortcoming of cumulative records lies in the
fact that some teachers, because of their feeling of infallibility
or apathy or like emotional factors, may on occasion evaluate
their students' progress adversely and thus likewise affect their
future academic standing.   It often happens that, in order to
circumvent their obligations, some teachers fail to study the
intellectual and emotional qualities of their students, and hence
consult only accumulative records which contain all kinds of
possible inaccuracies.   It is no wonder, therefore, that because
of such attitudes, some teachers undermine the characters and

personalities of their students.

Access to cumulative records should be limited to the principal, whose duty is to check them and see to it that inaccurate information is eliminated from them. Otherwise, the values of these records are negative.

The cumulative record in many schools is limited to the pupil's achievement and attendance, but no information about his personality, character, home background and extra-class participation. In many schools, the information is not satisfactorily recorded; therefore the cumulative records are not used by the homeroom and classroom teachers very extensively. The record should be kept up-to-date. Individual counseling requires constant reference to the cumulative record.

The cumulative records should contain any standardized tests. Some classroom tests can be filed. Such concrete evidence is just as important to a teacher whose problem is to help a learner. The cumulative record shows changes in behavior and the ways in which the individual is overcoming weaknesses and limitations noted at an earlier time. The process of selecting of items for permanent cumulative record contributes to the teacher's better understanding of individuals and serves as one additional basis for the planning of the next step. A good permanent cumulative record gives a picture of the growing learner.

The teacher in a particular instructional area assumes responsibility for developing the permanent record, and receives from other teachers pertinent items which they may have noted in their contacts with the pupils.

The best type of cumulative record lists facts to secure a maximum of information in minimum space.

The best type of cumulative record lists facts to secure a maximum of information in minimum space, and at the same time displays significant information for quick interpretation.

Cumulative records are of three types: 1. The pocket or folder type, where a wide variety of record cards are kept together; 2. a central record card, where all data are copied; 3. a combination of the two, where part of the record is copied on the folder and the remainder filed inside. In the interest of minimum clerical work, permanency, and utility, the first type is adapted to the individual school system.[1]

The types of information should be recorded.

The following information should be recorded:

1. Photographs of the student at various ages.
2. The family background, home and neighborhood environment.
3. School achievements.
4. Attendance record by grades.
5. Standardized test records of intelligence, achievement, aptitudes, interests, and attitudes.
6. Personality ratings or personality test records.
7. A health history, including physical examination data as well as list of diseases, dates when contracted and treated immunization.
8. Extra-curricular activities and hobbies.
9. Unusual experiences and achievements.
10. Evidence of leadership (statement of fact, not of opinion).
11. Anecdotal records.
12. Records of interviews and conferences.
13. Work experiences.
14. Vocational choices, preferably through the use of an interest inventory in addition to student's statement of vocational choices.
15. The student's own future educational plan.
16. Drop-outs and reasons for them.
17. Schools transferred to.
18. Grades completed in other schools (if any).
19. Personal appearance.
20. Citizenship and social traits.
21. Leadership qualities.
22. Personal honesty and ethical behavior.
23. Interest other than vocational.
24. All placements made by the school.
25. Follow-up services, and developments evidenced, references made, and results of referrals.
26. The grade record, including failures as well as subjects dropped.[2]

1. Flaum, *op. cit.,* p. 366.
2. *Ibid.,* pp. 364-365.

These records must be kept up-to-date by continuous contributions of all data that will help build a growth picture of the individual. The core teacher keeps the personal files for his own groups.

The student may have four or more teachers besides his core teacher. They might well meet at least once each week, and undertake such tasks as sharing information about students, developing new curriculum areas, sharing results of experiments in teaching methods, planning contacts with parents, etc.

The conference may also draw other personnel into discussions of pupil's problems and their possible solutions. A regular report might be transmitted to the core teacher by all teachers of the same grade. The core teacher will study the information, and use it in counseling interviews with parents. Interviews and conferences with parents provide many significant leads for better guidance. These conferences are three-way affairs between teacher, pupil and parent. The conference can also include planning next steps for each participant, all directed toward further growth of the learner. The teacher must consider how to open discussion of pupil progress, how to use data from the pupil's cumulative record.

Reports of Progress

If the teacher is to carry out his reporting responsibilities effectively, there are a number of skills he should develop.

He will need to learn to use whatever reporting system is in operation in his school. He should also become skilled in developing a variety of contacts with parents in addition to the periodic formal report that goes home. School personnel have developed many ways of communicating with learners, parents, and others. Some use a system of letters, parent-teacher conferences, etc. More frequently, a system of letter grades, ratings, or percentages is in use. The philosophy of the school system often determines the method of communication adopted.

The teacher will be required to learn to use whatever communication system is in operation in his school. However, there are many problems connected with the assignment of grades of which

the teacher should be aware. Each learner should be helped to
measure his achievement in terms of his own goals and abilities.
Strengths should be acknowledged frankly and praised gener-
ously. Weaknesses should be faced with equal frankness and
plans should be made to overcome them, where possible. The
stress should be on the future, not on the past. Strengths and
weaknesses should be analyzed as a basis for the next steps.
When difficulties are faced, learners should be helped to see
that something can be done about them.

The teachers must help to develop high standards of performance — challenging inaccurate statements, requiring learners
to use their textbooks or some other source, encouraging more
accurate observations, helping learners take effective notes.
Similar procedures characterize the development of fundamental
skills.

The reports should help learners develop skills in self-evaluation. One of the important characteristics of the forms in which
learners are developing effective appraisal skills is the number
of times that teacher and learners appraise work together. There
may be group discussions, when everyone examines his own
paper and reports on his difficulties, or sessions when a teacher
works for a few minutes with each individual in turn. If the
teacher does not want to waste the time of some individuals and
to fail to give the appropriate help to others, he must identify
the special needs of his class, see where regular classroom activities are already providing ample practice and where supple-
mentation is needed, and decide what explanations and experiences will best develop the understandings important to the
maximum progress of his learners. There are also sessions where
individual enterprizes (reports, themes, poems, notebooks)
are offered for group criticism. The teacher must help learners
to develop powers of self-evaluation and self-direction.

*Reports of progress should relate individual differences to ac-
cepted behavioral goals.*

This kind of statement can be written and shared at any time
that the teacher feels it would be of interest to the parent.

An important area of learning for every child is to recognize
realistically the progress he is making, his limitations and stren-

gths. He needs to be helped to see his competencies in the light of standards generally held. When parents and students can realistically relate individual growth to generally accepted standards and values, more adequate decisions will be made regarding school work.

Reports of progress should *not* be made for all pupils at the same time. Not all pupils will reach the point of needing to evaluate their progress and plan next steps at the same time. Preparing a large number of reports in a limited time often results in a tendency to use cliches rather than definitive statements.

Reporting student progress toward the goals of the schools is an important aspect of modern education.

When such reports are carefully constructed to include all important objectives, they are far more meaningful than the subject mark alone. It must be granted that this form of reporting does require considerably more time than marking the grades, but it is a much more effective method.

The most effective method of reporting is the personal conference, highly valuable because it provides face-to-face contacts with parents. In a friendly social atmosphere, parents, teachers, and the pupil may examine records, test data, and examples of pupil work, discussing all significant aspects of the child's development.

Failure to use periodic school-to-home reports other than report cards often leaves parents in a quandary.

Along with daily homework, the teacher can send home an accumulation of papers which the child has produced for arithmetic, spelling, or writing, so that the parents can see concretely the trend in the child's work. Along with conferences with parents, and report cards, the folder of completed work is a way of demonstrating the nature of the child's progress or lack of it.

The parent-teacher conference has been recognized as one of the most effective ways to report pupil progress.

One of the most commonly used plans for conferences in the high school is to hold an "open house." Parents may go from teacher to teacher in their classrooms. The conference must be based on the interpretation of report cards, standardized tests, and reports from other teachers. In this situation, the parent has professional assistance in educational problems, and the teacher assumes the role of an advisor. A successful conference plan requires a strong training program for the teachers.

Many reporting systems use two types of marks — one for achievement and one for progress or effort.

For *achievement* the usual letter type is used. The other is for *effort* and is numerical.

For achievement:

A — Outstanding progress
B — Better than expected progress
C — Average progress
D — Less progress than expected
F — Little or no progress

For effort:

1 — Superior
2 — Satisfactory
3 — Unsatisfactory

The weakness of marks and reports lies in the fact that it is very difficult for teachers to rate pupils on many of the important qualities which the schools seek to develop.

A progress report on a printed form is sent home periodically for each pupil.

The teacher writes a brief note or letter describing a pupil's progress in a given subject. Teachers have two groups (home-room) which sometimes include seventy students; it is then difficult to have conferences often. For that reason, a progress report is sent home. Although the new reporting procedures have taken a variety of forms, they usually provide for the following:

1. An evaluation of pupil progress in terms of the objectives of the total educational program and the various subjects in that program.
2. An evaluation of pupil progress in terms of the ability of the individual child rather than on the basis of a uniform standard for the group.
3. An analysis of the child's progress toward specific objectives in a subject, rather than one over-all mark for the subject as a whole.
4. An evaluation of the pupil's progress on aspects of development such as attitudes, character, and personality qualities, citizenship traits, and study habits.
5. Separate report forms for the different subjects.
6. Less frequent reports to parents than with the traditional report cards, but a more detailed report when one is made.
7. Teacher-pupil conferences to discuss with the individual pupil the progress he is making.
8. Teacher-parent conferences to discuss the child's progress in school. In some schools, such conferences are held at regular intervals, but in others they are at the request of either the teacher or the parent.[1]

Students' Reports of the Way They Study

Students' reports of the way they study indicate that certain methods are used more often by good students than by poor students.

One of the most extensive surveys of this kind in grades 4 to 12 reported the ten most significant methods of study characteristic of high scholarship:

1. Have a clear notion of the task before beginning the work of a particular study period.
2. Make complete sentences while writing.
3. Seek to master all the material as progress is made from lesson to lesson.
4. Study and understand the meaning of a chart or table.
5. Try to interrupt work at a natural break in the printed material.

1. Gruhn, William T., and Douglass, H.R., *The Modern Junior High School* (New York: The Ronald Press Company, 1956), p. 321.

6. Do not take notes while reading.
7. Work out concrete examples to illustrate general rules and principles.
8. Have on hand the materials required.
9. Use the facts learned in one class in preparing for another.
10. Read each topic in a lesson until it is clearly understood.[1]

Skillful supervised study provides instruction in how to study a particular assignment. As assignments become more creative and emphasize problem-solving and research, the classroom, library, and laboratory become the most effective places for study.

SUMMARY

In this chapter we have discussed the goals of guidance. Guidance is essentially a process of helping the individual find purposeful direction in his learning. The goals of helping pupils to understand their problems and to assist each other in solving them are guidance goals.

Educational guidance first of all deals with choices of subjects to study. Guidance services are indispensible in any high school program based on a recognition of and provision for differences among students. In secondary education, which is officially considered as a college preparatory function, the guidance activities should be enlarged.

---

1. *Guided Study and Homework* by Ruth Strang. From the NEA Journal, October, 1955, pp. 399-400.

FOR FURTHER STUDY

Adams, J.F., *Counseling & Guidance.* New York: The Macmillan Company, 1965.

Alberty, Harold, *Reorganizing the High School Curriculum.* New York: The Macmillan Co., 1953.

Alexander, W.M., and P.M. Halverson, *Effective Teaching in Secondary Schools.* New York: Rinehart and Company, Inc., 1956.

Bossing, N.L., *Principles of Secondary Education.* Englewood Cliffs: Prentice-Hall, Inc., 1955.

Faunce, R.C., *Secondary School Administration.* New York: Harper & Brothers, 1955.

Flaum, L.S., *The Activity High School — The Principles of Its Operation.* New York: Harper and Brothers Publishers, 1953.

Gordon, I.J., *The Teacher as a Guidance Worker.* New York: Harper & Brothers, 1956.

Gronlund, N.E., *Measurement and Evaluation in Teaching.* New York: The Macmillan Company, 1965.

Gruhn, W.T. and H.R. Douglass, *The Modern Junior High School.* New York: The Ronald Press Company, 1956.

Guided Study and Homework by Ruth Strang. From the NEA Journal, October, 1955.

How to Pass Graduate Record Examination; Advanced Test: Education. New York: College Publishing Corporation, 1967.

Jenkins, D.H. and Ronald Lippitt, *Interpersonal Perceptions of Teachers, Students, and Parents.* Washington, D.C.: The Division of Adult Education, National Education Association, 1951.

Johnston, E.G., Mildred Peters, and William Evraiff, *The Role of the Teacher in Guidance.* Englewood Cliffs, N.J.: Prentice-Hall, Inc., 1959.

Jones, A.J., *Principles of Guidance.* New York: McGraw-Hill Book Co., Inc., 1951.

Kelley, J.A., *Guidance and the Curriculum.* Englewood Cliffs, N.J.: Prentice-Hall, Inc., 1955.

Krug, E.A., *The Secondary School Curriculum.* New York: Harper & Brothers, 1960.

McDaniel, H.B., *Guidance in the Modern School.*   New York: The Dryden Press, 1956.

Stratemeyer, F.B., H.L. Forkner, M.G. McKim and A.H. Passow, *Developing Curriculum for Modern Living.*   New York: Columbia University, Teachers College, Bureau of Publications, 1957.

CHAPTER VII

GUIDANCE — "B"

Counselors

Each secondary school should have special counselors with only minimum teaching responsibilities or without any classes at all.

The counselors are concerned with the techniques of staff leadership, cooperative group processes, and in-service education of classroom teachers.

The following functions that appear to call for a counselor:

1. To coordinate the group and individualized instruction which is the principal responsibility of the classroom teacher.
2. To administer programs for promoting a better understanding of the student, through the securing of adequate data.
3. To aid in vocational placement of students, in the part time work program of the school.
4. To deal with difficult cases of physical or psychological maladjustment which requires special training and skill of a psychiatric nature.
5. To maintain a follow-up of graduates and drop-outs, and to interpret data regarding such a follow-up for the purpose of improving the guidance program and the total school program.[1]

The counselors should be selected with regard to their major task, which is likely to be helping teachers and students.

They can have a dynamic effect in developing the guidance program. One way to achieve better communication is for the

1. Alberty, Harold, *Recognizing the High School Curriculum* (New York: The Macmillan Co., 1953), p. 335.

special counselor to have at least one core class of his own. He should see himself as one who earns his status by being helpful. Together with other guidance teachers he should seek to provide in-service education in such areas as:

1. Understanding the growing, maturing child.
2. Understanding the forces in the community and the family that help mold the pupil's personality.
3. Understanding the influence of the peer group in shaping his attitudes and behavior as well as the part the learner plays in the interaction of himself in the matrix of his social environment.
4. Personal skill in the observation and analysis of pupil behavior in the milieu of these complex factors that enter into his growth and development as a person.
5. Ability to participate effectively in group processes, counseling pupil and parent.
6. Ability to define and solve school problems, which are regarded as basically a form of action research.[1]

Within schools, the classroom teacher must work with specialists in the mental or physical health of children.

These specialists are an integral part of effective school administration. The modern trend is for the specialist, if he is dealing with any concerns of the child which can profit from school help, to consult with school personnel, especially with the classroom teacher and with principals.

The *psychologist* is a specialist in child development, in tests and measurements, personality development, and in general problems of learning. He is also likely to be professionally prepared to do individual or group counseling with children and to consult with parents. Psychologists may come to the school to give lectures, hold conferences on general topics of child development. Psychologists may do a variety of testing, interviewing, or developmental studies on children. Psychologists who work with children will, however, have a major interest in the individual child and will have much to offer in the way of specific help.

Any specialist working with children ought to have some know-

---

1. Gordon, Ira J., *The Teacher as a Guidance Worker* (New York: Harper and Brothers, 1956), pp. 10-12.

ledge of the child's school setting. The more the school and the private practitioner can work together, the greater is the likelihood of helping all concerned.

The school must face and work with reality. It must be careful to see that, in its efforts to impose a realistic discipline on the youngster, it does not turn the outside professionals and the school away from the vital issue of helping the child.

Specialists are available to give help as needed in the core programs.

The work of each grade group centers in a core program, with time for special courses, short-term projects, and individual activities under the guidance of specialists. The teacher responsible for core programs has rather broad academic and cultural backgrounds, with some specialization in one or two fields. The teacher-specialists are responsible for homeroom activities and general guidance of the students in their core group; all have at least two periods weekly for work with individuals, for record-keeping, and for the many other activities.

There are teacher-specialists in art, music, mathematics, science, foreign languages, industrial arts, vocational education, home economics, business education, health and physical education. Almost all specialists also teach core classes. Their classrooms are equipped as laboratories where it is possible for an entire class to work easily, or for individuals and several small groups to work at the same time.

The specialists are available to give help as needed in the core programs. They meet with classes in their homerooms, or remain in the laboratories, where individuals or groups come for help on problems being studied in the core. This requirement is met by arranging the schedules of specialists. Part of their day can be devoted to *service units*, and part to *service on call* to the core classes. In addition, some part of each specialist's schedule is allotted to the guidance of individuals with special interests.

The guidance counselor must be able to stimulate and maintain interest in the guidance program throughout the whole school.

The guidance counselor must be able to secure the cooperation of teachers and administrator in order that each one will
feel a sense of responsibility toward the guidance needs of the
students.   Outside of the school, he must be able to work har-
moniously with community welfare agencies, social service
agencies and with other institutions.   He must have contacts
with various personnel managers in industry and small business
in order that usable work-school vocational programs may be
developed.

*The guidance counselor should be an expert in conducting inter-
views, and administering and interpreting tests.*

He must have a real understanding of students as individuals
and be able to inspire confidence in them.   He must be fair
and objective, but must never be shocked or condemn students
because of their behavior or problems.   He must be able to create
an atmosphere in which students are aware of his personality
as being helpful, understanding, kind, and friendly.   He creates
a situation in which the student feels a sense of freedom for
self-expression.

*Individual conference and counseling should provide the counse-
lor with the opportunity to know the student as an individual.*

The most vital function of the guidance counselor and one of
the most effective means of doing individual guidance is through
the individual conference.   Before meeting with the student, the
counselor should prepare himself by studying all the available
data on the student that his cumulative record provides.   He
should develop a flexible plan of approach, but must allow the
student to take the initiative in beginning the interview.
    The counselor must be careful in this situation to do the follow-
ing things:
    1. He must gain the confidence of the student by creating a
        sincere, friendly relationship.
    2. He must be concerned with the student's plans and prob-

lems.

3. He must use all facts which he has in order to help the student to understand his problems.
4. He must retain an impersonal, objective, yet sympathetic role during the interview.
5. He must convince the student that he wants to help him.
6. He must help the student develop constructive objectives.
7. He must help the student develop confidence in himself.
8. He must make the student feel that he is welcome to return for further discussions.
9. He must help the student face his problem and not let him stray from it.
10. He must help the student express himself clearly and fully.
11. He must use questions which the student understands skillfully and directly.
12. He must not embarrass the student nor make him feel that the interview is a form of punishment or a confessional.
13. He must keep a record of each interview but not take notes during the interview.
14. He must keep the student's confidence by not talking about him outside the conference.
15. He must carefully note the changes in physical and emotional reactions of the student to various questions as possible indicators for latent problems or difficulties which need to be investigated.
16. He must be sure that before the interview is closed both he and the student are aware of what has happened and what is to be done in the future.[1]

The guidance counselor uses standardized objectives tests as additional background for understanding the student.

The most common of these tests are the achievement tests, and personal attitude and adjustment tests. The test scores must be kept in strict confidence, but the student should be able to see his test scores.

The guidance counselor must interpret these test scores in terms of what they seek to test and should also relate each score to other test scores on a comparable basis.

---

1. Flaum, L.S., *The Activity High School — The Principles of Its Operation* (New York: Harper and Brothers Publishers, 1953), pp. 359-361.

The counselor also helps the student develop confidence in himself, develop his own objectives, and make his own decisions in order to solve his problems.   All counseling techniques must be adjusted to the problem and personality of the student.[1]

The consultant's activities are necessarily related to the problems that arose out of the administrative approach.

The consultants are usually employed to assist the administration and to help teachers, especially production committees, at points where the execution of plans is difficult.   The consultant must be concerned primarily with training situations and activities by which teachers and laymen learn to perform.

The consultant in his role will encourage, through his technical knowledge and skill, a mutual exploration of situations, helping the staff to formulate its own difficulties more adequately.   At this point, the consultant can be of a great help by suggesting ways of gathering and interpreting needed data.

The consultant can provide many services for groups.

He can stimulate interest in curriculum improvement and develop enthusiasm for tackling various educational problems.   A consultant can help organize a group, can focus its consideration on the resources available to it, can indicate alternative ways of attacking a specific problem.   Or the consultant can serve as a teacher for individuals and groups who are to participate in service activities.

The consultant should be an individual who is sympathetic, understanding, and willing to begin with a particular group at the level at which he finds them.

The consultant should have two kinds of competencies — *one* in the actual problem area in which the group is working, and the *other* in the combination of attitudes and skills that enable him to use his special ability to help the group.[2]

Consultants may be found among teachers and others within the school system itself, also among laymen.   Many universities

1. *Ibid.,* p. 362.
2. Stratemeyer, *op. cit.,* pp. 696-697.

and colleges have special organizations from which specific consultation services can be secured. Some of the workshops, conferences, and other professional meetings sponsored by colleges and universities are especially designed to provide consultant services.

Many community organizations, agencies, and institutions have specialized personnel who are willing and able to provide planning assistance.

The Conception of Discipline

Discipline may be thought of as organization of one's impulses for the attainment of a goal.[1]

The student must come to look upon the school as but one aspect of the total, and the school discipline must reflect the larger implications of life for the student. He must conceive of discipline as constructive and concerned with the development of those attitudes and habits of conduct that contribute to the social well being of the student. The correct techniques of management and method, moreover, must be regarded as the principal agency of good discipline.

"Modern" youth has but intensified the prevalent, somewhat natural opposition, to control from above.

Two principal methods of handling school discipline are recognized:

1. By direct control it meant those steps that must be taken to correct an overt act once it has been committed. The main purpose of direct control is to restore the class or student to normal schoolroom activity.

2. The indirect means of control contemplates primarily the prophylaxis ideal. Under this plan the work of the school is so organized that an overt act does not occur, except as ideal conditions cannot be provided.[2] The ideal of the school is to achieve such working conditions that direct control will be reduced to a minimum.

1. Sheviakov, George V. and Redl, Fritz, *Discipline for Today's Children and Youth* (Washington, D.C.: Department of Supervision and Curriculum, N.E.A., 1944), p. 4.
2. Bossing, Nelson L., *Teaching in Secondary Schools* (Boston: Houghton Mifflin Company, 1952), pp. 491-493.

The teacher who emphasizes the direct modes of control is seriously in danger of losing sight of importance of method.

It is easy to over-emphasize the place of direct control in education. The teacher should impress the class with unquestioned ability to deal with every situation that arises.

Correction of any sort represents an unfortunate situation. Under no circumstances should correction take place under the stress of emotion. Therefore, correction should be impersonal. In most situations, it is possible to have private conferences with the student over matters that need correction. If the school can instill correct attitudes through experience, it will have contributed materially toward a wholesome civic atmosphere in the school and in the community. It is a maxim of discipline that, when correction is necessary, the offender should suffer severely as a result of the offense.

There are *two* types of pain that may be inflicted — *physical* and *mental.* In the secondary school it is assumed that physical pain will not be inflicted. The most common means of inflicting pain is mental. The teacher needs to exercise extraordinary wisdom in the application of mental suffering appropriate to the nature of the individual.

In discipline, the individual should increasingly assume responsibility for himself, his decisions, and his actions.

In this case, the homes and schools need increasingly to test ways of exerting their influence so that learners have an opportunity to practice self-discipline. Good teaching makes the learner capable of teaching himself, so the best discipline should result in people responsible for their own control. Self-control is a requirement in any classroom.

Effective learning requires good discipline in the external process of education, and in the learner.

The child is not well-ordered or disciplined at the start. He has to develop these ways of behaving. He sees, in time, and as his experience accumulates, that an ordering of his life is important.

Good discipline is a way of achieving team work toward goals. Without good discipline the team is chaotic, the school room is a waste of everybody's time.

Not only is good discipline important in achievement, it is equally important in affecting the way we feel about ourselves and, indirectly, the way we feel about others.

By "bad" discipline we refer to discipline that is too harsh, too quickly administered, over-generalized, and also, which emphasizes the person rather than his deed.

Good, modern, discipline should be unobtrusive. Good discipline should be based on a firm and reasonable program of learning. The teacher has to know about the problems of the withdrawn child as well as the problems of the overactive child. The practical difficulty here lies in how to apply discipline to the problems of the child. Most of us have at some time stretched our imagination to its limit in order to appeal to the child, to his wanting to learn. Our intentions to educate are good but our aim is poor. We have to set goals. We have to keep them clear. We have to let children know what is expected of them. We need to take a long, careful look at our children, at our ways of teaching them. We should not wait until the child goes astray educationally, loses interest, or fights back. To discipline properly one must know when to leave the child alone to work out his own solutions.

Reasoning is important in conduct and self-control.

There is no precise age of reason, no precise time at which a child becomes susceptible to reason and keeps this susceptibility thereafter. Ability to reason depends upon intellectual ability or willingness to face facts. A child may reason very clearly in one situation and very poorly in another.

Sometimes teachers with good intentions and good aims over-discipline the child.

If too much correction is placed at the child's disposal, he is thereby confused. The teacher may be too cautious, too attentive, even if corrections are given in good spirit. Teachers who

mean to instruct the student would do well to consider the fre-
quency and importance of their comments. Sometimes the mistakes the child makes carry with them sufficient correction. If
the consequences of his actions are already clear enough to the
child, this is the best lesson he can learn.

A characteristic of poor discipline is its defeating nature.

Poor discipline is damaging to the child's self-respect. If a
child is slow in catching on to a number of important aspects of
his daily living, it does not, of course, follow that he is "dumb,"
but it does follow that techniques may need changing.

Fear is an example of the effect of bad discipline. If children
behave well only out of fear, then teachers would be poor indeed.
The accuser is thereby likely to lose status and the respect of the
one he is trying to control.

Punishment is usually a bad form of discipline.

From a modern pedagogical viewpoint, discipline should not
be equated with punishment, but with properly directed learning,
with purpose and control. With the presentation of clear-cut
alternatives, the child knows what will happen to him with either
course of action.

*The teacher is able to accomplish much more by not applying
physical punishment.*

The task of the school is first to introduce the method of so-
called "moral suasion"; with the help of this meritorious method,
the teacher is able to accomplish much more than by compelling
students to perform their duties by applying physical punishment. At all costs, ambition must be awakened in children, paired
with a feeling of duty which will be an internal force that at
every moment will compel them to deal properly with their
tasks.

Unreasonable sternness of parents or teachers never turns out
for good, for they lose their authority in the eyes of their children. And, in a large degree, their children and pupils lose con-

fidence in them. Physical punishments greatly blunt the minds of children and, furthermore, develop stubbornness and even brutality. They kill ambition and meritorious feelings. They are opposed to the spirit of the fullest development of personality. Physical punishments are an old resource of incapable teachers who not only did not know how to teach and educate, but who probably actually did not want to undertake their work seriously.

If the occasion actually arises that no argument can penetrate the mind, and the taut nerves of a child can be quieted only by corporal punishment, it must be only as a last resort. At the same time, there is the right to demand from parents or teachers at this moment that they be guided by the criteria of healthy reason, and not give reign to their exasperated nerves. There have been cases where children have been crippled for life because of corporal punishment.

Corporal punishment is the only effective means of control which some students recognize.

Mistakes do happen with the best of intentions. In the final analysis, it must become clear to the teacher that every situation is unique and demands its own solution. The teacher who reveals a genuine faith in the good intentions of the student will find that confidence honored. A quiet, serious conference with the student, in which the wise teacher asks well-directed questions that lead the student to discover for himself the seriousness of his behavior, is the most effective way of correcting a fault constructively.[1]

Today, education stresses the cooperative nature of the education task between home and school. Where a spirit of cooperation has existed that has involved the total educational situation, the home should be a source of great assistance.

The need to work with parents is usually considered fundamental to the improvement of the child's behavior.

Parents may vary widely in their degree of insight, intelligence, motivation, or cooperation, but they have far more immediate continuous impact on the child's life than anyone else. On the

---

1. Bossing, *op. cit.,* pp. 500-502.

whole, there are reasonable parents and effective assistants to the teacher in solving classroom problems.

In the case of the youngster who is lagging in achievement for whatever reasons — the teacher may consider some of the following actions:

1. Set up a program of reporting to the parents every week or two as to the child's classroom progress.
2. Do not let the child use postponement as a total dodge to getting out of school work. Both teacher and parent should obtain as much agreement as possible on how to handle specific situations.
3. Suggest a series of home work lessons which a parent can supervise, protecting the child from distractions such as television.

The parents have to be interested in the school. The professional educator has to carry a greater responsibility. Any experienced teacher knows that discussions with parents can sometimes flare up into emotional scenes, where feelings are hurt. A cool, objective review of the problems at hand is sorely needed. There are some general procedures to follow in most instances requiring home-school cooperation:

1. A program of homework and a method of controlling disciplinary infractions have to be worked out with teacher and parent participation.
2. The set of expectations put to the child have to be fully agreed upon and supported by home and school.
3. The teacher must, of course, know the parents' attitudes and predispositions, if he has to consider what can be done in the school or classroom to improve the child's situation.
4. Even if the teacher is correct in a difference of opinion with parents, it is mostly an empty correctness that cannot provide a constructive solution. The teacher has always tried to work with parents.

The teacher has to do more than present learning materials, or reports on the child's progress. The brief conferences could acquaint the parents with the problem and possible solutions.

It is very important for learners to have the security of consistent leadership.

In classrooms where there is consistent support, learners are expected to follow through on a number of reasonable agreements. A consistent teacher disciplines himself in the behavior he expects his group to achieve. Skillful teachers build many insights into the value of disciplined behavior while saying very little. Teachers make an important contribution to learners' growth in discipline by the kinds of persons they are. To build effective relationships with other persons you must understand your own aspirations and needs. As the teacher tries to understand why his learners behave as they do in given situations, he must learn to look objectively at the motivation for his own behavior.

Discipline should be learned by teacher and learners. If the teacher wants his learners in his classes to grow, he must grow in self-understanding, and in his own ability to meet his needs.

Techniques for Obtaining Good Discipline

Psychological tests are useful ways of learning about the child's achievements, interests, and abilities.

Children respond differently to different adults and to different approaches. The teachers should consider these differences, knowing each child well in terms of his achievement. The teacher can apply the disciplined learning more judiciously and constructively. He can take advantage to get off to a good, firm start, keeping his attention on the primary purpose. The purpose is not to threaten the children but to let them know the main business of school work and to clarify their role in it. This is not the place to enter into detailed discussion of tests and measurements; it is sufficient to state that this area of knowledge is a *sine qua non* if the other points made are to be used effectively.

The teacher's viewpoint and his expectations as to what the child should do must be reaffirmed to the child periodically.

The teacher should not naively assume that, just because he is doing a good job, he is a good teacher; that the child will respond with one hundred per cent cooperation. Some children do not need more than a slight push of encouragement to be able to go on their own. But most children must have rather sustained attention, otherwise they feel the teacher no longer cares. The teacher's viewpoint and his expectations as to what the child should do must be reaffirmed to the child periodically. He needs support of his attitudes, his skills, his knowledge. It is logical, then, to find it necessary to support the child's efforts at learning. Left alone, most children will not automatically refurbish their attitudes, skills and achievements.

In setting the requirements for the child, try to make them as clear as possible without too much verbal explanation.

The less the teacher talks, the more he imparts to the child by his attitude. The whole task here is to emphasize the emotional development in terms of successful classroom living. This same emphasis, would obtain, of course, for any other aspect of education. The subject matter is important as an instrument of knowledge about the world, but it is equally important as an instrument of knowledge about one's self. No evaluation of self or of subject matter can arise without the child having the contact with tasks, obligations, and/or problems which are posed as part of learning. Thus, discipline is a method of working, a habit of mind, a set of criteria by which to study and judge.

How Achievement is Facilitated by Good Discipline.

Efficiency of learning in the classroom depends on a disciplined routine. Get the first presentation over efficiently. Once the mind has taken in an idea or an impression, it is much easier to stimulate and teach. If the subsequent presentations are worked out as carefully as the first impression, they will likewise be successful.

Immediate concentration, proper selection of, and attention

to stimuli do not guarantee achievement. Immediate focus on the material at hand is certainly good but not all that is necessary for learning. A child may focus well for a few minutes, then lose interest.

The problem of sustaining attention requires flexibility of approach and correlation of material to the child's mental development. To sustain attention, one has to keep the child at the task.

The teacher has to be careful to see that the student distinguishes between negative practice with a purpose, and simply poor practice that has only negative results. The teacher who requires the child to write one hundred times, "I must pay attention in class," thinks he is helping him to concentrate, but he is worsening both his general attitude toward the classroom activities and his skill in applying himself. Rote memory can be overstressed in the same way. A wrong emphasis in rote learning exists in not applying the to-be-learned materials better.

Failing the child at the end of the year is probably not a good device to obtain discipline or achievement.

Our concern is with teaching the child good study habits and attitudes. Passing and failing are problems integral to achievement. But these achievement problems are basically matters of daily self-discipline. If a child does not, or can not, succeed after efforts have been honestly and diligently been made, then failing him or, better, trying to cope with his lack of achievement in some more constructive way is fully indicated. It should be clear that teachers have no objection to failing a student when maximum effort has been made by the student and others to help him complete the work acceptably.

Perhaps, at the high school level, a failure in a course can have more constructive effects. Because of the student's age, the obligations he has may be clearer to him. Teachers should guard against the common tendency to use failure as a retaliation.

Adolescents need both inspiration and direction.

First, students need to have background information for almost any important topic. If teachers can't give students all the facts, they can suggest resource materials and sources of information. *Second,* an adolescent's interest has limits, which can be stretched as a result of quality instruction. Effective teachers prescribe study activity based on general understanding needs.

Calculated effort for independent study.

Teachers who stimulate student-assumed study have to make a strong effort to get the job done. Self-assumed study, except in a few cases, does not occur without teacher encouragement. The importance of teachers cannot be underscored enough in all phases of the independent study operation.

There are *three* principles to keep in mind in this regard:

1. It is required that the staff be willing to spend countless hours with individual students. Independent study motivation requires individual instruction of each student.
2. Teachers need to define the diverse methods of possible investigations. The teacher's job is to teach processes and procedures which the learners can apply to topics of investigation.
3. Teachers have to know the student's personalities to be able to make use of individual interests.

Independent study in any form must never be used as punishment.[1] Learning is the internal rearrangement of complex systems of perceptions, attitudes, feelings, skill, and knowledge. A teacher is more than a store of related facts. He needs to be a highly skilled expert in stimulating personal growth and behavior.

The Importance of Concentration

Two broad courses of action have usually been followed in handling children with concentration and achievement problems.

One has been based on the attitude of "let the child alone; she's already been pushed too much." The lack of concentration is attributed to tension or repressed feelings which, in turn, are considered to stem from some kind of mistreatment or misunder-

---

1. Beggs, David W. *A Practical Application of the Trump Plan,* (Englewood Cliffs, N.J.: Prentice-Hall, Inc., 1964), p. 126.

standing by parents. This type of home condition, it is maintained, is expressed in various ways, and may show itself in school work ability.

A frequent prescription along this line is: If pressures made him too tense to concentrate, then perhaps reducing the pressures will naturally lead him to move toward better concentration and school work.

A *second* alternative actually follows from the first, that of reducing school and home pressures as a necessary beginning point, but also submitting the child to play therapy so as to allow him to work off his already accumulated tensions. The play therapy routine is often complex, and may take a long time and bring one or both parents into therapy. The reasoning behind it is that the child has to be drained, so to speak, of his tensions so he can gain freedom to do his work unhampered by emotional constrictions.[1]

Emotions become dominant factors in classroom problems.

Some problems with children's behavior cannot be solved quickly. It often takes time to determine whether a given course of action is useful. The bright children can often get by at school with minimum effort. Their ability to learn just enough to pass leads ultimately to poor work habits and to emotional problems. The point here is that poor work habits themselves can lead to emotional problems. Gradually the typical youngster is brought into more demanding programs as he moves up the educational ladder. He finds after a while that he cannot keep up, not because of poor ability in the average case — or primary emotional problems, — but because he is lacking in habits of perseverance and efficient work. He then begins to feel inferior and to develop a failure pattern instead of a success pattern. The consequences seem evident. He continues with his failures and negative attitudes; he looks for others to blame for making him this way. He is reinforced in not taking responsibility for himself and his educational or emotional plight. He continues with as soft programs as possible and ultimately may accept a lower, less happy, less challenging level, below his true abilities.[2]

1. Phillips, E.L.; Wiener, D.N.; Haring, N.G.; *Discipline, Achievement, and Mental Health* (Englewood Cliffs, N.J.: Prentice-Hall, Inc., 1960), pp. 85-86.
2. *Ibid.,* pp. 88-89.

Repeated effort is required, accompanied by evaluation of reasons for success and failure.

Repetition of efforts is generally fruitful when certain conditions are achieved:

1. The learner sees a real purpose in making these efforts.
2. He comes to understand the reasons for the success and failure of his efforts.
3. He is helped to redirect his efforts in such ways as to make them more effective.

The modification of behavior involves a series of progressive efforts toward goals. It may take years to succeed in such efforts, when the goals are basic and the obstacles great. Unless the learner continues to believe in the goals — to feel a genuine need or purpose for his striving — he is unlikely to achieve them. In short, he must have *motivation*.

The word "motivation" is intended to mean a recognized goal that is intrinsic in an experience because it satisfies a need or desire felt by the learner. In this sense, one is motivated to engage in an activity when he has a purpose that it fulfills. It is a far different thing to develop learning experiences that fulfill needs than to decide first what the experiences should be and then set out to arouse an appetite for them. This interpretation of motivation suggests an individual drive to achieve a purpose, to pursue an interest, or to solve a problem.[1]

The Child's Relationship with His Peers

Each class is composed of different individuals; each has its unique pattern of interpersonal relationships.

There is a challenge to find even better ways of guiding learing, as well as that of meeting the unpredictable aspects of every learning situation. Establishing favorable reactions to his own personality is a most rewarding task for the teacher. Flexible surroundings and a wealth of instructional materials even more conducive to learning provides the general psychological atmos-

1. Faunce, *op. cit.,* pp. 57-65.

phere which affects the relationships of teachers and pupils.

It is not the teacher's role to interfere and save the sensitive child but rather, at first, to apply his skills to modify an aggressor's attitudes.

The more sensitive and less resourceful child is perhaps most often the victim of unfair play, and such children are in greatest need of adult help.

A more persistent common problem is that of the child who simply needs to develop more respect for his peers and his elders. Parents should give support to the teachers, and direct the distressed child toward solving the problem; but they are overwhelmed by their feelings, and cannot rise to an objective, problem-solving attitude.

It is occasionally necessary to send children home from school if they are disruptive.

The teacher has to learn to view the child's socially disturbing behavior as something that can be changed. The step of sending a child home from school for the remainder of a day requires some forethought. Teacher, principal, and parent must agree that this procedure is useful. The teacher may give the child one warning about his conduct, telling him that he will be sent home if he continues to disobey. If he does continue to do so, the teacher can take him to the office where the parent can be called. The important issue here lies with its proper execution, with careful planning of the conditions under which it will be carried out.

The interest of teachers should be in helping children to mature socially. The teacher can move toward bringing the overly rebellious child into sufficient conformity.

Perhaps every school has an "isolation room" in which to put children who are disruptive of ordinary routine.

The purpose of isolation is twofold: (1) to bring a halt to the disruptive behavior which a given child is displaying; and (2) to teach the child that the teacher has a resource and can move effectively in a way related to his obligation.

It should be emphasized, however, that the "isolation room" should be resorted to only in extreme cases and should be considered very cautiously, because if used indiscriminately it could affect adversely the psychological development of children. Reaction to such disciplinary action depends upon the emotional make-up of the children involved. Children with melancholy and choleric inclinations will experience it very deeply and might be affected by it for a long time. Staying in an "isolation room" forces the child to meditate and analyze. In most cases the end result of such mental activity will be negative. The child might easily lose self-confidence, prestige in the eyes of both his teacher and his fellow students, and might shut himself in and become stubborn. It might also happen that the child will take the isolation room for granted and regard any type of punishment as meaningless.

SUMMARY

Each secondary school should have special counselors with only minimum teaching responsibilities, or without any classes at all. The counselors should be selected with regard to their major task, which is likely to be helping teachers and students.

It has been our position that most problems of learning and achievement can be remedied, not by mechanical devices that end all problems, but by painstaking and persistent efforts to keep the student to his task in firm, fair, intelligent, and rewarding ways. Growth toward maturity is a slow process. Problems have to be solved in a slow, and careful manner.

FOR FURTHER STUDY

Adams, G.S., and others, *Measurement and Evaluation in Education*. New York: The Dryden Press, Inc., 1956.

Adams, J.F. *Counseling & Guidance*. New York: The Macmillan Company, 1965.

Alberty, Harold, *Recognizing the High School Curriculum*. New York: The Macmillan Co., 1953.

Anderson, V.E. and others, *Principles and Practices of Secondary Education*. New York: The Ronald Press Company, 1951

Beggs, D.W., *A Practical Application of the Trump Plan*. Englewood Cliffs, N.J.: Prentice Hall, Inc., 1964.

Bossing, N.L., *Teaching in Secondary Schools*. Boston: Haughton Mifflin Company, 1952.

——————, *Principles of Secondary Education*. Englewood Cliffs: Prentice-Hall, Inc., 1955.

Bradfield, J.M., and others, *Measurement and Evaluation in Education*. New York: The Macmillan Company, 1957.

Craig, R.C., *The Psychology of Learning in the Classroom*. New York: The Macmillan Company, 1966.

Faunce, R.C., and M.J. Clute, *teaching and learning in the junior high school*. San Francisco: Wadsworth Publishing Company, Inc. 1961.

Flaum, L.S., *The Activity High School—The Principles of Its Operation*. New York: Harper and Brothers, 1953.

Gordon, I.J., *The Teacher as a Guidance Worker*. New York: Harper & Brothers, 1956.

Hill, G.E., *Management and Improvement of Guidance*. New York: Appleton-Century-Crofts, 1965.

Krug, E.A., *The Secondary School Curriculum*. New York: Harper and Brothers, 1960.

Miller, C.H., *Guidance Service*. New York: Harper & Row, Publishers, 1965.

Patterson, C.H., *The Counselor in the School*. New York: McGraw-Hill Co., 1967.

Phillips, E.L., D.N. Wiener and N.G. Haring, *Discipline, Achievement and Mental Health*. Englewood Cliffs, N.J.: Prentice-Hall, Inc., 1960.

Ross, C.C., and others, *Measurement in Today's Schools*. New York: Prentice-Hall, Inc., 1954.

Rosser, N.A., *Personal Guidance*. New York: Holt, Rinehart & Winston, Inc., 1964.

Sheviakov, G.V., and F. Redl, *Discipline for Today's Children and Youth*. Washington, D.C.: Department of Supervision and Curriculum, N.E.A., 1944.

Smith, Eugene, Tyler, R.W., *Praising and Recording Student Progress*. New York: Harper & Bros., 1942.

Stefflre, Buford, *Theories of Counseling*. New York: McGraw-Hill Book Co., 1965.

Strang, Ruth, *How to Report Pupil Progress*. Chicago: Science Research Associates, Inc., 1955.

Stratemeyer, F.B., H.L. Forkner, M.G. McKim and A.H. Passow, *Developing a Curriculum for Modern Living*. New York: Columbia University, Teachers College, Bureau of Publication, 1957.

Thomas, R.M., *Social Differences in the Classroom*. New York: David McKay Co., 1965.

Travers, Robert, *How to Make Achievement Tests*. New York: Odyssey Press, 1950.

CHAPTER VIII

THE EDUCATIONAL PROGRAM

An Important Aspect of the Educational Program

An important aspect of any good educational program is designed to provide these educational experiences that will best utilize the present drives and motivations of the learner in activities, and direct his growth toward the ends desired by society.

The ends of education are inherently social ends, determined by the requirements, the problems, and the aspirations of the society of which the student is a member. Consequently, the curriculum must be selected with reference to both the present desires of the child and the demands of society. Curriculum planners should give careful thought to the understandings and abilities one needs to function effectively as an individual and as a citizen.

Information beyond the maturity level has no place.

The specific situations of every-day living, and the meaning it has and can have for the particular learners determine the exact content or subject matter to be used. The activities in which learners engage will vary from some that are very simple to some that are quite complex. How simple or how complex will depend on the insights of which learners seem capable and the experiences for which they are ready. Information beyond the maturity level of the group has no place. When solutions to everyday problems are approached through carefully planned actions, there are opportunities for growth in understanding for generalizations basic to problem-solving.

Daily planning helps both teacher and learners take an immedi-

ate look at the next steps.

The teacher's role in developing experiences with learners is that of a guide. This planning involves a study of the learners. The teacher brings more insight to pupils' suggestions and possesses sufficient security to allow greater freedom in counseling the learners. The teacher should also be prepared to lead the discussion so that first steps are taken in working on the problem.

The major purpose of pupil-teacher planning is to discover the meaning learners see in an experience. Learners who know why they are engaging in an activity do not avoid it or treat it lightly.

Learners must also learn how to appraise the possible values in an experience and how to anticipate problems. A variety of aids should be used to keep plans clear and to help learners carry through effectively.

Skills in planning will vary with the maturity of learners and with intellectual ability. Participation in planning is equally important for the youngest learner and the college youth, for the slow learner and the intellectually gifted, but each will contribute according to his maturity and ability. Through sharing in scheduling their activities, learnes grow in ability to estimate how much time will be needed for a given activity, to recognize the value of budgeting time, to use time efficiently in carrying out plans, and the flexibility needed to meet the demands of the developing situation.

As learners work with the problems and situations of everyday living, the teachers have responsibilities to help learners develop wider and deeper insights by bringing new aspects of the problem to their attention; to make materials available and to suggest sources of information pertinent to the situations with which learners are dealing. Gifted youth particularly tend to like activities which increase their insights and understandings of basic concepts, relationships and processes.

Skills are Important for Curriculum Improvement Activities

Some curriculum development activities require specific skills which the participants may lack. Curriculum planning has been viewed increasingly as a group process because it is possible in groups to build an atmosphere which stimulates and supports new behavior. An effective group can provide a climate for growth, for acquiring new values and behaviors.

The curriculum should consist of a wide variety of purposeful activities based on the present capacities, interests, and needs of learners.

The demands and requirements of society must naturally be taken into account. But the educator must never forget that his first duty is to help the child at each stage of development. The ends and objectives of education are social, having their source not in the purely private needs of individuals but in the ideals and demands of society.

The practical application of educational planning is of evident importance.

At a time when the demand for access to education everywhere grows tremendously, it is obvious that the scarce resources should be stretched to their maximum effectiveness. Moreover, the needs of technological and industrialized societies impose the necessity for matching educational output with professional manpower requirements.[1]

Curriculum Leadership

Leadership is conceived as a functional role, played by an individual at a particular time in a particular group of people.

Leadership is being exercised when a group member is helping the group to define and to meet its needs. The leadership in a group may pass from person to person as the group deals with different problems or with different aspects of a single problem.

In general, it can be said that the role of functional leadership requires a high degree of professional knowledge with respect to the school and the field of social influence within which it

---

1. Bereday, George Z.F. & Lauwerys, J.A., *The World Year Book of Education, 1967* — Editor's Introduction (New York: Harcourt, Brace & World, Inc., 1967), pp. xiii-xiv.

operates.

The primary role of curriculum leadership is to extend the group's skill in the identification of problems, the discussion of ideas, and the formulation of decisions for action.

Curriculum leaders may supply needed expertise in the selection of procedures for changing the curriculum. Creativity in instructional improvement depends on the development of leadership among many individuals — students, teachers, administrators, and persons in professional organizations. The curriculum leader who recognizes that his major concern is in mobilizing the energies, interests, abilities, and initiative of individuals must give attention to the significance of human relations; must find means to motivate and inspire individuals to acquire and use skills.

The value of providing for school visitation as a means of encouraging and stimulating professional growth.

Such visits should include detailed pre-planning, practice in and refining of observational skills, and disussion of observations after the visit.

Supervisors work with teachers, administrators, parents, and other community persons in varied ways, depending upon the particular problem faced.

In working with a teacher, the supervisor may secure desired instructional materials, participate in classroom activity, observe the teaching situation, and may also help in organizing groups studying diverse aspects of the program.

Workshop and Similar In-Service Training

A workshop refers to a full-time program for at least four weeks, organized primarily around problems of the members, and usually with participation in some common social activities.

The term "work conference" is used to refer to a full-time program for two or three weeks, involving group work on special problems, supported by lectures and discussions which may be scheduled in advance, and usually including some social activities.

The term *"conference"* is used to describe a single meeting called to deal with a specific topic, or a series of meetings extending up to one week in length, involving lectures and discussions scheduled in advance, and possibly accompanied by small group work on special problems.

The *clinic* is somewhat similar in that it, too, is set up to provide an opportunity for learning and problem-solving under expert help. Clinics adapt the procedure used in medicine of presenting specific problems to specialists for analysis, assessment, and help in solving them. One or more consultants or experts may supply the needed direction and assistance in analysing difficulties and in suggesting possible steps for the solution of a particular curriculum problem. Thus a group of teachers may work with a remedial reading specialist who guides their activity in diagnosing individual difficulties.

Workshops, work conferences, and *conferences* may be generalized or specialized, providing opportunities for groups or individuals to work on specific problems. They may be conducted in a local school, for a particular school system, on a college or university campus, or sponsored by a regional or national professional organization.

Workshop and similar procedures can have particular value for groups of teachers working toward a curriculum. Clinics can have value as teachers identify problems in working with children and youth on life situations.[1]

Many teachers encourage learners to engage in projects which call for repeated applications of skills they have helped learners to develop.

In addition to specific practice sessions in class, independent work by learners through assignments, and practice that daily

1. Caswell, Hollis L. *Curriculum Improvement in Public School Systems* (New York: Bureau of Publications, Teachers College, Columbia University, 1950), pp. 62-63. Quoted in: Stratemeyer, *Developing of Curriculum...,* pp. 686-687.

experiences provide, many teachers encourage learners to engage in projects which call for repeated applications of skills
they have helped learners to develop. Some of these projects
may be relatively independent of their on-going classroom work.
Often they call for a large measure of creative activity. English
teachers, for example, may encourage learners to seek positions
on the school paper, where the pupils may be required to write a
variety of articles, proofread, edit, interview, practice many
skills which will further their competence in English and be a
source of personal accomplishment for the individual. Speech
teachers will want their pupils to engage in the all school speech
activities, like the debating club or the speakers' bureau. Physical education teachers should encourage those pupils who need
further opportunity to develop their physical skills to engage in
intramural and intermural sport activities. Hobby clubs may
provide the needed motivation for pupils with basic manual and
mechanical skills to practice in order to be truly skilled perform-
ers. These suggestions are all closely tied to the schools' extra-
class program.[1]

*Fundamental Skills and Their Development and
Homeroom Functions*

*Skills should be developed through situations where learners
can see the need for them.*

Learners should be helped to grow in understanding the principles underlying effective development and use of skills. Meeting these criteria requires programs of skill development that are
flexible in terms of individual abilities, that use every appropriate opportunity during the school day. Tests will be used flexibly as resources of information, rather than followed lesson by
lesson. Children must express themselves clearly if others are
to understand them and they, in turn, must listen critically. Lack
of proficiency must be interpreted in terms of maturity — one
would not hold the same standards for each child.

Part of the planning should include consideration of the skills

1.   Carter, William L.; Hansen, C.W.; McKim, M.G., *Learning to Teach in the
Secondary School.* (New York: The Macmillan Company, 1962), pp. 247-248.

needed and the learners' present effectiveness in their use.

There must be provision for the orderly development of skills, as situations requiring skills become more demanding, more complex and more accurate methods are needed.

To develop skills in terms of the demands of new situations, teachers must be thoroughly familiar with the techniques that contribute to competence in each skill area, the ways in which these techniques are interrelated, and the times at which they are most suitably emphasized. The teacher senses when the demands of the situation call for increased skill, and whether the learners' present maturity will make additional growth possible.

Proficiency in skills is attained only with practice.

However, practice must be planned in relation to individual needs and to the total amount of experience. Many valuable opportunities for practice are provided through situations in which the skill is actually needed.

In the occasional situations which demand maturity well beyond that of the learners, the skill aspect of the problem would be solved by the teacher.

Children who are at somewhat the same level of development work together. The others may come together in a wide variety of groupings. Flexibility in grouping allows individuals to proceed at their own rates. The materials used for practice will be any which prove helpful in explaining the process but will be used in relation to the situation faced.

Textbooks and supplementary books are needed if the skills are to be developed.

Plans are made for skill practice just as they are made to follow up any other concern. Periodic checks on progress through discussion and a variety of informational tests will be needed.

School equipment should be selected and used so as to contri-

bute to skills.

Within the classroom a wide variety of resources should be available: pictures, films, filmstrips, recordings, collections, models, charts, maps, etc. Materials used to develop skills in reading, computation, and language should be flexible. Books to aid in the development of skills, like reference books, and small paperbound books on single topics can be very useful.

School materials should be selected, stored and so arranged as to make possible easy communication between groups, classrooms and laboratories for special work. Space should be allotted within rooms for small groups and individuals to work on special interests.

The school has a responsibility to guide learners in the use of the community resources.

Children go on excursions, use the various institutions of industry, and use various forms of community transportation. From the exhibits and pamphlets prepared by local agencies come a series of pictures or a display showing the steps in the development of a product. As community members with whom children associate, they can supplement the work of the school. The doctor, nurse, engineer, lawyer, and farmer contribute information about the occupations they represent.

Other possibilities are found in the public library's special services exhibits; the programs of the various recreational centers can provide other valuable experiences.

A class which is to publish the school paper may profitably study local papers.

In the course of the discussion many different questions will be raised. Homeroom sessions in high school sometimes serve this same purpose. The homeroom functions as:

1. *An administrative unit* (Roll-taking, announcements, locker issuing, drives, etc.)
2. *A unit of the school community* (Representative base for student council, place which students call "home").

3. *An instructional agency* (Based on learner's interests and needs).
4. *An agency for counseling* (Guidance files in homeroom).
5. *An avenue for group guidance* (Educational, vocational, personal-social).
6. *An agency for parent-teacher relationships* (Parent conferences, parent room organization, home calls).
7. *A means of improving human relations* (The goal: understanding and accepting others).[1]

Research and Experimentation

Research is a way of seeking answers to meaningful questions through systematic gathering of evidence about causes, and reflects on problems.

Experimentation is a specific research procedure that calls for the testing of a specific idea to determine whether it has the desired results in practice.[2]

Research involves a careful, systematic search for more accurate answers to questions. Research usually aims at the establishment of basic generalizations or truths which practitioners will apply to their activities. An individual teacher can use research techniques in attacking a problem which he faces in his classroom. One teacher may be dissatisfied with some aspects of the teaching-learning situation and may undertake research to find ways of improving it. Research is viewed as a flexible process, not a fixed formula to be followed step-by-step.

Of the many conditions which foster research and experimentation in the school situation, one of the most important is a climate that will provide sufficient security for individuals to feel free to discuss their real concerns and problems. In identifying problems, it is important to raise questions and not to state answers, for ready solutions may suggest that fundamental causes are being overlooked. The hypothesis must be tested. Testing a hypothesis means actually putting the change into practice and observing the results. The selection of the techniques and procedures for assembling test data requires an understanding of the nature of evidence.

School faculties may also find it necessary to study coopera-

---

1. Johnston, Edgar G. and Faunce, Roland C., *Student Activities in Secondary Schools* (New York: The Ronald Press Company, 1952), pp. 74-80.
2. Stratemeyer, *op. cit.,* p. 705.

tively problems of scheduling and of how to make the school community an effective learning environment. Cooperative studies will be needed to develop more effective evaluation procedures. Teachers who are involved in the research process will actually use many of the data-gathering techniques that they already use in the process of studying learners. The wise selection and use of consultants can facilitate all phases of research. An important means of acquiring research experience is for the individual teacher to explore a problem which concerns him in his own situation. Interdisciplinary studies are needed, and the significant insights of specialists in fields other than education should be analyzed and interpreted.

Schools Today Reflect a New Responsibility

There are differences in the degree to which there is emphasis on specific knowledge and skills and on the methods of work through which these specifics are acquired.

To provide an education that will function effectively in the lives of children, there is need to re-examine the basic curriculum problems. Courses of study show great diversity as to both the range of specific knowledge and skills needed by all learners and the ways used for developing them. Teachers and other curriculum planners must do more than outline the broad goals and the specific knowledge, understandings, and skills which make up the scope of the curriculum. Decisions must be made regarding the ways in which those understandings and skills are to be related and grouped for teaching. Decisions must be made regarding the order in which proposed learnings are to be developed.

The common desire is to plan and implement a school which will furnish the knowledge necessary for a well-rounded education.

Although sound concepts about learning enter every curriculum issue, they are central to the question of how to teach, how to guide curriculum experiences, and how to help teachers translate what they know about the learning process into classroom behavior.

Every aspect of education — defining the role of the school, deciding what to teach, determining the basis for organizing the curriculum, selecting ways of guiding experiences, evaluating pupil growth — requires a choice among alternatives. The individual teacher must become a curriculum worker constantly examing, testing, and evaluating his own practices and procedures as these effect the total educational program. The world demands men who have developed a way of living which tests new ideas, explores new concepts, and re-thinks the application of principles in new situations. Not what an individual knows, but how he uses what he knows as he faces problems of daily living, is a fundamental consideration in developing a curriculum. Thinking men, willing and able to use a scientific approach to the solution of individual and social problems, are essential. A scientific approach implies the habit of seeking reliable information, of distinguishing between fact and fiction; of coming to reasoned conclusions on the basis of careful study of all available data; of evaluating conclusions in the light of new evidence.

The responsibility of the school is to help develop deeper insight as the maturity and experiences of learners permit.

The school can contribute to this end by helping children to see the true worth of each individual; by teaching them to appraise their work with honesty.

The school must be a place where children can learn how they can develop the flexibility of mind imperative to successful living. Each learner has his own unique pattern of capacities. A range of abilities within each class and a variation of ability levels within each individual must be assumed and planned for.

Each learner grows according to his own pattern; his development follows a recognizable sequence.

Each child develops according to his own speed. Readiness for school activities does not depend on maturation alone; experience background also influences learning; through teaching methods it is likely that the immature learner will progress.

To give guidance in selecting experiences that will best achieve the goals, the curriculum worker must understand how learning takes place. There are many activities appropriate for the general maturity of learners, suitable to his particular capacities, and of interest to him. Readiness for learning is related to the developmental process, of helping the learning to acquire the skills and experience needed for undertaking the new activity.

SUMMARY

An important aspect of any good educational program is designed to provide those educational experiences that will best utilize the present drives and motivations of the learner in activities, and to direct growth toward the ends desired by society. Consequently, the curriculum must be selected with reference to both the present desires of the child and the demands of society. Curriculum planners should give careful thought to the understandings and abilities needed to function effectively as an individual, and as a citizen. The curriculum should consist of a wide variety of purposeful activities based on the present capacities, interests, and needs of the learner. Curriculum leaders may supply needed expertise in the selection of procedures for changing the curriculum; to provide an education that will function effectively in the lives of the children.

The common desire is to plan and implement a school which will furnish the knowledge necessary for a well-rounded education.

FOR FURTHER STUDY

Audio-Visual Materials of Instruction, Forty-eigth Yearbook, Part I. National Society for the Study of Education. Chicago: University of Chicago Press, 1949.

Boyles, E.E. *Pragmatism in Education.* New York: Harper & Row, Publishers, 1966.

Bereday, G.Z.F. and J.A. Lauwerys, *The World Year Book of Education, 1967*—Editors Introduction. New York: Harcourt, Brace & World, Inc., 1967.

Billett, R.O., *Fundamentals of Secondary School Teaching.* Boston: Hougton-Mifflin Company, 1940.

Bossing, N.L., *Teaching in Secondary Schools.* Boston: Houghton Mifflin Company, 1952.

Carter, W.L., C.W. Hansen, M.G. McKim, *Learning to Teach in the Secondary School.* New York: The Macmillan Company, 1962.

Haag, J.H., *School Health Program.* New York: Holt, Rinehart & Winston, Inc., 1965.

Hudgins, B.B., *Problem Solving in the Classroom.* New York: The Macmillan Company, 1966.

Johnston, E.G. and R.C. Faunce, *Student Activites in Secondary Schools.* New York: The Ronald Press Company, 1952.

Kinder, J.S., *Audio-Visual Materials and Techniques.* New York: Chanticleer Press, 1949.

Stratemeyer, F.B., H.L. Forkner, M.G. McKim and A.H. Passow, *Developing a Curriculum for Modern Living.* New York: Columbia University, Teachers College, Bureau of Publications, 1957.

Walters, Everett, *Graduate Education Today.* Washington, D.C.,: American Council on Education, 1965.

Wiles, Kimball, *Supervision for Better Schools.* Englewood Cliffs, N.J.: Prentice-Hall, Inc., 1967.

EDUCATION

VOL. III

THE
PRINCIPLES
OF
MODERN CURRICULUM
IN THE CLASSROOM

*The
Principles with Their Interpretations
and
Suggestions*

CHAPTER I

THE CURRICULUM

Curriculum Concepts

*The curriculum consists of all the activities engaged by stu-
dents which are provided, supervised, or directed by the school
to achieve or carry out given purposes of schooling.*

The *curriculum* is really the entire program of the school's
work. It is *everything* the students and their teachers do.

The term "curriculum" is not limited to the outline of the
content to be taught, but is used to include all of the learning
of students which is planned by and directed by the school to
attain its educational goals. This definition covers the formulation of educational objectives, the planning, use, and organization of learning experiences, and the appraisal of student
learning. It also includes not only the learning activities carried
on in the classroom and laboratory but also those at home or in
extra-curricular situations.

A major step in most theories of curriculum development is
the formulation of the educational objectives of the school. It
includes objectives relating to home life, personal-social relations,
civic life, occupations, and the like. It includes not only knowledge and intellectual abilities, but interests, attitudes, social
and recreational skills.

The present shift in school objectives is toward a more dis-
criminating selection, toward the kinds of learning which involve
intellectual skills, which require sequential experiences.

Modern Approach to Learning

The modern approach to learning closely intertwines the
larger aspects of the curriculum with methods in the total pro-

cess of learning. Organized classroom instruction is a necessary part of the curriculum, but the curriculum includes more than organized classroom instruction alone.

The older conception of education placed primary emphasis upon memory processes and acquisition of knowledge. The new, modern concept of education is the process through appropriate experience situations. Therefore, curriculum must be highly flexible in content and organization. The curriculum now focuses attention upon what kind of experiences the learner should have, rather than upon the subject he should study. All activities should be selected with a knowledge of the maturation level. Consideration should be given to college entrance requirements.

Two broader areas of experience learning that are finding ready acceptance into the content of the modern curriculum are the so-called *work-experience* and *extracurricular activities.*

The work-experience is primarily a device to strengthen the effectiveness of vocational education. The out-of-school work-experience approach gives the high school student the chance to develop, through his part-time work, connections that may lead to a full-time job upon graduation.

The experience-centered approach is in line with the principles as guides to a good secondary school.

Teaching is a problem-solving activity; it is fundamentally the finding of best solutions for those everyday problems confronting teachers in behalf of students. Good training supposedly will be brought automatically into being by the pressure of methods from within. The more one knows about the elements of learning, the more able one becomes in planning and executing during teaching time the processes most influential upon progress. A school usually selects some phase of the curriculum for study by the faculty for the year or over a period of years. The class period is allotted to a teacher in order that learning may be kept moving forward. The approach can be based on various inclinations possessed by learners.

The common learnings should satisfy the needs of the young people and make provision for adjusted experiences to individual differences of children.

The curriculum needs to be rich in experiences in constructing, organizing, evaluating, and making direct contact with the community. Pupils in secondary schools ought to work on tasks in which they can succeed, the accomplishment of which will contribute to their security.

The secondary school should give many opportunities for investigation of different points of view.

The best teaching ranges up and down through many levels of experience from direct to abstract and back again.

This is possible not only with learning materials, but with learning activities. But, more effectively, the organization of the curriculum provides for the students' seeing relationships among different experiences.

Visual aids, verbal illustrations, recall of past experiences, demonstrations, developmental discussions, interpretations, and other types of sensory experiences can be utilized. Class time must be devoted to the building up of experiential backgrounds from printed or verbal materials.[1]

The subject-centered approach. — Measurement of progress in learning is by the amount of subject matter acquired. Learners pass or fail on the basis of the amount of subject matter learned.

Four major types of organization can be identified:

1. *The organization by separate subjects.* Here, the scope and organization of school experiences are designed in terms of the subjects to be studied.
2. *The organization by subject fields or groups of related subjects.* — history and geography as social studies; physics, chemistry, and biology as the natural sciences.
3. *The organization in terms of broad areas that cut across subject fields.* These are areas of living or major social functions, so organized as to include every major aspect of life in which learner must function effectively.
4. *The organization emerges from the needs or problems faced by the group* (scope, organization, nor sequence

---

1. Andersen, Vernon E. and others, *Principles and Practices of Secondary Education* (New York: The Ronald Press Company, 1951), pp. 75-78.

is specifically outlined and pre-planned by grade).[1]

Ad. 1. The very nature of this design, by separate subjects frequently used at the college level, tends to focus learnings on the relationships inherent within the subject, rather than on interrelationships among subjects. Pupil-teacher planning and unit activities are not foreign to classrooms operating under this organization. The systematic acquaintance with the cultural heritage, a major goal for curriculum designs, build around separate subjects.

Ad. 2. The scope of the curriculum is still determined by the traditional subjects, but the organization brings together the content of related subjects. Specific topics or concepts within the broad area indicate the sequence from grade to grade.

Designs in which related subjects are grouped are more widespread at the elementary than at the secondary or college levels. Steps in the direction of grouping subjects are found in high schools in courses in general science, communication arts, and in certain types of "core," combining two or more specific subjects.

Ad. 3. Two major patterns have emerged within this general approach — the *first* is a curriculum designed to deal with all major areas of human activity; and the *second* is a design focused on selected problem areas relating to personal and social concerns of children. In each of these patterns, subjects are drawn whenever and wherever they contribute the needed facts understandings, and concepts. Both approaches make specific proposals for curriculum scope, organization, and sequence in advance of the teacher's work with learners. Sequence is usually designated by assigning specific points of focus to different grade levels, using psychological studies of the maturing learner to determine placement.

Ad. 4. In each of the preceding types of curriculum design, scope and sequence are outlined grade by grade, although more flexibility is allowed when areas of study cut across subjects. Here, educators concerned with helping children to draw all needed subject-matter areas to solve their problems of daily living, while still capitalizing on pupil purposes, backgrounds, and capacities, advocate a curriculum design that frees each teacher to develop experiences in terms of the purposes and needs of his particular class. The organization for a particular

1. Caswell, Hollis L., and Foshay, A.W., *Education in the Elementary School* (New York: American Book Company, 1951), pp. 257-268.

group depends on the ways in which problems become focal with them, and sequence is a matter of starting with learners where they are and taking them as far as the new problem or situation demands. This type of design is also one that provides greater opportunity to adjust to the special capacities, problems, and purposes of individuals. This curriculum design is one that demands a very high quality of teacher preparation. It calls for expert understanding of learners, and for breadth of knowledge, as well as for ability to help children focus facts from many sources on a single problem.[1]

Essential difference between subject- and experience-centered approach.

The essential difference is that the learner's development is considered first; then, the experiences to develop those behaviors are planned and subject matter is used to lead to desirable outcomes, and to develop desired attitudes.

In the experience approach, the subject matter is selected during the learning situation to meet the needs. In the subject approach, the selection may come entirely from such sources as the State Department of Education, the central administration of the school, or some other sources. In the experience approach, the teacher needs to be better trained, and needs to have a better understanding of adolescents and life outside the classroom than in the subject approach. He must make a constant study of the behavior of his learners to observe their growth; he must study their abilities, interests, and previous school background. Here, the Handbook on Curriculum Study offers the following list of principles:

1. The curriculum will be effective to the degree that it accurately mirrors the dynamic nature of environment and the "inevitability of social change."
2. Basic social change is in the direction of increasing social complexity and cooperative endeavor.
3. For purposes of curriculum development, society is here conceived as a democracy in which the growth and welfare of the individual and of the social group is regarded as of transcendental importance.

1. Stratemeyer, Florence B. and others, *Developing a Curriculum for Modern Living* (New York: Bureau of Publications, Teachers College, Columbia University, 1957), pp. 91-105.

4. The school is one of the agencies of society for the continuation and recreation of itself.
5. Experiences are the fundamental basis of learning.
6. Growth processes in individuals and in society are of continuing interaction between individuals and society.
7. There is a wide range of differentiation among individuals
in interests, understandings, appreciations, abilities, ability to learn.
8. Effective curriculum development must be comprehensive
and continuous.[1]

Efficient teaching results from teaching the proper subject
matter at the proper time by proper method. To reach this point,
teaching must be based on sound principles of learning. Curricula that violate the principles of learning are wasteful.

*The basic principles of curriculum development, which underlie
the activities of learners, are essentially the same at every age.*

Curriculum planners who would provide for youth's special
needs have some unique problems to solve, however. Because
learners at this level have the ability to grapple with life situations with greater depth and breadth of insight, the help of *specialists* must be available for longer periods of time. Variations
in interests, coupled with maturing intellectual ability, compli-
cate the problem of securing effective balance between general
education and specialized education — of providing the *extended
experience* required by youth with special talent, interest, or
concern. In varying degrees, depending on the concerns and
maturity of individuals, there are also problems of providing
extended acquaintance with specific subject fields. The specific
learning experiences and their organization will vary with emerging maturity.[2]

*If curriculum builders wish pupils to develop clear concepts,
they should provide many experiences with the materials they
wish the pupils to learn.*

The more and varied our experiences are, the clearer our concepts become. To develop good concepts one must guide pupils,

1. *Handbook on Curriculum Study,* Curriculum Series, Bulletin No. 1 (State
of Oregon, Department of Education, December, 1937), pp. 75-82.
2. Stratemeyer, *op. cit.,* p. 579.

rather than tell them. Learners need to manipulate both materials and ideas; to see them in different contexts; and to watch them work. Drill and practice are both essential in the learning of skills and in learning for retention. *Meanings* and *relationships* can be utilized to make subject matter easier to learn. Subject matter that lacks meaning also lacks interest. It is difficult to keep *motivation* high when a pupil is learning such material.

The goals of learners can be made to fit the curriculum — to some extent.

Goals or purposes determine not only what we do but what we perceive and what we understand and how we react to situations. Teachers can influence the goals pupils select, and can cause them to change their goals, to discard less desirable goals in favor of better ones. When a child works for an intrinsic goal, he works because he wants to work, or because the product of the work is valuable to him. Subject matter that has intrinsic value to learners has longer staying power than that learned because of extrinsic values. Not all our needs are felt needs, and learners must learn some things, whether they like to or not. In such cases, one must turn to extrinsic goals. Everything a man does consciously he does in relation to some goal. Immediate goals seem to be more effective motives than are deferred goals. The teacher in the classroom must depend upon immediate goals as motivation for the students' daily class work, but to build curricula for immediate goals is not necessary. Setting goals that are beyond one's capacities tends to discourage and frustrate learners, because they cause failures. But repeated failures are liable to cause emotional problems. On the other hand, goals that are set too low provide no challenge and may cause discontent. Presumably, curriculum standards should be neither too high nor too low for any learner. Learners' goals can be changed, and sometimes must be changed, to meet goals set by adults. Consequently, curricula need not be tied to learners' transitory interests. Each curriculum should be so differentiated that each learner, no matter what his abilities and interests, will be challenged to put forth his greatest effort. Pupils should be given ample opportunity to solve problems, to investigate independently, and to think originally. The curriculum that concentrates only on the academic is doing only part of the job. The content of the curriculum needs to be meaningful to the pupils and valuable to them, both now and in the future. The curriculum should follow an orderly sequence, increasing in difficulty and complexity as the child becomes ready. The curriculum should be free to the child, so that he can realize his full potential.

The Subject Curriculum

The subject curriculum is an organization of the content of education into subjects of instruction.

The distinctive characteristics of subject curriculum:

1. In the subject curriculum, the content is selected and ordered in such a way as to discipline the student in those classifications and arrangements of ideas that have proved most beneficial in locating and investigating new problems of specialized research. By becoming disciplined in subjects such as mathematics, history, English, and science, the student acquires the ideas, facts, and skills by which he continues to grow when his school days are over.

2. The other distinctive characteristic of the subject curriculum is that it emphasizes expository discourse and techniques of explanation.

Exposition is a form of discourse in which ideas are stated and elaborated so that they may be understood. The main ideas are ordered and explored and, when convenient, illustrated. At least four kinds of exposition are found in the subject curriculum:

1. Proceeds from the simple to the complex.
2. Is an expository order based upon prerequisite learnings. This principle is followed particularly in subjects consisting largely of laws and principles, such as physics, grammar, and geometry.
3. The form of exposition which proceeds from the whole to

the part.   Geography frequently begins with the globe, with the idea that the earth is a sphere.
4. This kind of exposition is chronological.   Facts and ideas are arranged in a time sequence, so that presentation of later events is preceded by discussion of earlier ones. This is the organization followed in history courses.

Teaching procedures and techniques are largely based upon language activities — lectures, discussions, questions and answers, written exercises, oral reports, term papers, and the like. Most of these activities tend to emphasize the meaning of terms in their relation to other terms.   Hence, the subject curriculum tends not to use such activities as painting, cartooning, modeling, designing, constructing, and the like — for these are seldom suited to the purposes of instruction.

Other characteristics of subject curriculum:

1. The subjects may be required of all students, required only for certain specified groups, by certain individuals, or by anyone. Those responsible for planning the subject curriculum have determined in advance that some subject matter shall either be required or elected by specified individuals or groups.   Since the subject curriculum is planned in advance, it is necessarily planned for someone.   Therefore, the designation of these individuals and groups who are to enter certain courses of the curriculum is only to be expected.

2. The program of general education is determined in the subject curriculum by making some subjects constant in all programs of study.   These constants do not, of course, constitute all of the common experience areas.   There are assembly programs, fire drills, and other all-school functions that provide common learnings.   Nevertheless, it is true that the required courses do comprise the major share of the general education program.

3. *Requirement of subjects does not mean identical experiences for all students.*   Teachers of a subject curriculum know about individual differences and understand the necessity of taking these into account in the teaching process.

4. *Required and elective subjects are determined in advance.* In order to plan course offerings, it is necessary to determine

in advance which courses to offer, the number of sections of each, the people who are to teach them, and the people who are to enroll in them. It is also necessary to decide the grade level at which each course is to be offered, and to select the students who are to be required to take, or are free to elect each course at each grade level.

5. *Elective courses, differentiated assignments, and special programs care for individual differences in interest and ability.* Adjustment of instruction to interest and ability of students is made in the subject curriculum partly by elective subjects and partly by differentiation of assignments within subjects. If a boy is interested in farming, he may take courses in agriculture. Variations in ability may be provided for by differentiated assignments in which the faster learners participate in more as well as different activities.

6. *This curriculum may or may not be given deliberate social direction.* No teacher can carry on the instructional process without moving in some social direction. The first choice of direction is made in the determination of educational goals.[1]

One of the most difficult tasks of curriculum building is the selection of subject matter appropriate to the objectives of instruction.

Changes in objectives require changes in content.

As an individual acquires the knowledge available to him in the subjects, he takes on the ways of thinking peculiar to these subjects.

He learns to think as the physicist thinks when he studies physics, as the historian thinks when he studies history. If he does not learn so to think, the fault is to be found in the instruction and not in the curriculum pattern.

In any kind of curriculum whatever, some things are emphasized and others are excluded. There is always some sort of selection, and whatever is selected is necessarily separated from other things.

The subject curriculum assumes that the subjects are a con-

1. Smith, *op. cit.,* pp. 230-238.

venient and efficient way of classifying knowledge for use in helping children learn the answers to their questions and to ask new and more advanced questions.

But even more, it is the function of instruction to push back the horizons of children, to expand their ideas, and to show them new possibilities. As they take on new knowledge, children develop new ways of looking at things, and new and enlarged interests and ideas.[1]

The Correlated Curriculum

The correlated curriculum is a subject curriculum in which two or more subjects are articulated, and relationships between or among them are made a part of instruction without destroying the subject boundaries.

The views of Herbart laid great stress upon *concentration*, by which he meant complete absorption in an idea or object of thought, and *correlation*, by which he meant the reinforcement of the idea by related and supporting conceptions. These conceptions emphasized interest, meaning, and relation, which led his followers to the notion of concentration and correlation of studies. In their view, concentration was interpreted as the grouping of subjects around a central study, and correlation was interpreted as the support of the topics of this central subject by related studies. This interpretation is also the substance of the current significance of correlation. For example, history and geography may be taught so as to reinforce each other, or courses in science and mathematics may be conducted in such a way that the mathematics becomes a useful tool in science, and the scientific data and problems become material for study in mathematics courses.

Characteristics of the correlated curriculum.

There are three kinds of correlation, depending upon the kinds of subject matter involved: *factual, descriptive,* and *normative.*

Factual correlation is illustrated in the articulation of history and literature when the historical facts are studied with a view

1. *Ibid.,* pp. 250-252.

to enriching the enjoyment of the reader. Another illustration is found in the subjects of history and geography when the facts of geography are studied as the setting of a historical event.

Descriptive correlation is illustrated in the use of generalizations common to two or more subjects. Psychology can be correlated with history, or with any of the social studies, by employing psychological principles to explain social events.

Normative correlation is attained in much the same way as descriptive correlation, the chief difference being that the principles are social-moral, rather than descriptive. For instance, American history and literature may be correlated at some points through the social-moral principles constituting the theory of democracy.

The extent of correlation between subjects depends upon the inherent relations of the subjects, convenience, and the knowledge and wisdom of the teachers.[1]

The Integrated Curriculum

The term "integrated" is used to distinguish this curriculum from the type which is set up in divisions by subjects. Moreover, it is organized in such a way that the teacher may find readily at hand the proper aids and subject matter content for directing the learning processes, to the end that better unification of effort and greater integration of learning may be achieved.

Distinctive characteristics of integrated curriculum:

1. The integrated curriculum is planned to provide better selection and organization of teaching materials and to promote better methods of teaching and learning.

2. The integrated curriculum organizes the educational program in such a way that the child will be the focal center for growth and development.

In constructing the integrated curriculum, the organizing determinants are derived from an interpretation of life needs, rather than from fixed subjects to be learned.

The learning becomes effective only to the degree that the whole child is interested. The integrated curriculum attempts to

1. *Ibid.*, pp. 252-254.

bring about the transmutation of subjects and lesson-reciting into life experiences, so that learning may become both more natural and more effective.

The course of study should have sufficient enrichment and flexibility.

The course of study should have sufficient enrichment and flexibility so that the teacher may continue the varied learning processes, whether they be securing information, developing certain attitudes and appreciations, or cultivating certain skills. Moreover, pupils should be recognized as individuals, and permitted to progress in accordance with their learning ability and the amount of time available.

This varied plan of teaching may involve large groups at times, and small groups at other times.

The relative amount of class instruction, of small-group teaching, of individual assistance, of routine drill, and of individual and self-directed effort must be left to the judgement of the teacher.

The integrated curriculum has been set up in course-of-study units.

Such units are for the guidance of the teacher, and indicate where the materials of instruction are to be found, and in what ways the outcomes may be realized. At times the major emphasis will be upon enrichment of meanings and understandings, at other times upon the drill or the use of techniques sufficient to promote growth in thinking and learning.

The integrated curriculum is based on the philosophy which defines education as "creative grappling with the situations which the world continually puts before us."

The individual must and does act in response to the problems or situations with which he is faced. It is the task of education to set up its program in such a way that the child may and will

develop the ability to consider intelligently and face courage-
ously certain life problems with some skill in finding possible
solutions.

*It should be understood that integrated curriculum presents a
somewhat new organization of subject matter.*

The integrated curriculum presents a somewhat new organization of subject matter involving changed methods of teaching,
along with other changes which require time for training teachers
and adjusting organization.

The integrated curriculum enabled the teachers to shift more
easily from the teacher-assigned task to the teacher-pupil directed activities.[1]

The Activity Curriculum

Essential characteristics of activity curriculum:

1. The activities are planned cooperatively by students and the
teacher. Children are thus engaged not solely for the knowledge
gained but also for the satisfactions, methods, and disciplines
resulting from participation in the planning process.

2. The curriculum may or may not have deliberate social
direction. No educational program is socially neutral. The first
basis for the selection of curriculum content is the interest of
children. These interests have been conditioned by the radio,
television, motion pictures, comic books, newspapers, homes,
the church, and other mind-forming agencies. If the teachers
in an activity curriculum understood and held such a value system, then the activity curriculum would be devoted deliberately
to social ends.

3. The problem-solving is the dominant method. In the activity
curriculum, the teaching-learning process consists largely of
problem-solving. The major values of this curriculum are not to
be found in the answers to problems but in the learnings inherent
in the activities of problem-solving. The subject matter from
almost every field of knowledge is used in the activity curriculum,
because the interests of children lead to problems requiring a

1. Oberholtzer, Edison E., *An Integrated Curriculum in Practice* (New York:
Bureau of Publications, Teachers College, Columbia University, 1937), pp. 7-17.

great diversity of content.

4. Special classes and out-of-class activities are often necessary to care for children's individual needs. The school recognizes a responsibility to help the child who wants to pursue an interest beyond the domain of a particular project.

5. The special subjects provide for specialized interests. While the individual is motivated to learn the skills of arithmetic, writing, and speaking, or others by the need to engage in certain activities, activity programs have found a need for time set aside for further development of these skills. It must be understood that these specialized subjects grow from the demands of pupil interest and need.[1]

Principles of Activity Curriculum

The primary principle of the activity curriculum is that the interests and purposes of children determine the educational program.

What is taught, when it is taught, and the order in which it is learned go back to what is required for the realization of children's purposes.

According to the theory of the activity curriculum, children are always actively engaged in doing something.

The principle that the educational program is to be shaped by the interests and purposes of those to be educated gives a special place to subject matter in the educative process. This principle implies that subject matter is a means of fulfilling the purposes and aspirations of the individual or social group. The activity program does not visualize any undue coercing of individuals to follow the interests of the group. If a child found his individual interests compelling, he would not be forced to go along with the group.

The teacher plays a unique role in an activity organization. His first responsiblity is to locate the dominant interests of individuals and of the group, for the activity program is bound by these no less than the subject curriculum is bound by subject matter lines. However, once these interests are apparent, the teacher's influence is felt in cooperatively helping the children to select the most worthwhile of these for study.

1. Smith, *op. cit.,* pp. 275-281.

*A second distinctive principle of the activity curriculum is that
"common learnings" result from the pursuit of common interests.*

Children, like adults, usually have mutual interests and individual interests at the same time. It frequently happens that individuals prefer to pursue their personal interests rather than those shared by the group. Again, individuals may not agree as to which of the interests mutually entertained should be followed. At this crucial point in the development of an activity program, the ability to reach agreement about the interests to be pursued will depend upon whether or not the children have enough shared values in which to ground their opinions.

*The third distinctive principle is that the activity curriculum is
not planned in advance.*

Since child interests provide the starting point for instructional planning, it follows that the activity curriculum cannot be pre-planned.

While the teacher cannot plan the curriculum in the sense of determining in advance what the children are to do, he is responsible for several major tasks for which planning is necessary:

1. He must work with individuals and groups of individuals to discover their interests.
2. He must guide them in evaluating these interests and in making selections from among those which are considered.
3. He must help the individual or group to plan and to carry out the activities required in the pursuit of these interests.
4. He must guide the individual or group in assessing what they have accomplished.

All of these responsibilities require that the teacher make plans for his own activities in the classroom. He must decide how he can best help the children plan what they will do, how they will do it, and how they will evaluate the results of their activities. Materials and equipment must be available, and possible ways of seeking out the interests of individuals and the group must be explored. Categories of interest based on research studies and practical experience are often included in descriptions of activity programs. Such categories are the result of investiga-

tions of areas in which children at certain ages may find fundamental interests.[1]

Guidance and Curriculum

*The children are intensely active in meeting the complexities
in the world of their everyday experiences.*

The children's interests are, for the most part, limited to the
present. Their motives are derived from the normal course of
their daily living. Preparation for the future should not be neglected; for such preparation is the result of effective participation
in activities.

*Children must adjust to the physical and cultural environment
into which they are born.*

They can accomplish this most effectively by studying as directly as possible those aspects of their environment relating to
their everyday affairs. Observation embraces those activities
that have to do with the exploration of the environment and with
the adjustment of children to it. The environment stimulates
them to observe, to ask questions. They ask about trees, plants,
insects, etc.

*Play — As an area of children's activity, it should be developed
on a parity with any other category of children's interests.*

Playing with *water*, pouring, wading, watching objects in water,
building water-wheels, watching the action of water on land.
Playing with *air*, sailboats, windmills, airplanes, etc. Playing
with *reflectors*, mirrors, prisms, lenses, which develop problems
in light, color, etc. Experience with magnets, batteries, tele-
phones, electric motors, electric lights, etc.

The *handwork* is the subject in elementary school. It is based
upon the constructive activities in which children normally engage. That children like to make things, to construct, to contrive,
is a matter of common observation. It bears out the fact that
children's interests are very diversified, and tend to be distri-

1. *Ibid.,* pp. 274-275.

buted over a great variety of objects and events. Children show interest in first one thing and then another; they change from one activity to another as their interests lead them, without the least hesitation.

The stories included in the program must be such as will give immediate enjoyment.

The general types of reading materials used are indicated in the following list:
1. Fables, fairy tales, myths, legends, wonder stories.
2. Travel, including sightseeing, exploration, scenery, and customs.
3. Nature.
4. Industries.
5. History and biography.
6. Fiction and humor.

Among the activities included in this category are dramatics, singing, drawing, and looking at pictures.

Present knowledge of children's interests rests upon practical observations, shrewd guesses and empirical generalizations. A considerable amount of understanding of interests has resulted from practical experience in building activity curricula and in observing the free behavior of children.

The activities, the things children can do will vary in appeal to children of different ages.

Children in the first grade may be interested in building and decorating a playhouse, but the second and third grades these same children may be more interested in building and studying appropriate window displays. Activities embody meanings, values, and skills, and require all sorts of instructional materials.

Guidance and curriculum are closely related in at least five ways:

1. An unsuitable curriculum will create more problems than a large staff of counselors can correct.
2. An inadequate curriculum will block effective guidance.

3. Insights gained in the guidance of individual pupils should be used in curriculum modification.
4. Many phases of guidance may lead toward curriculum modification.
5. Guidance through groups is an important part of the curriculum.

Guidance techniques also serve as a source of insights into curriculum needs:

1. Through *observation,* teachers can see where pupils' interest is high, where apathy prevails, where class work is too hard or too easy for individual children, where a particular learning process has been well or poorly analyzed.
2. Through testing, teachers see where pupils are underachieving or over-achieving.
3. Through *subjective compositions* by the pupils, teachers gain insights into the effectiveness of the curriculum and methods of instruction.
4. Through *follow-up studies,* often made by guidance workers, teachers may become aware of poor instruction in English.
5. Through *interviews* in which, for example, retarded readers have told how they were allowed to sit in class and do busy work, without receiving any help.

Child study, curriculum, and guidance interact with one another. Child study uncovers needs for educational experiences which the curriculum can supply. Through guidance, individual pupils are helped to choose and succeed in experiences that help them to develop their potentialities.[1]

1. Strang, Ruth, *How Guidance Relates to the Curriculum—The Personnel and Guidance Journal,* January, 1954, pp. 262-265.

SUMMARY

The learnings of the secondary school are organized into a curriculum in order to further the needs of both the individual and society. The old social demand was for college preparation. Now, less than one-third of the high school students go on to college, but the college-preparatory curriculum predominates.

The two approaches represent fundamentally different points of view: the *first* begins with the subject matter to be learned; the *other* with the desired development of the student.

The experience approach can be used most effectively in the area of the common learnings. In some areas of specialized learnings, it is more difficult to apply an experience approach.

The proposed curriculum fosters growth, social relationships, and helps an individuals use their learnings as guides in dealing with life situations.

FOR FURTHER STUDY

Alexander, W.M., and Paul Halverson, *Effective Teaching in Secondary Schools.* New York: Rinehart and Company, Inc., 1956.

Anderson, Vernon, *Principles and Procedures of Curriculum Development.* New York: The Ronald Press Company, 1956.

Anderson, V.E., and W.T. Gruhn, *Principles and Practices of Secondary Education.* New York: The Ronald Press Company, 1951.

Baldwin, Orrel, *The Way We Live.* New York: Noble & Noble Publishers, Inc., 1964.

Beck, R.H., W.W. Cook, and N.C. Kearney, *Curriculum in the Modern Elementary School.* Englewood Cliffs, N.J.: Prentice-Hall, Inc., 1953.

Butler, F.A., *The Improvement of Teaching in Secondary Schools.* Chicago: University of Chicago Press, 1954.

Carin, Arthur, and R.B. Sund, *Teaching Science through Discovery.* Columbus, Ohio: Charles E. Merrill Books, Inc., 1964.

Caswell, H.L., and A.W. Foshay, *Education in the Elementary School.* New York: American Book Company, 1951.

Cay, O.F., *Curriculum: Design for Learning.* Indianapolis: The Bobbs-Merrill Co., Inc., 1966.

Handbook on Curriculum Study, Curriculum Series, Bulletin No. 1 (State of Oregon, Department of Education, December, 1937).

Herrick, V.E., D.W. Andersen, and J.B. Macdonald, *Strategies of Curriculum Development.* Columbus, Ohio: Charles E. Merrill Books, Inc., 1965.

Hurley, B.D., *Curriculum for Elementary School Children.* New York: The Ronald Press Co., 1957.

Nason, L.J., *How to Study the Right Way.* New York: Cornerstone Library, Inc., 1965.

Oberholtzer, E.E., *An Integrated Curriculum in Practice.* New York: Bureau of Publications, Teachers College, Columbia University, 1937.

O'Donnell, Mabel, *Real and Make-Believe.* New York: Harper and Row, 1966.

Smith, B.O., W.O. Stanley, and J.H. Shores, *Fundamentals of Curriculum Development.* Yonkers-on-Hudson, N.Y.: World Book Co., 1957.

Strang, Ruth, *How Guidance Relates to the Curriculum — The Personnel and Guidance Journal,* January, 1954.

Strategy for Curriculum Change. Ed. by Robert R. Leeper. Washington, D.C.: Association for Supervision and Curriculum Development, 1965.

Stratemeyer, F.B., H.L. Forkner, M.G. McKim, and A.H. Passow, *Developing a Curriculum for Modern Living.* New York: Columbia University, Teachers College, Bureau of Publications, 1957.

CHAPTER II

THE CORE CURRICULUM

Features of the Core Curriculum

The core curriculum represents an experimental approach to the selection and organization of some of the common learning materials in the high school curriculum around the significant problems of youth.[1]

The core curriculum grew from two widely different emphases in educational thought:

1. The organization of subject matter into a unifying core of studies was believed to be a way of enriching the content with greater meaning by making the interrelations of subject matter more evident.

2. It became clear that the educational program must emphasize the clarification and maintenance of common values. The society became fragmented and divided by the forces released by science and technology.

Two features of the core curriculum distinguish it from all other forms of curriculum organization.

1. The core curriculum emphasizes social values. The universal elements of the culture give society its stability and unity. The core of the universals consists of the basic values or rules by which the people govern their activities. By these rules they decide what is good or bad, desirable or undesirable.

The values that make up the stable and vital aspects of the universals constitute the heart of the core curriculum.

The *aims* of a subject curriculum are conceived in terms of understandings or skills achieved in the study of organized fields of knowledge. The need for these understandings and skills is

1. Mills, Hubert H. and Douglass, H.R., *Teaching in High School* (New York: The Ronald Press Co., 1957), p. 271.

justified partly on the basis of their value to individuals as specialists. For instance, if a man knows mathematics, he will be able to study physics.

2. The structure of the core curriculum is fixed by broad social problems or by themes of social living. Just as the structure of the subject curriculum is shaped by the requirements of explanation and research, and that of the activity curriculum by the interests of children, so the structure of the core curriculum is determined by the way in which social issues are grouped.[1]

Departures from the subject-matter organization of the central courses of the curriculum (those subjects required of all students) were sometimes referred to as experiments with the core curriculum.

The subjects that are considered necessary for graduation became known as "required" subjects or "constants"; the other subjects considered of special value only to particular students are listed as "electives" or "variables." The *constants,* when grouped together, are called the *general curriculum,* or *common learnings.*

"Constants" (state requirements) for high school diploma are: English, American history, physical education, plus course requirements for curriculum students are taking.

"Constants" for college preparatory course — liberal arts are: minimum of two years of mathematics (preferably elementary algebra and geometry), two years of a modern language (French, Latin, Spanish, German or Russian); plus state-required subjects (English, American history and physical education), plus electives to meet required amount of credits for graduation.

"Constants" for college preparatory course — science majors are: four years of college preparatory mathematics, physics, and chemistry; two years of a modern language (one or more), plus state-required subjects, plus electives.

The "required" courses are frequently referred to as the "core" of the high school curriculum.

The difference between the "core program" and the "core curriculum":

The *core program,* emphasizing the development of the com-

---

1. Smith, *op. cit.,* pp. 311-317.

mon competencies needed by all, and the *other division* emphasizing the development of special competencies based upon the recognition of individual differences in interests, aptitudes, and capacities; the entire curriculum utilizing consistently the same basic principles of learning, teaching methods, and problem organization. The *core curriculum* refers to a form of the experience curriculum organized into a closely integrated and interrelated whole with one division.[1]

In the core program, teaching is essentially a matter of guiding the learner in a way that will enable him to meet new situations and adjust to them effectively. In each core group are included pupils of varying abilities and interests. In secondary schools in which the cores are carried on successfully, pupils are placed heterogeneously in core classes. The daily core-class period is usually longer in the junior high school, because junior high pupils have a greater need for general education, and senior high school students need more specialized studies.

In some schools, two or more teachers act as instructors of the class, one of them serving as coordinator of the work.

The learning materials are selected by the teacher and the students.[2] These materials are then organized around comprehensive units of learning. A wide variety of learning materials and experiences appropriate to the study of a particular problem are utilized, such as textbook and library materials, audio-visual aids, fields trips, etc.

In the *methods* of instruction, emphasis is placed upon problem solving techniques, including cooperative student-teacher planning, student research, and group discussions. In the class period, students engage in various types of study activities, such as individual reading, planning and preparation by individuals

1. Bossing, Nelson L., *Principles of Secondary Education* (Englewood Cliffs, N.J.: Prentice-Hall, Inc., 1955), p. 412.
2. The participation of students in the selection and planning of teaching material should not be understood as a process whereby the teacher consults his students as to what material should be considered. This is an *indirect* method of teaching. By giving the students a chance to participate in the planning, those in charge of teaching give them also a chance to think, to verbalize, to express logically their thoughts, and finally to arrive at correct conclusions. Moreover these students acquire social habits, but most of all they learn to adjust their varying opinions intelligently. It goes without saying that the result of such mutual planning will be considerably influenced by the teacher's intention, because it is he who initiates such planning.

However, in order to make such planning optimally fruitful, the teacher must be appropriately prepared for it, and the students must be intellectually mature. Otherwise, such planning might easily become a waste of time.

and committees for reports, exhibits, etc.

Evaluation of the work of the members of the core class is made by: self-evaluation, tests, observations of student behavior, skills, and attitudes.

What Is It?

Many types of core programs are new to school practices. Subjects combined in the core are correlated but not fused. For example, the teaching of American literature may be correlated with the teaching of American history. The group may be taught both subjects by one teacher, or each subject by the appropriate subject teacher.

In recent years, many attempts have been made to clarify the concept of the core as that term is applied to the high school curriculum. Some of the fairly common definitions are: a group of required subjects, a combination of two or more subjects. It is a fact that many terms such as the following are used synonymously with core: common learnings, general education, unified studies, self-contained classrooms, basic courses, fused courses, and English-social studies.

The conception of core most likely to transform and improve general education in the high school is: a group of structured problem areas, based upon the common problems, needs, and interests of adolescents, from which are developed teacher-student planned learning units or activities.

Following are some of the principal characteristics of an effective adolescent-problems core program based on this conception:

1. It deals with the area of general education, and hence is directed primarily toward the development of the common values, understandings, and skills.

2. Since it provides for general education, it is required of all students at any given level.

3. It utilizes a block of time sufficiently large to deal with a broad, comprehensive unit of work, with homeroom and guidance activities, and with individual instruction.

4. It is based upon the common problems, needs and interests

of youth as ascertained by the teaching staff and the core teacher, in cooperation with his students. It draws freely upon all pertinent resources, including logically organized subjects or fields of knowledge.

5. It has a clearly defined but flexible scope and sequence based on pre-planned problem areas derived from the major values of democratic living, and the common problems, needs, and interests of students.

6. Instruction is based upon learning units derived principally from the established problem areas which are planned, carried forward, and evaluated by the teacher and students.

7. It is supported and reinforced by a rich offering of special-interest activities — both formal and informal — designed to meet the particular needs of students, and to develop their unique capacities, interests, and talents.

The difference between the two types of programs is to be found in the fact that the *core program* deals with the area of *general education,* and hence finds its scope and sequence in the broad areas of living, while the *special-interest areas* deal with a content determined by the *particular field.* *Both* types of learning experiences are essential to a well-rounded education.

Actually, a good core program cannot be developed without the help of a subject specialist in planning resource units or guides in core classroom teaching at points of need, and in teaching his special field with constant reference to what goes on in the core so as to reinforce and enrich the core program.[1]

Essential Features

The core curriculum has four essential features:

1. The core areas are required of all students. The common learnings they consist of are believed to be essential for all members of the society, regardless of ability, social status or vocational plans. They are designed to provide all youth with a common social orientation and to foster social reintegration.

2. Activities are cooperatively planned by teacher and pupils — the idea that children should have a large share in the location,

1. *A Sound Core Program—What It Is and What It Isn't,* by Harold Alberty. From the *NEA Journal,* January, 1956, pp. 20-22.

selection, and definition of problems to be studied, as well as in planning the activities by which the problems may be solved; the way children accept the problems as their own responsibilities. The theory of the core curriculum recognizes the principle of personal involvement as an essential element of effective teaching.

3. Provisions for special needs and interests are made as they arise. The core curriculum is a more flexible organization than the subject curriculum. It is, therefore, more responsive to the interests of individuals. By the same token, the structure of the core curriculum is not based primarily upon the interests of individuals, as is the activity curriculum, and thus needs more special arrangements to care for those interests. Each area of the core program is fraught with possibilities for the stimulation of specialized interests, but provision for further development of these specialities is to be found, for the most part, in courses outside the core program.

The core curriculum does not include a number of activities commonly found in the school.

4. Skills are taught as they are needed. According to the theory of the core curriculum, learning to read, write, spell, use arithmetic, work with others, think effectively, or perform adequately, and a host of other skills, should be motivated by a feeling of need on the part of the individual. The core program, however, provides the problems and experiences that create the need for various skills.[1]

The core consists of a number of logically organized subjects or fields of knowledge, some of which are correlated. Four types are representative of what most writers describe as core type and core curriculum.

> *Type A.* Each subject retains its identity in the core; that is, subjects are correlated but not fused. The group may be taught both subjects (e. g. American history and American literature) by one teacher or each subject by the appropriate subject teacher.
>
> *Type B.* Subject lines are broken down. Subjects included in core are fused into a unified whole around a central theme.

1. Smith, *op. cit.,* pp. 318-324.

Type C. Subjects are brought in only as needed. The core consists of a number of broad pre-planned problems usually related to a central theme. Problems are based on predetermined areas of pupil needs, both immediate felt needs and needs as society sees them. Members of the class may or may not have a choice from among several problems; they will, however, choose activities within the problems. *Type D.* Subjects are brought in only as needed as in "C". There are no predetermined problem areas to be studied. Pupils and teachers are free to select problems on which they wish to work.[1]

Harold Alberty, in analyzing the current uses of the term, found that programs called *core* could be fitted into six basic categories.

1. The core consists of a number of logically organized subjects or fields of knowledge, each of which is taught independently.
2. The core consists of a number of logically organized subjects or fields of knowledge, some or all of which are correlated.
3. The core consists of broad problems, units of work, or unifying themes which are chosen because they afford the means of teaching effectively the basic content of certain subjects or fields of knowledge. These subjects or fields retain their identity, but the content is selected and taught with special reference to the unit, theme, or problem.
4. The core consists of a number of subjects or fields of knowledge which are unified or fused. Usually, one subject or field (e. g., history) serves as the unifying center.
5. The core consists of broad, pre-planned problem areas, from which are selected learning experiences in terms of the psychobiological and societal needs.
6. The core consists of broad units of work, or activities, planned by the teacher and the students in terms of needs as perceived by the group.[2]

---

1. Wright, Grace S., *Core Curriculum Development: Problems and Practices*, U.S. Office of Education Bulletin, 1952, No. 5 (Washington, D.C.: Government Printing Office, 1952), p. 8.
2. Alberty, Harold, "Designing Programs to Meet the Common Needs of Youth," *Adapting the Secondary-School Program to the Needs of Youth*, Fifty-second Yearbook, Part I, National Society for the Study of Education (Chicago: University of Chicago Press, 1953), ch. 7, pp. 119-120. Quoted in: Leonard H. Clark and others, *The American Secondary School Curriculum* (New York: The Macmillan Company, 1965), pp. 143-144.

Characteristics of a true core:

1. *The core must be common to all pupils.* The true core program is for all pupils, and all pupils are involved in it.
2. *The core occupies a large block of time, perhaps as much as one third to one half of the school day.* Because of the need for greater flexibility and scope in core programs, the double- or triple-period class is probably the most common characteristic of courses called core curriculum.
3. *The core is guidance-oriented.* Because a true core has to do with the problems and immediate concerns of youth, it is usually considered an excellent medium for guidance activities. Because it gives pupils and teacher an opportunity to get to know each other well, the long block of time lends itself admirably to teacher counseling. Both individual and group guidance services are integrated to the core.
4. *The true core is problem-oriented.* The content of a true core program consists of the problems of youth and society. Ideally the pupils and teachers have a great amount of latitude in the choice of problems.
5. *The core ignores subject matter lines but rather considers all knowledge to be its province.* The true core utilizes the method of problem-solving throughout. To carry this method out successfully the problems that the pupils investigate must be real, live, open-ended problems. Creative learning rather than instruction is the rule for the true core program.

    Therefore the subject matter of the core program does not fit into any one subject field or discipline. Usually much of the content comes from the language arts and the social studies, but the scope of the core is not limited by these fields and may well include any other, or all others, of the academic spectrum.
6. *The core involves pupil-teacher planning.* Problem-centered courses require teacher-pupil planning because an essential element of problem-solving is the forming of the problem. Whatever the broad areas prescribed for the particular grade, the pupil and the teacher in the program work out together the problems to be solved, the scope and sequence, the methods and procedures to be used in studying them,

and criteria for evaluating the success of their study and the conclusions or solutions arrived at.

7. *In the core, subject matter and skills are taught as they are needed rather than in any fixed sequence.* Because the problems of youth and society determine the subject matter of core programs, the specific skills and concepts are not taught in any fixed order, but rather are taught as they are needed. To many this seems to be a very dangerous technique.

8. *The true core requires considerable teacher preparation.* Core programs must be taught in relation to the other courses in the curriculum. To place the core in a separate compartment, isolated from the other subjects in the curriculum, violates the basic principle on which core theory is founded. Therefore core teachers and the teachers of specialized subjects must plan with each other so that they all can profit optimally from each other's work. In addition, the flexibility of the problem approach makes it imperative that the teacher be more than well-prepared in order to cope with the many contingencies that may arise.

9. *In the core individual differences are provided for by method rather than by curricular structure.* Core programs are common to all pupils, but the pupils do not all study identical subject matter. Differentiation to suit the needs, interests, and abilities of the pupils is provided by one variation or another of the unit method.

Ordinarily the unit includes class activities that can be shared by the entire class and a large number of activities that must be done individually or in small groups in laboratory fashion. The laboratory approach gives the pupils plenty of opportunities to plan their own work, to explore facets interesting to themselves, and to work at their own speed. The laboratory approach gives the teacher plenty of opportunity to confer with individuals and to help them with their problems.[1]

---

1. Clark, *op. cit.*, pp. 144-147.

Block-of-Time Classes

Although true core programs are not very common, block-of-time courses are quite popular, particularly in the junior high school grades. By block-of-time classes we mean classes that meet for double- or triple-class periods, and combine or replace two or more subjects. Ordinarily, the term "block-of-time class" is reserved for general education courses, that is, courses required for all pupils.

Three kinds of block-of-time classes:

1. The subjects retain their identity, although scheduled together in a multiple period. In this type of block of time, the courses taught within the block of time may or may not be correlated.

2. In the second type of block-of-time class, the subject matter of the subjects taught has been integrated into a unified course.

3. The third type of block-of-time course is the true core curriculum described in the preceding section.

As a rule, the subjects of the block-of-time courses are taught as separate, distinct subjects.

Methods in block-of-time courses do not differ from methods used in other good secondary-school courses, except that perhaps the long periods may lend themselves to more variety than the ordinary periods do. The classes are not likely to be problem-centered any more than other academic classes are. When problems are used, they are more likely to center around problems of subject matter than problems of youth.[1]

Block-of-time classes are common in the junior high schools of the country but are much less frequent in the high schools. At present, although the block of time is popular in the junior high school, the current pressure on subject matter, and the increased stress on the structure of the disciplines may be reversing the movement toward the block of time, even at the junior high school level. The block of time has certain definite advantages in the junior high school grades:

1. The block of time in grade seven makes an admirable transition from the self-contained classroom of the elementary school

1. *Ibid.,* pp. 156-157.

to the departmentalization of the secondary school.

2. The block of time makes it particularly helpful in the pupil's transition from the elementary school to the secondary school in that it reduces the number of teachers the pupil must face. Similarly, the block of time reduces the teacher's load. For instance, a teacher who has two double-period block-of-time classes of thirty students each teaches only to sixty pupils, whereas, if he taught four thirty-pupil classes of English or social studies, he would have one hundred-twenty pupils. This reduction allows him to learn to know his pupils better and should make it possible for him to teach them more effectively. In addition, this more intimate contact makes it possible for the teacher to carry out the guidance function more adequately.

3. The block of time also lends itself to more effective teaching. Because of the long period, one can utilize films, field trips, laboratory work, and other activities too long for single-period classes. The long period gives them time to get some real work done. The block-of-time format gives flexibility to organization for teaching.

Nine-tenths of the block-of-time classes are subject-centered courses differing little from ordinary courses. Ordinarily, block-of-time classes are not experience-centered; they should not be condemned for faults alleged to experience-centered core curricula. Like the core curriculum, block-of-time teaching does require exceptionally well-prepared teachers.[1]

Interdisciplinary Seminars and Service Units

Interdisciplinary Seminars — a variation of the unified studies approach that may or may not utilize a block of time is the interdisciplinary seminar. The program consists of a series of lectures on current topics concerning the humanities and the social sciences given to the entire senior class by outstanding lecturers, and followed up by class discussion and other assignments in regular class-size sections.

Service units are developed on a short-term basis when needed

1. *Ibid.*, pp. 158-161.

to clarify a particular part of work being considered in the core.

The type of service from specialists is giving help on a short-term basis to individuals and groups. Service units are for students who have talents and interests requiring extended or intensive work, as well as for those who need remedial assistance.

Typical Core or Block-of-Time Schedule[1]

Period	Name Monday	HR. 8-1 Tuesday	RM. B-6 Wednesday	Thursday	Lunch A Friday
1	Core or Block	Core or Block	Core or Block	Core or Block	Core or Block
2	Core or Block	Core or Block	Core or Block	Core or Block	Core or Block
3	Core or Block	Core or Block	Core or Block	Core or Block	Core or Block
4	Math.	Math.	Math.	Math.	Math.
5	Home Arts	Science	Science	Science	Science
6	Home Arts	Music	Typing	Music	Typing
7	Phys. Ed.	Phys. Ed.	Phys. Ed.	Phys. Ed.	Phys. Ed.

Unified Studies. A number of schools have integrated the subject matter of the block-of-time program into a completely new course. These fully integrated courses go by many different names, and differ from other courses only in that the subject matter is served up in different portions. We may call these integrated courses *unified studies* or *unit core programs.*

1. *Ibid.,* p. 149.

The *teaching method* of the unified studies courses is quite likely to be some form of the unit method. Sometimes the teaching is academic, but frequently it features problem-solving. Integrated courses are less likely to be taught traditionally than other block-of-time classes are.[1]

The Advantages

There are several advantages of following this planned organization of instructional material.

Among the most important advantages may be mentioned the following:

1. This type of approach to learning activity almost invariably generates a higher degree of pupil interest and makes unnecessary the resort to threats and rewards or any other artificial and indirect motivation.
2. The flexibility and opportunities for different kinds of activities among the youngsters make valuable contributions toward the adaptation of learning to individual capacities and abilities and needs.
3. It provides needed training in the application of subject matter and learnings to the problems of life.
4. It is a splendid training situation for social education among the learners working together in the cooperative situation, with the necessity for give and take, for leadership and followership, and for other valuable social experiences.
5. It tends to shift the responsibility for the success of the learning activities more to the student and less exclusively to the teacher.
6. It provides for much more teacher cooperation and teacher and interdepartmental planning and coordination.
7. By reason of the large block of time occupied in the daily schedule and the fact that the teacher has ordinarily only two or at the most three core groups, the use of the core plan reduces the number of students with whom the teacher must get acquainted and also the number of homes of parents with which the teacher should make contact. It is thereby possible for the teacher to know a great deal

1. *Ibid.*, p. 157.

more about each individual and to render much better guidance.

8. There is much more emphasis upon critical thinking, evaluation of materials, planning, and evaluation of the program, and less exclusive emphasis upon following directions and learning verbal materials to be recited to the teacher or tested by him.

9. The core arrangement provides for a larger block of time, usually two hours, thus eliminating the necessity for student shifting at the end of the class period to another subject involving new orientation.

10. The teacher of the youngsters in a core curriculum group is the sponsor of those youngsters and does a great deal of group guidance and outside of the group a great deal of personal, individual guidance with the students in his core group or groups.[1]

The Opposition

In spite of the many arguments put forth in its favor, the core has aroused much opposition.

1. It leaves out essential subject matter. By essential subject matter the critics usually mean factual information and skills that they believe fundamental to scholarship and to preparation for adult life.

2. The core includes so much varied subject matter that to expect any teacher to have all the competencies a core teacher should have is unreasonable. A really good core teacher needs a breadth and depth of liberal and specialized education that is hard to find.

3. The pupils in the core program lose the values inherent in the content and method of the subject fields because the core program violates the structure of the disciplines. In core programs, pupils do not have sufficient opportunities to acquire skills in the methods of history, criticism, science, and other disciplines, and so will grow up to be intellectual cripples.

4. It dilutes the curriculum with content that its critics feel is not worthy of secondary education. In their estimation, real

1. Douglass, Harl R., *Secondary Education* (New York: Ronald Press Company, 1952), pp. 179-180.

life problems such as boy-girl relationships, budgeting, and family relationships reek of anti-intellectualism, and so should be barred from the secondary school.

5. The core is soft and leads to undisciplined behavior and slovenly habits of thinking.[1]

The core curriculum does not encompass the entire curriculum. Ususally it consists of a block of time amounting to two or three periods per day, replacing the social studies and the English language arts in the curriculum, and perhaps also serving as a medium for conducting the guidance program. Less frequently, the core program also replaces general education courses in science, mathematics, and art. However, teachers of art, music, mathematics, science, and other subjects are sometimes called in as consultants by the core teachers whenever the problem areas to be studied in the core curriculum make it seem desirable.[2]

The core curriculum is a natural replacement of the homeroom.

The core curriculum accepts extracurricular activities on a par with all other learning activities. In the core curriculum, therefore, there are no longer extracurricular activities, but only learning activities of many types. The homeroom was a device created within the framework of the subject curriculum to make possible a closer acquaintance between key teachers and pupils, so that the pupils could receive more careful counseling, primarily with regard to their educational ebjectives.

More Important Requirements for Effective Operation of the Core Curriculum

Teachers should have a broad general education and specialized training.

The function of the teacher in a core program is to facilitate the process of personal growth. The teacher must be thoroughly disciplined in methods of thinking appropriate to socio-moral problems. He should also be trained in a specialized field of knowledge. The specialized electives will require that some teach-

1. Clark, *op. cit.*, pp. 151-152.
2. *Ibid.*, pp. 147-148.

ers have specialized training in at least one field. It should be noted that teachers who work in the core program are frequently called upon, especially in the smaller schools, to teach in their specialties in addition to their duties in the core program.

The teacher has the responsibility for becoming informed concerning the soundness of the psychological, educational, and sociological principles upon which the program is based. It is important for the teacher to know and respect subject matter, but it is of equal importance that he be able to recognize it as a means to an end in the solution of personal problems.

The NEA committee on the preparation of core teachers.

The NEA committee on the preparation of core teachers for secondary schools has formulated this list:

Understanding the adolescent and meeting his needs.

Observing and classifying kinds of behavior; e. g. aggressive, withdrawing, submissive. Analyzing behavior so as to construct hypotheses about needs of an individual.

Prescribing remedies for particular cases.

Altering a situation so as to provide for meeting the needs of an individual.

Keeping-records about developments in behavior.

Using the major fields of knowledge as resources.

Identifying major social, economic, and political problems or issues.

Using major fields of knowledge in solution of current problems.

Relating various fields of knowledge to a problem area.

Locating and using materials, persons, places and other resources in helping solve current problems.

Organizing resources in appropriate form for later use.

Providing leadership through understanding and use of democratic process.

Classifying, analyzing and prescribing for group needs as these arise.

Clarifying thinking and valuing processes.

Orienting a class in use of the planning process, including formulation of goals, identifying hypotheses to be tested, gathering facts and information, evaluating results.

Using counseling and guidance.

Listening to and "drawing out" the counselee.

Making suggestions without dominating.

Waiting patiently for results.

Structuring classroom situations to help individual personalities.

Interpreting data from tests and other sources.

Organizing and using learning materials.

Selecting and organizing materials around broad problems of current concern.

Predicting problems of adolescents.

Gauging student interest, reading power and development levels in selecting materials.

Devising varied opportunities for students to utilize resources.

Cooperating with administrators, librarians, fellow-teachers and local citizens in developing resource materials and opportunities.

The effectiveness of the core-class work is depended upon many factors, the most important being the teacher.[1]

Activities in Class

It is essential that the teacher know the basis of grouping of his class.

Various methods of teaching may be employed in the core curriculum, but the cooperative problem-solving method usually predominates.

The activities in a class in which students and teacher engage in cooperative problem-solving include the following:

1. Association for Supervision and Curriculum Development, *Preparation of Core Teachers for Secondary School* (Washington, D.C.: National Education Association, 1955), pp. 45-46.

1. *Selecting a particular problem.* In selecting a particular problem, the class will explore the various problems to ascertain their importance and general interest.
2. *Analysis of the problems.* The students will need to make frequent reference back to the original statement of the problem. The main problem will be broken down into a series of small problems.
3. *Getting information from various sources.* Various committees may be formed and given the responsibility of getting information from various sources. This step involves the use of books, films, interviews, field trips, etc.
4. *Panel discussion and conclusion.* Various aspects of the problem may be presented to the class in the form of panel discussion by the committee, and later should be followed by general class discussion. Conclusions may be offered by individuals and committees and subjected to modification and acceptance by the entire class.
5. *Plans of action.* The class should decide whether further action is necessary, and the class should make plans for a definite course of action.[1]

Buildings and Equipment

Buildings, grounds, and classrooms should be large and flexible enough to permit pursuit of group activities.

Buildings and classrooms to house a core curriculum would follow the general pattern of those required for an activity curriculum. The rooms must lend themselves to whatever problem is studied. Floor space must be more ample than in the conventional classroom, for the core curriculum requires workrooms. Furniture should be strong and easily movable.

Corridors should be large, well-lighted, and decorated by student groups or displaying student work.

The grounds of the school should also be large enough to lend themselves to the varied requirements of a core curriculum. There should be space for a play area, and flower and vegetable gardens.

1. Mills, Hubert H. and Douglass, H.R., *Teaching in High School,* 1957, pp. 280-281.

The equipment and materials for a core curriculum are of functional utility.

The core program needs those supplies required by the problems arising. There will be occasions for textbooks, in the sense of a copy of the same book for each child. Several copies of the most valuable reference books may be required. A library should be located in each large school where materials for use in each major area of the core program are collected for distribution. The equipment and materials needed in the specialized courses are very important. The rooms adapted to these purposes will take on the form of well-equipped laboratories. The building should have several general purpose or activity rooms.

All the arrangements require a flexibility of administration.

Equipment and materials can be ordered in advance with fair assurance that they will be needed and used.

The teaching staff and the public must see the value of the core curriculum.

When a new organization and new methods are established to replace the ones the members of the community have known so well, the school is faced with a new task. The public relations program of the school must be continuous and effective.

SUMMARY

The core curriculum, or the core program, represents an experimental approach to the selection and organization of some of
the common learning materials in the high school. Within the
framework of this concept are established ideas and practices to
meet emergent demands for a new general election.

The core consists of a number of logically organized subjects
or fields of knowledge, some of which are correlated. The core
curriculum accepts extra-curricular activites on a par with other
learning activities. In the core curriculum, therefore, there are
no longer extracurricular activities, but only learning activities
of many types.

The function of the teacher in a core program is to facilitate
the process of personal growth.

FOR FURTHER STUDY

A Sound Core Program — What It Is and What It Isn't, by Harold
Alberty. From the NEA Journal, January, 1956.

Association for Supervision and Curriculum Development, *Preparation of Core Teachers for Secondary Schools.* Washington,
D.C.: National Education Association, 1955.

Bossing, N.L., *Principles of Secondary Education.* Englewood
Cliffs: Prentice-Hall, Inc., 1955.

Bruner, J.S., *The Process of Education.* Cambridge, Mass.:
Harvard University Press, 1960.

Clark, L.H., R.L. Klein, J.B. Burks, *The American Secondary
School Curriculum.* New York: The Macmillan Company,
1965.

Curriculum Office, Philadelphia Public Schools, *A Guide to the
Teaching of Literature in Grades 7 through 12* (tentative).
Philadelphia: School District of Philadelphia, 1960.

Douglass, H.R., *Secondary Education.* New York: Ronald Press
Company, 1952.

Gwynn, J. Minor, *Curriculum Principles and Social Trends.* New
York: The Macmillan Company, 1960.

Holland, J.G., and B.F. Skinner, *The Analysis of Behavior.* New
York: McGraw-Hill Book Company, Inc., 1961.

Hunt, M.P., and L.C. Metcalf, *Teaching High School Studies.*
New York: Harper, 1955.

Mayer, Martin, *The Schools.* New York: Harper and Row,
Inc., 1961.

Mays, A.B., *Principles and Practices of Vocational Education.*
New York: McGraw-Hill Book Company, Inc., 1948.

Mills, H.H., and H.R. Douglass, *Teaching in High School.* New
York: The Ronald Press Company, 1957.

National Council of Teachers of English, *The English Language
Arts.* New York: Appleton-Century-Crofts, Inc., 1952.

Smith, B.O., W.O. Stanley and J.H. Shores, *Fundamentals of
Curriculum Development.* Yonkers-on-Hudson, N.Y., 1957.

Smith, Paul, *Creativity — An Examination of the Creative Process.* New York: Hastings House, 1960.

Townsend, E.A., and P.J. Burke, *Learning for Teachers*. New York: The Macmillan Company, 1962.

Travers, R.M., *Essentials of Learning*. New York: The Macmillan Company, 1963.

Weiss, M.J., *Reading in the Secondary Schools*. New York: The Odyssey Press, Inc., 1961.

Wright, G.S., *Core Curriculum Development: Problems and Practices*. U.S. Office of Education Bulletin No. 5, 1952 (Washington, D.C.: Government Printing Office, 1952).

CHAPTER III

THE PROCESS OF CURRICULUM IMPROVEMENT

Ways to Curriculum Improvement

Classroom and all school activities offer many ways to help learners develop efficient methods of working.

The task of the teacher as a faculty sponsor of one or more activities should be to decide how the projects undertaken by learners can best contribute to their growth. The teacher will find that there will be many problems through which he can help students learn to make efficient use of personnel. Within committees there will be problems of how to organize the work, so that the best use is made of the time and energies of each individual. There should be additional lessons in using time wisely.

Assemblies, homeroom programs, interest groups, and school publications offer many opportunities to enrich class experiences. Service responsibilities to the school, participation in athletic, music, or dramatic activities, represent positive means of helping learners feel that they are respected and needed by those with whom they work. The basic understanding that the welfare of all the members of the group depends upon the degree to which each person carries out his particular responsibilities is one of the most important learnings that comes from the experience of participating in co-curricular activities. Such activities are valuable means of expanding learners' skills in cooperative problem-solving.

Each secondary school should build a schedule that will make it possible for every learner to carry his required and elective courses, and to participate as fully as his interests, abilities, and time will allow in the co-curricular program.

The total school setting should be directed toward learner growth. Since the classroom teacher has daily contact with the learners in his classes, he should know them best and be able to offer learners help in many of their problems. This success in helping learners discover their problems, and guiding them progressively toward accepting more and more responsibility for their solution, will depend in great measure upon the quality of human relationships in his classroom.

The effectiveness of any program of curriculum improvement must be measured in terms of actual changes in learning experiences.

The ways in which the quality of learning is improved are many. There must be, in addition to the informal gains made by capable teachers, a systematic, organized curriculum program which unites the efforts of teachers, students, and varied individuals. This approach stress the significance of involving in curriculum processes the people who are closest to the educational experiences of children.

Changes in social forces necessitate changes in school programs; new insights into the nature of learning require modifications in existing practices. Continuous curriculum improvement is important. The school is a social institution whose vitality is dependent on the quality of the relationships among the people who teach, learn, and live within it. The school system has evolved rules and regulations, laws, and guides which effect the organization and instructional program of classes.

Any change that will facilitate the achievement of desired goals is legitimately part of the curriculum improvement process.

Some kinds of curriculum improvement activities simply require the individual teacher's desire to test new ideas. Consultants and special resource people may be needed. Money and favorable working conditions are very important if individuals are to devote time and effort to curriculum improvement. There must be involvement of individuals and group participation. Leadership is needed, and efforts must be coordinated. While flexibility in organizational pattern is desirable in achieving improvement under any curriculum design, it is essential when the curriculum develops around the life situations learners face. Opportunities must be provided for teachers of different grades to work together.

In curriculum building, we should emphasize such things as the skills of thinking and learning.

The fact that one must deal with the whole child does not necessarily imply that the curriculum should contain all learning in all fields of knowledge. Curricula should depend less upon telling, and turn to emphasizing creative learning and self-realization. Each learning depends upon and should be based upon previous learning. Therefore, curriculum builders should take care in developing effective learning sequence.

Curriculum Activities of Teachers

In improving the experiences of learners, curriculum activities of teachers may be:

Task-centered — working on a particular, definite job, such as the selection of books and other teaching materials for a classroom library. Here the task is clearly defined, and the individual or committee directs attention to ways and means of completing the assignment.

Idea-or policy-centered — aiming at the clarification of concepts or exploration of ideas, such as proposals for the use of out-of-school resources.

Idea-centered is closely related to the task-centered focus; attention here is on the exploration and examination of ideas, and the formulation of guides to action.

Problem-centered — using the methodology of identifying, refining, and working toward solutions of problems. For example, a faculty stresses possible causes of increased student absenteeism, or a teacher tries to improve parent-teacher conferences by analyzing present sessions. Groups engaged in action research or appraisal frequently operate with this kind of focus.

Production-centered — producing particular teaching-learning materials or equipment, such as kindergarten-grade-three committee which prepares a resource guide for its own use, a committee that develops a list of films available locally, or a teacher who builds a radio trouble-shooting board for his science classes. Some kind of product is the goal.

Skill-centered — pointing at the development of certain essential and desired skills, such as the acquisition of new techniques for teaching elementary science, for observing children's behavior, or for conducting small-group meetings. These activities usually provide opportunities for acquiring new skills through practice.

General education or appreciation-centered — focusing less on a particular phase of the educational program and more on general cultural and professional development. Broadening travel, art appreciation courses, and forums on critical issues in education illustrate this kind of purpose.

These various foci of attention and practice are typical, however, of the range of activities that should be encouraged in an organized program for curriculum development.[1]

Cooperative action research is an approach to improve a real situation through a systematic examination of the situation itself.

Changes in the curriculum involve, first and foremost, changes in the thinking and behavior of teachers. Cooperative curriculum research depends, to a great extent, upon the leadership in public schools and in teacher-training institutions.

The research pattern evolves as teacher and consultant test their perceptions of a real situation. The problems lead the consultant and the teacher, working together, to the gathering of data that will aid clarification of the problem.

The appropriate outcome of cooperative action research is the development of principles of analysis and method.

Curriculum improvement is the result of changes in practices by individual teachers.

The teacher needs the emotional support of a group of associates. The group must be one in which he is free to verbalize his ideas, obtain criticism without feeling defensive. The members

---

1. Miles, Matthew B. and Passow, A.H., "Training in the Skills Needed for In-Service Programs," *In-Service Education for Teachers, Supervisors, and Administrators.* Fifty-sixth Yearbook of the National Society for the Study of Education, Part I, p. 353 (Chicago: The University of Chicago Press, 1957). Quoted in: Stratemeyer, *op. cit.,* pp. 672-674.

of a group protect each other from attack. Such cooperation should be between selected single teachers or groups of teachers with agencies and individuals in the community.

Some educators themselves have been responsible for impending educational progress and community understanding. Only through wide-spread public support and participation can the schools find the strength and prosper.

To meet multiple demands involved in curriculum change, specialized personnel resources are essential and should be available.

While expertise is certainly essential in bringing about change, the role of consultant has shifted to emphasize the resources, skills, and materials that should be made available to individuals and groups working to improve learning experiences. The resources can assist in curriculum development if effectively applied to teaching.

How we learn. We learn through our experiences. Not all experiences result in learning, of course. In order for learning to be efficient, the experience should be novel, vivid, and meaningful. One learning builds on another. Consequently, it follows that learning should follow an orderly sequence. A child who does not understand simple division should not be expected to succeed with long division. He must learn the prerequisite skills before he is ready for the new one. Incidentally, the completion of prerequisite courses is no proof that the youngster has the background necessary to make him ready to learn a particular subject. The curriculum that makes the most of the principle of readiness must indeed be a flexible one.

No classroom teacher can be a scholar in the many areas of human knowledge and experience.

To his own abilities should be added many contacts with the experts who know the up-to-date and truly significant knowledge and resources. We have to find the best ways to bring the scholar into curriculum development. His influence needs to be felt with regard to the selection and proper emphasis of content.

*Improved instructional practices are the result of preservice
and in-service education programs for teachers.*

There are many approaches to the improvement of curriculum.
Each has a limited usefulness, and each is correct as far as it goes:

1. A "professionally minded" teacher, with some administra-
tively provided consultant help, will bring about improvements
in his teaching.

2. "Working Committees" on the faculty are freed to deal
with significant instructional problems.

3. "Cooperation" with the community.

4. To send teachers to summer workshops to get "the word,"
and this leads to anything from a new direction maintained
through the support of the "internalized" workshop group to
all sorts of new problems of communication, and of being out-
of-step with the home group.

5. Through studious application of a well formulated method.
This provides a set methodological concept, but it gives little
guidance at the most important point — namely, in deciding
just what the objectives should be.

Each of the approaches recognizes that individual growth of
teachers is required for originating new and better curriculum
ideas; that the individual teacher must be supported emotionally
by other people during the creative act, and also in maintaining
his new practices.[1]

Participation of Lay Persons

*Lay persons can participate in curriculum improvement in many
different ways.*

Lay persons have been assigned various important roles in
program-planning. The rationale for lay involvement stems
from a basic belief that persons affected by decisions should participate in their making; that the combined intelligence of many
individuals will result in better problem solution. The purposes
of lay participation in curriculum planning, then, are increasing
understandings, sharing of resources, and utilizing competencies

1. Thelen, Herbert A., *Group Dynamics in Curriculum Improvement,* "Educational Leadership," Vol. XI, No. 7 (April, 1954), pp. 413-417.

wherever located.

Lay persons can help in establishing policy by serving on advisory councils and committees which are dealing with various policy problems. They can contribute in planning activities by working on coordinating councils, acting as resource consultants in areas where they have special competencies, securing and preparing materials for use by teachers and pupils, and participating directly in the various programs and procedures for curriculum improvement. Lay persons may also help in the teaching-learning process rather directly by working with teachers and students in various service and informational roles.

Student participation has taken the form primarily of cooperative planning of learning experiences, rather than involvement on organized curriculum development programs.

The faculties enable students, particularly at the secondary school level, to meet with committees dealing with such problems as analyzing needs of youth and setting school policy.[1]

A Systematic Approach to Curriculum Change

Systematic methods should be employed in solving such curriculum problems as the grade replacement of materials, the identification of child and adolescent needs, and the development of effective methods of teaching.

The school tends to shape the attitudes of teachers toward curriculum change as well as their perception of what is educationally possible and desirable.

Curriculum change is a form of social change; any modification of the curriculum change will affect the wider community. In such an operation as curriculum change, it is helpful to take a broad analytical perspective of the total picture. It must begin with selected aspects of total school-community situations. Usually it will begin with some specific situation that requires attention. Where circumstances permit, the situation may be expanded so as to require a broad school-community diagnosis. In either case, a group of persons will be formed to deal with the situation. The group will survey the specific situation to identify the diffi-

1. Stratemeyer, *op. cit.,* p.679.

culties. If the plans do not work according to anticipation, they are then revised.

All persons involved in research must share in planning it, or else the program developed by the research may not work in practice.

The Participation of Teachers and Students in Planning of the Program

The teachers and students should share in planning the program from start to finish.

In almost every step of curriculum change, working committees composed of appropriate members drawn from laymen, teachers, and students will be directly engaged in policy-making.

The selection of educational objectives, the materials and methods of instruction, and the administration of the school necessarily require choices among values. The teachers should be more competent in this area than other members of the community. The systematic approach stresses not only wide participation but also the use of psychological knowledge and human relations, skills in planning and controlling the processes of curriculum change.

Power in the schools should be concentrated for any effective plan for curriculum development.

A faculty should strive to perfect its own procedures of working together as a faculty. The faculty should examine its machinery for policymaking, for resolving differences of opinion about important educational issues, for assuming its share of administrative responsibilities. The task of keeping everyone informed about what is going on in a program of curriculum development requires a plan of communication. Each person should be able to perceive the curriculum program as a whole, and thereby maintain his sense of direction.

In any program of curriculum development, there will arise technical questions about basic principles and procedures of curriculum construction, about the determination of the scope and sequence of the curriculum.

The consultant, through his technical knowledge and skill, will encourage a mutual exploration of the situation, helping the group to formulate its own difficulties more adequately and to work out plans for dealing with them. But consultant services can be used most effectively if a local staff has defined its problems with care, and has reached the point in its deliberations.

Any effort to change the curriculum will encounter the forces of educational and social structures through individuals affected by the change.

In any school-community situation, there will be points of both satisfaction and dissatisfaction among parents, pupils, and teachers regarding the school. The simplest way of ascertaining the opinions of parents, pupils, and teachers is through the use of questionaires and interviews. It is important to know at what points in the welfare scale either the satisfactions or dissatisfactions tend to concentrate. The curriculum will not be changed until the forces that shape the decisions of the superintendent and principal are changed.

Several forces originating outside the local community impinge upon the existing curriculum to keep it at its present level of development.

There are state laws specifying that certain things be taught; rules and regulationgs of state departments of education concerning what will be accepted for credit and under what conditions it will be accepted; requirements of accrediting and certificating agencies; and admission requirements of colleges and universities. Then there are state-wide and nationwide pressure groups, which frequently influence the school against making changes believed to be detrimental to these groups. These requirements and influences can be presented as forces opposing certain curriculum changes. Frequently, these forces can neither be changed in direction nor reduced in strength as far as the local school personnel is concerned.

This is especially true of the requirements of state laws, of state departments of public instruction, of accrediting and certificating agencies, and of universities and colleges. In these instances, the outside influences must ordinarily be taken as part of the given circumstances within which curriculum change must be made.

As soon as the first change of curriculum has been made, the fears and uncertainties, the satisfactions and dissatisfactions of those concerned should be ascertained. This sort of diagnosis should be kept up throughout the entire span of change, down to and including the point at which the new equilibrium is finally established.[1]

Ways of Getting Under Way in a Program of Curriculum Revision

The curriculum change is a form of learning; it proceeds best when teachers become involved in problems that are real to them.

There are many ways of getting under way in a program of curriculum revision; these include carrying on such activities as studies, visits, readings, and self-surveys by local faculties, and then utilizing the resultant data as a basis for arousing discontent with the existing program:

1. Have the faculty apply the "Evaluative Criteria" (prepared by the Cooperative Study of Secondary School Standards Committee) to your school.

2. Engage some outside agency (e. g., a university survey committee) to survey the curriculum.

3. Have the faculty survey the school's curriculum.

4. Encourage the faculty to visit, or otherwise discover, what was done in one or more schools which have successfully initiated a program of curriculum development.

5. Interest the faculty in examining the "literature of high school criticism" in order to determine for itself which of these criticisms are valid, and consider which of the valid criticisms could honestly be applied to the local school.

6. Read and discuss with the faculty one or more idealized descriptions of imaginary curricula (e. g., "Education for All

---

1. Smith, *op. cit.,* pp. 496-497.

American Youth"), comparing the resultant "picture" with the practices of the local school.

7. Enumerate with the aid of the faculty the full range of the major types of learning experiences and services (e. g., help in choosing an appropriate vocation, learning how to spend money wisely, preparation for wise parenthood, acquiring a variety of avocational interests and skills, placement service, etc.) which they think the local school should ideally provide.

8. Cast the numeration noted in Method 7 above into a formal questionaire, and give this inventory either to former or present students, or both, in order to discover how much, if any, of each type of help was or is being received.

9. Encourage teachers to attend summer school curriculum courses.

10. Encourage teachers to attend curriculum workshops.

11. Encourage teachers to attend state, regional, and national conferences of leaders in their respective school enterprises (e. g., National Council of Teachers of English, National Vocational Guidance Association, etc.).

12. Encourage teachers to attend curriculum conferences, held by universities or other agencies.

13. Have a study made in which the socio-economic status of the pupils in each year of the high school are compared with similar data of the fifth-grade populations of all "feeder" schools.

14. Have a study made to determine the socio-economic status of all pupils who "belong to" or who "take part in" each classroom or student activity of the school.

15. Have a study made of cost to pupils (e. g., books, dues, fees, etc.) attending the school, projecting these findings against the average family income in the community.

16. Have some member of the faculty report to his fellows the findings of the published researches bearing upon the types of data noted in Methods 13, 14, and 15 above, inviting the staff to estimate the degree to which these findings are probably true of the local situation.

17. Have the faculty familiarize itself with recommendations of the various national professional organizations which concern themselves with any aspect of the secondary school curriculum.

18. Encourage teachers to make intensive case studies of a small number of pupils in order to discover the ways in which the school is and is not meeting the needs of these youngsters.

19. Have the felt needs and problems of all youth in the school studied through appropriate inventories.

20. Have the faculty study thoroughly the social and psychological foundations of secondary education in order to determine what responses the school should include, and how these can most effectively be engendered.[1]

The Conditions

In order to appraise experimental studies of curriculum patterns, it is necessary to understand the conditions that must be satisfied by research on this problem.

These conditions are:

1. The theory of the curriculum pattern to be tested must be stated unequivocally.

2. The conditions (social, psychological, educational, and physical) under which the curriculum pattern is tried out must be desribed in detail.

3. The anticipated results of the curriculum theory must be stated as hypotheses derived from the theory.

4. Data must be collected to ascertain whether or not the hypotheses derived from the curriculum theory were borne out by observed facts; for, as these hypotheses are tested out, confirmed, or invalidated by observation, the theory is affirmed or denied.

The general conditions of any complete theory of curriculum organization involve such a multitude of variables that research workers may choose to test only one or two aspects of a curriculum pattern.

Practitioners have frequently attempted to apply the results of experiments without creating the conditions within which the new technique or procedure could yield the results claimed for it in the experiment.

1. *Guide to the Study of the Curriculum in the Secondary Schools of Illinois* (Springfield, Ill.: State Department of Public Instruction, 1948), pp. 25-26.

The experimenter must be aware of, and state accurately, not only the factual conditions of an experiment, but also the consequences which must follow from the execution of experimental operations.[1]

The curriculum worker is usually interested, not only in the learning products resulting from a new curriculum design, but also in a comparison of these products with those resulting from some older and better understood alternative plan.

Thus, investigations are common which attempt to compare "traditional" and "new type" curricula with respect to their effects upon student behavior.[2]

The Approaches

In the history of curriculum development, three approaches have been employed: the administrative, the grass-root, and the demonstration.

The Administrative Approach. The superintendent of schools, recognizing the need for curriculum development, sets up machinery for accomplishing the needed revision. He arranges the faculty meetings in which the need for curriculum improvement is presented, and he asks the board of education to approve a curriculum development program. Then a *steering committee* is appointed, consisting of administrative officers and teachers. This committee, working closely with the superintendent, performs a number of functions; and it usually prepares a statement of general objectives covering the entire school system. These formulations become the curriculum development manual for the remainder of the faculty.

In addition, the steering committee works out plans for training teachers in curriculum work. It determines the number of consultants to be employed and the kinds of activities best calculated to familiarize teachers with the theory and practice of curriculum building.

The plans finally worked out by the steering committee usually provide for a number of committees, consisting largely of teachers, and referred to as *production committees,* to prepare new courses of study in keeping with the objectives and guiding principles laid down by the steering committee.

Finally, the courses of study must be tried out and installed. This responsibility is ordinarily assumed by an *installation committee.* This committee interprets the new courses of study to teachers and principals who were not directly involved in the preparation of the new guides.[1]

The Grass-Roots Approach. Failure of the administrative approach was attributed largely to the fact that it did not enlist the interests of teachers in the task of curriculum revision. The teachers did not become personally involved in such a way that changes in the curriculum were perceived by them as being of constructive consequence. The grass-roots approach attempts to find ways of involving all members of the staff in the problem of curriculum building, from the first to the last stages of the process. In its most comprehensive form, the grass-roots approach is community-wide. It embraces not only teachers but also students, parents, and other members of the community. This approach is based upon four general propositions:

1. The curriculum will be improved only as the professional competence of the teachers improves.

2. The competence of teachers will be improved only as they become personally involved in the problems of curriculum revision.

3. If teachers share in shaping the goals to be attained, in selecting, defining, and solving the problems to be encountered, and in judging and evaluating the results, their involvement will be most nearly assured.

4. As people meet in face-to-face groups, they will be able to understand one another better, and to reach a consensus on basic principles, goals, and plans.

In this pattern of curriculum development, the function of the central administration is to provide stimulating leadership, free time, materials, and whatever else the various schools may need.

The grass-roots approach also makes wide use of consultants, as well as bulletins and study guides issued by the central ad-

1. *Ibid.,* pp. 426-428.

ministration on such topics as child development, community needs and resources, social and economic conditions, and innovations in curriculum theory and practice.[1]

The Demonstration Approach. The demonstration approach has been contrived to produce changes in the regular program on a small scale. This approach discovers the consequences of a proposed change on a small scale before making the change in the whole school.[2]

The Teacher's Role in Improving Instruction

The teacher creates the type of learning situation that will determine the attitudes, understandings, skills, and appreciations that pupils develop.

The secondary school teacher is a permanent student of problems and conditions. Curriculum improvement occurs as individual teachers feel secure in trying out new procedures. The teacher determines what the curriculum will be like through the selection of materials to be used by the class. He can determine how to use the school library and other sources of information.

Progress in curriculum development will result from teachers' experimentation with new content, procedures, and materials. The teacher's freedom in planning the curriculum for his pupils will depend to a considerable extent on the policies established by the board of education, and any supervisors which the school may employ. In larger secondary schools, teachers usually have more to say about which books are to be purchased. In the smaller high schools there is less likely to be cooperative study of what the school is trying to do; textbooks are most frequently chosen by the superintendent or the teacher.

Education should be interpreted more fully as the dynamic process of guiding the experiences of students.

The philosophy of education recognizes the many variables in the teaching-learning situation. Examination of some of these variables will help the teachers perceive the need for a continuous quest for better teaching. Each teacher has to develop

1. Storen, Hellen F., *Laymen Help Plan the Curriculum* (Washington, D.C.: Association for Supervision and Curriculum Development, National Education Association, 1946), pp. 3-75. Quoted in: Smith, *op. cit.*, p. 428.
2. Smith, *op. cit.*, pp. 435-436.

procedures that seem to work well with all classes.   For example, procedures for conducting a discussion can be used successfully with different groups of the same general maturity, because they are aimed at getting the group members to define their own topics.

Improvement in the human relationships of the classroom consists of the increasing ability of the teacher to have effective relations with the students.   Increasing adaptability in relationships comes with growth in abilities to study individuals, and to identify oneself with others.   These abilities can be cultivated through further education of the teacher and his experience.

The teacher can teach with full use of present environmental factors and with some eye to the future environment.

Reading and keeping up with news, and participation in organized in-service education and curriculum planning programs are the teacher's best ways of continuing improvement.   The great body of professional literature and the varied possibilities of in-service education projects developed by school systems and teacher-education institutions gave most secondary teachers an opportunity for keeping up with developments in the teaching field.   Teachers who desire to improve their ways of working with learners need to keep abreast of professional research, general literature, and the best practices in order that their classes may have the advantage of the best materials and techniques available to them.

The teacher must carefully analyze the situation, identify the problem involved, weigh alternative solutions, and then try out something that appears a possible step toward improvement.

Improvement of instruction is in the improvement of the teacher himself.

The teachers become better teachers through improving ways of working with learners, the environment, and teaching materials.   Improvement is a process of learning and one in which the learner and the teacher must determine and seek his own goals. The improvement of teaching occurs as teachers improve themselves. As the teacher is finding ways of securing greater satisfation in his work, he inevitable is becoming more adept in his personal relations, and more open-minded about educational problems. The interpersonal relations of teachers and pupils are most critical in determining the quality of the educational process. The teachers, therefore, should regard their practices at any given time as simply the ones then used, and keep an open outlook for new and better practices.

The Teacher as a Professional Worker

The teacher as a professional worker shows evidence of planning for instructional activities.

He provides opportunities for learners to participate in planning instructional activites. The teacher as a professional worker gives evidence of increasing interest and skill in studying growth and development of individual learners. He provides opportunities for learners to participate in individual and group activities; adapts instruction to the needs of individual students; provides opportunities for pupils to participate in evaluating the results of instructional activities. He shows a willingness to cooperate with other teachers; participates in the in-service training program of the staff; changes plans and procedures in instructional activities when conditions suggest such changes; makes effective use of supplementary aids and community resources. He keeps records of pupil achievement, and cooperates in establishing relations with parents and other members of the community.

The teachers should try to verbalize their own beliefs about what is good teaching, and should check their beliefs against those of other teachers. They should recognize the necessity of evaluating their own teaching performance in the light of accepted concepts of what constitutes good teaching.

Every teacher is entitled to know by whom he is rated, and by whom he may be helped.

The teachers usually have at least one supervisory person to whom they can go for help without fear of being rated low because they express a problem. The supervisors promote their services, possibly to the extent of systematic classroom visits and conferences with beginning teachers. Teachers should expect clear-cut statements of purpose by supervisors who visit their classrooms, and who arrange for conferences and other opportunities for securing help. They secure help much more readily from supervisors when clear explanations are given of the duties and ways of teaching. The teacher has to invite the supervisor to visit his classroom and help analyze a problem, whenever the problem is one that can be seen by classroom observation. The teacher has to be sure that he clearly understands the supervisor's suggestions, and arrange for subsequent conferences if further explanations become necessary.

The help teachers receive from each other, from advisory personnel, and from other persons is usually available on the school staff.

The teacher's first responsibility in using these persons as aids in improving instruction is to know their identity and functions. Hence, an important part of the orientation program for teachers is that of clear identification of the special services available to help teachers. The services should be used as frequently as desirable and as early as possible.

Effective teaching uses learners continuously to seek improvement. When learners are involved in making plans, they, too, are responsible for their success. The greatest help learners can give is their participation in the classroom program.

Teachers seeking to get ideas, research, or materials bearing particular problems need to know the usual sources for identifying pertinent writings.

The in-service education activities which are widely available to high school teachers include professional reading, university courses, professional meetings, conferences, study groups, and workshops. Their professional training should result in such skills as the use of the *Education Index* to locate periodical literature, the *Review of Educational Research,* and the *Encyclo-*

pedia of Educational Research, to locate research studies, and other resources to find books. The librarian is ordinarily an invaluable asset to the teacher seeking improvement through better use of materials. The professional materials should be regarded as resources of high priority in efforts to improve teaching. The teachers can make their own collection by sharing their personal copies of professional magazines and books. There are many opportunities for professional reading — once on the job, and in the training program which is very helpful.

Professional Meetings

There are many types of professional meetings to provide specific help on instructional problems.

Most teacher organizations provide worthwhile in-service education opportunities through their programs for members. School systems are also developing many types of professional meeting to provide specific help on instructional problems. In addition to the annual meetings of national and state organizations, exhibits, and discussion sessions, there are the various local organizations with frequent meetings. Also, many schools and teacher organizations arrange various kinds of continuing study programs. These programs are designed to give help on system-wide or school-wide problems, such as reporting to parents, using local resources, and guidance of learners. There are varied types of programs, including plenty of opportunity for getting acquainted and for discussion. The teachers who participate in the meetings have the opportunity to suggest programs and to participate in planning. The participants use the opportunity to share their problems, feelings, contributions, and experimentation.

Courses for Teachers

A variety of courses for teachers is available in the teacher-ed-

ucation institutions.

Special courses are offered to give individual teachers help on specific problems. In many cases, however, teachers have considerable freedom in their choice of courses. Also, some college and university instructors organize their courses. They must make possible the participation of teachers in planning these courses, but at the same time the enrollees must assume some responsibility for the success of the course.

If opportunities to participate in planning are given, the teachers should take full advantage of them by suggesting the questions on which help is desired.

The Workshop Organization

The most common type of workshop valuable to in-service education for improving instruction is that organized and supported by the school system for its personnel.

The workshop organization provides for considerable activity in small groups organized around unifying factors, such as mutual problems, common interests, teaching fields, etc. Workshop participants usually identify in advance some of the instructional problems to be considered in the workshop. The organization and schedule of the workshop is maintained on as flexible a basis as possible, so that provision may be made for meetings and other activities which are desired by the participants. They are encouraged to criticize policies and procedures of the school system, and to make recommendations for improvement.

Experimentation in Teaching Methods

Good teaching method is always experimental.

Teachers who are guided by the modern view of teaching are always seeking such ways of working with their learners which are the most effective.

The process of experimentation is the scientific method of inquiry applied to teaching method.

Action research, or *research to guide action,* is characterized by Stephen M. Corey, as follows:

> Those who engage in action research do so primarily because they wish to improve their own practices. Action research is conducted in the heat of combat, so to speak. It is conducted by teachers or supervisors or administrators in order that they may know, on the basis of relatively objective evidence, whether or not they are accomplishing the things they hope to accomplish.[1]

Four steps are involved in classroom experimentation.[2]

1. Defining the problem.
2. Formulating a hypothesis.
3. Gathering data about the hypothesis.
4. Reaching conclusions from the data.

The teachers need to define problems for experimentation rather exactly. It is not enough to be dissatisfied with a situation; for experimentation to flourish, the teacher must inquire into the basis of the dissatisfaction, and ask ultimately what actions he may undertake to get a more favorable situation. The element of practicability must be given considerable weight in the teacher's classroom experimentation. Classroom action research has to deal with hypotheses that can be investigated in the present classroom situation. In classroom experimentation there are very real limitations on the types and extent of evidence teachers can gather.

Among the sources which may provide data for the teacher who is experimenting are the following:

1. Opinions of the teacher, other teachers, and special school personnel, pupils, and parents.
2. Observation of individuals and groups by the teacher and others.
3. Achievement records based on tests of various sorts.
4. Rating scales used by the teacher and others to estimate pupil behavior.
5. Evaluation of teaching made by pupils and observers.
6. Records of pupils' use of the library and other resources for learning.

1. Corey, Stephen M., *Action Research to Improve School Practices* (New York: Bureau of Publications, Teachers College, Columbia University, 1953), pp. 142-143.
2. Alexander, William M., and Halverson, P.M., *Effective Teaching in Secondary Schools* (New York: Rinehart & Company, Inc., 1956), p. 522.

7. Comparisons of pupils' work at various times.
8. Recordings of group evaluations of experimental practices.
9. Interviews with pupils to determine their reasons for individual reactions to experimental practices.
10. Inventories of pupils' activities.

Whenever experimentation is undertaken, it is a wise precaution to collect some systematic evidence regarding conditions which are related to the behavior it is hoped to change. Experimental teachers have only to join the quest for improvement and carefully take the steps just outlined as they find points in which improvement seems desirable.

The prerequisite for educational experimentation is an *educational philosophy* on the part of the teacher that experimentation is a necessary phase of teaching method. Without this philosophy experimentation is superficial and uncertain. Teachers who have the philosophy of education will put it to work under almost any teaching conditions.

Teachers should cooperate with each other in experimentation by undertaking joint experiments, relieving each other of routine duties at times, helping in the extra duties experimentation sometimes involves, and by providing counsel and assistance as requested.

Freedom of discussion prevails in faculty meetings, and teachers are encouraged to express their dissatisfactions and to work together in finding more satisfying conditions. Supervisory or other consultative assistance is available to help teachers organize and carry on experimentation.

Experimentation is an integral part of dynamic teaching. Experience in problem-solving processes will help learners become increasingly able to think through their own problems critically. Teachers should constantly be testing this theory through evaluating learners' growth.[1]

The First Task of the Teacher

The teacher should study each individual in order to identify

1. Alexander, *op. cit.*, pp. 523-527.

his concerns and potential creative abilities.

Each classroom setting is designed to help each learner achieve his maximum potential. It takes into account the capacities of every learner and meets the needs of the talented learner. There are special possibilities within the school program of which the teacher should become aware if he is to bend his resources toward education of the learner with a special gift.

The first important task of the teacher is to make a special effort to identify learners with unusual talent. He should use his own judgment in distinguishing between potential creative ability and better technical performance. The teacher has to look for the learner with originality, inventiveness and the depth of his insights.

With a little effort, the teacher in the content fields can develop a variety of individual projects and interests. Learners with exceptional talent should be urged to use the work period to pursue their special talents. The learner with writing talent may serve as a reporter for the school newspaper. There will also be ways of encouraging individuals to use their special talents in group projects. As a music teacher, he may help the learner with musical talent to learn how to transcribe his original melody. To help individuals develop to the full extent of their ability, he must provide the leadership and encouragement.

The talented learner deserves stimulating contacts with others who are gifted in his field. The teacher, in this case, has the responsibility of referring his learners for more expert help. Educators have inescapable leadership responsibilities. At times these may be to provide services not usually considered part of the school program; at other times, to guide the learners to the community agency already organized to give help.

Teachers should provide purposeful learning experiences — to help learners to see the purpose of what they are learning in school.

This is a point at which psychological research in the area of motivation has made a major contribution. The basic question is how to make the work more meaningful or purposeful. No matter what his grade level or his teaching field, he will need to develop skill in helping his pupils to establish vital purposes for what they learn.

Whether the curriculum design is organized around topics that permit all subject areas to be drawn upon as needed, so that each teacher works within a separate subject field, the teacher will find concern that learners be helped to develop awareness of interrelationships among subject fields.

Obviously, teachers under all curriculum designs need to stress the development of competence with fundamental skills.

The word "skill" as used in today's high school has come to be broadly interpreted. The teacher will be expected not only to work toward higher levels of performance in reading, language, or mathematics, but he must also emphasize listening skills, observing techniques, and group process skills. In his classes he will find some learners who have not achieved the competence in fundamental skills which he considers adequate for high school work. His task will be to recognize the variety of skills his learners need for competence in the courses he teaches.

The development of better educational experiences — either in his own classroom or as a member of a curriculum committee — will depend upon the effectiveness of his professional problem-solving skills.

In some school systems, what teachers consider to be a desirable program has to be balanced against what they feel must be taught for the purposes of passing college entrance examinations or other standardized tests. In some places, the concerns of certain community or pressure groups will determine, in part at least, the kind of program to be offered. In other, the number of students who elect certain specialized programs our courses will affect the school offering. Although such factors need to be reckoned with, lasting gains in terms of better programs for learners will be made only as more teachers become skilled in analyzing and solving educational problems.

The teacher needs to translate goals into behavior if he wishes to teach information effectively.

There are many ways of evaluating success in teaching information; the teacher must have clearly in mind the methods which will best accomplish the results for the work which he is teaching.

Teachers do not grow unless they actively seek new ideas.

The teacher must continue to acquire insights into human nature and into the society in which we live. If he is going to help his learners to understand what is happening in the world around them, he may have to set for himself a definite reading program. He will discover that, no matter how deep or how broad his acquaintance with his area of specilization, there is much that he does not know.

Teachers must find the creative potential of each learner, whatever his level of ability, and develop it to the fullest in all aspects of school activity.

The first task of the teacher is to recognize the creative possibilities in all aspects of the secondary school curriculum. In guiding their learners' growth in creative expression, as in guiding their growth in any other aspect of development, the teachers must know precisely what their goals are. They must also be able to help their learners to develop personal insights and standards without blocking their freedom of self-expression.

Creative expression demands skill. Learners need to be helped to develop the techniques that will facilitate their efforts in creative expression. The teachers have an obligation to help their learners acquire the skills and the ways of working that will make it possible for them to express themselves in satisfying ways. The teacher who does the best job in developing creativity in the learner meets him where he is, and by patient encouragement brings him to higher levels of attainment. Proficiency comes with maturity and with careful teaching. Books, plants, pictures, musical equipment, etc. — all of these contribute to the richness of a student's insights into the world of knowledge.

The teacher should urge each learner, regardless of intellectual level or talent, to make his contribution in his own way.

If teachers are to help their learners find in their creative experiences sources of personal satisfaction, they must plan their work with them so that there will be an opportunity to explore, to pursue special interests, or to complete individual projects. Therefore, the teachers should plan carefully with their learners the schedule of class activities which will give proper emphasis to creative expression. Many factors will influence what they should plan, where they should begin, and how far they should go. It depends on the learners — their imagination, and previous experiences in creative work. Very important, however, will be the way in which the teachers view the possibilities for creativity. Specific opportunities for creative expression in their classrooms exist in a variety of ways. The teachers should really be stimulating their learners to creative expression, to individual enterprises on which learners are working on their own initiative.

Individual differences and the general maturity level of the learners must be taken into account in every aspect of the school program.

As with planning any other aspect of the program, the first step will be to survey the capacities and needs of the learners. The objective test records will probably be available to help the teacher survey his learners' present fundamental skills, and to know better their individual interests and talents. The best way to discover creative talents consists of activities which stress doing. Among the most profitable are reporting and writing. Regardless of the subject or the age level, the teacher will soon begin to identify something unique about each learner if he observes his group wisely. There is probably no better way of discovering organizational ability than by an oral and written report, or working cooperatively in groups on a variety of experiences, such as panels and committees for various projects.

A series of exploratory activities can be useful in uncovering special talents and interests, as well as revealing reading needs, language deficiencies, and lack of study skills. The nature and extent of the exploratory activities may vary according to the subject, the time available, or what the teacher wants to find out, and his own talents and insight.

The first step in considering the types of experiences they need is identifying the creative potentials in his learners and the technical level at which they are now operating. The teacher should look at the opportunities inherent in his regular class activities. There are many opportunities for creative expression in the classrooms, and the teacher has one problem in planning his program — that of deciding which to choose.

Special days may offer opportunities for special activities — school celebrations, musicals, athletic contests, etc. There will also be some demands from the school community for help with assemblies, scenery for a play, and events such as Christmas, or a program around their special needs and interests. Depending on the teacher's sensitivity and imagination, regardless of the subject area he is teaching, all learners can have the experience of a well-balanced program.

Each class and each subject should contribute something in accordance with the potentialities of the subject. The teacher's own professional judgement, rather than the textbook, should be the guide when it comes to deciding what activities should be stressed and what help should be given. He should have some idea of what his learners can do, what their present level of proficiency is, and what the next steps should be. The teacher should combine the knowledge of his subject with his study of the learners in his class to form the place of departure for every new adventures in creative skills, and he must make final decisions on how best to realize the creative potential of the learners.

In helping learners become more skilled in creative expression, too, there will be times when he will want to help his learners to arrive at established concepts and principles.

In fostering growth in creative expression, much will depend upon the sensitivity with which the teacher guides the efforts of individuals.

The teacher who is concerned about creativity recognizes latent abilities in pupils, and takes steps to insure that these are released and developed. Many potentially creative learners need to be pushed. No one can teach creativity, but a sensitive teacher can help a learner to express himself. Such teachers are able to sense what a learner is trying to express in his creative effort and to give him the opportunity that makes it possible to express and do things in his own way. The important function of the teacher is to secure the learner's maximum participation in pupil-teacher planning — a situation in which learners, in degrees appropriate to their maturity, share in determining the rules of conduct in class, help in selecting specific problems which they wish to solve, and suggest ways in which they plan to attack them. Learners must have freedom to plan, to carry out their plans, to accept their errors as learning experiences, and to move on to better achievements. The teacher should not allow learners to make choices which he knows, in the light of his own experience, are not going to yield good results. Sharing experiences and achievements with learners, not every teacher can achieve the same results, but every teacher should be a developer of creative expression.

A responsive group in a permissive atmosphere will stimulate its members to engage in many day-by-day creative efforts.

There is joy in sharing with others, and a wealth of stimulation from working with one's friends on cooperative projects. There is in classrooms a wealth of creative expression and a multitude of ways of sharing creative efforts. These include sharing art exhibits, music festivals, and cantatas of other days. In the classroom, everybody shares, and skillful teachers also use group-creative efforts as a means of stimulating individuals. Individual suggestions should be considered, but acceptance always depends upon the purposes. Each student likes to do something which is different and to get some recognition for it. The teacher should use his professional judgement in helping learners to plan a job that is reasonably within their present level of skill. A learner should be working on his own creative efforts and learning better techniques at one and the same time. The teachers should find ways of helping learners decide exactly what they want to express, and should provide them with skills they need to convert their imaginations into concrete and worthwhile results.

Helping learners to grow and develop deeper values is an extremely important role in the total pedagogical process.

The role of teachers in helping learners to grow in many kinds of understandings, and to develop deeper values is an extremely important one in the total pedagogical process. The role of teachers is not to equip their learners with a set of rules by which they may judge their life and all efforts, but to help them develop insights into many elements that contribute to the good result. If the teachers want to help their learners to develop deeper insights, they must start with learners where they are. The teachers should help them take an objective look at their work and encourage them to think. But learners will not grow in insight unless they are working with teachers who are concerned with these aspects of growth. The learners will grow as teachers help them to achieve their goals, to set their own standards, and to identify their own strengths and weaknesses.

The role of teacher is complicated, of course, because each learner has his own unique perceptions, and each react in different ways. Only the acquaintance with learners is helpful in sensing what new experiences might be provided.

The Teaching Method

Teaching method embodies the teacher's efforts in teacher-pupil relations to bring about individual and group problem-solving activities.

The method itself, the way of solving problems reflectively, becomes content for teacher and learner alike, to the point where many pupils will learn how best to solve their own problems. This *scientific method* is really the only way of learning, and must be the basis of the teaching method.

1. Subject matter is *what* we teach; method is *how* we teach.
   The *ends* are learning; the *means* the way we achieve such
2. learning.

3. The *product* is the outcome of a learning experience; the *process* is how we provide for the experience to take place.

The scientific method is what most people today mean by a sound intellectual method, and discussion is one example of what people mean by a pedagogical method. A *pedagogical method* is a method by which a teacher teaches truth. The intellectual purposes of education can be achieved only when teachers use pedagogical methods which stimulate and direct scientific thinking in learners.[1]

There is a distinction between technique and method.

The former we may consider as a specific way of doing a particular task in the methodology of education, for example, the technique of organizing a committee of learners, or of conducting a discussion. The latter is defined as the process of teacher guidance of pupils' activities.

The critical intellectual activity we call reflection is most effective as a method of problem-solving.

The individual does not just happen onto a solution; he tries out, reflectively, various possible solutions until he arrives at the solution which he has no reason to reject.

Direct teaching of facts does not always change attitudes.

Attitudes are emotionalized sets of predispositions that influence our behavior with reference to all situations or objects to which they are related. Our attitudes are, at least in part, determined by our concepts. In large measure, what we believe about something will decide what our attitude toward it will be. Thus it is that changes in beliefs also change attitudes. Hence, one can use direct teaching of facts to teach attitudes.

However, direct teaching of facts does not always change attitudes. Concepts alone do not determine attitudes. Emotions are also involved. A strong attitude may continue to influence a person even though intellectually his beliefs have changed. Even though lectures can be very effective, as a rule, to change

1. *Ibid.,* pp. 7-10.

another person's attitudes by this method is extremely difficult.
To change attitudes, one must provide many favorable associations. Because young people tend to imitate the attitudes of persons whom they can admire and identify with, good examples
should be provided. Group opinions exert great pressure on the
attitudes of individuals. In addition, group discussions seem to
give one an opportunity to convince oneself. In short, although
direct teaching has some value in the building of attitudes, to
be most effective the teacher must resort to more devious methods.[1]

*The full resources of the classroom have not been utilized unless
there have been opportunities to observe an experienced teacher
at work.*

The points in the teaching sequence at which observation is
provided, and the specific purposes of the student and teacher
make a difference in the effectiveness of the experience. The
observation periods can be profitably interspersed, however,
with short-term responsibilities as desirable ways to help the
student-teacher to establish himself with the class. Beginners
also need the reassurance of having seen the general techniques
used by their cooperating teachers in planning, handling a remedial lesson, helping a special committee, and presenting a
completely organized lesson.

Observation can also be used to help both student-teacher and
cooperating teacher gain a better understanding of individuals.
Such experiences can add much insight into the needs of individuals. Obviously, any observation is more valuable when its
purpose is clear. The problems which suggest the need for observation should be identified ahead of time in conference, and
some rules for good observation thought through. Such conferences are essential. These brief contacts, however, do not provide
the time required to help a student think through all the complex
problems that confront him. Occasionally, the student-teacher
and cooperating teacher agree to use a lunch hour for this purpose, or to meet after school once a week.

It can be helpful to the student-teacher to have opportunities
to talk with school personnel with whom he may be expected

1. Clark and others, *op. cit.,* pp. 58-59.

to work a year hence: the principal, the counselor, the attendance officer, or visiting teacher. It is often enlightening to the student-teacher to sit in on conferences regarding an individual learner, so that he can have first-hand experience with some of the problems faced in working cooperatively with parents, cooperating teacher, principal, counselor, and visiting teacher.

Conferences

Conferences can also serve to help the student-teacher look forward to the time when he will be in charge of his own classroom. Perhaps the most important guide for conducting a conference in which the student's teaching is to be analyzed is that he needs to know where he is succeeding, as well as where he needs to improve. Cooperating teachers should not hesitate to analyze frankly with students the dark places in the day's work. The student-teacher should be encouraged to offer his reactions to the way various activities unfolded. Starting a conference with concerns uppermost in the student's mind does not exclude the discussion of other topics.

The student-teacher who can analyze in general terms what went wrong in a situation is not always the person able to make a concrete suggestion about what to do next. The suggestions made in conference must be specific enough to give the student a sense of direction. Discussion of specific classroom events will offer many opportunities to help him to grow in understanding himself. He can be helped to take a major step toward becoming a professional person if he can learn to evaluate his work objectively. But cooperating teachers are not trained counselors. They can bring to the student-teaching relationship their own expectations.

The Effect of Distribution of Practice

The general rule — that the more distributed the practice, the more rapid the learning — must be qualified.

The effect of distribution of practice is conditioned by psychological realities and by the skills the individual is trying to learn.

The length and distribution of class periods usually have been determined with little regard to psychological realities. The most frequent pattern of distribution at the high school level is a fifty- to sixty-minute period, five times a week, for one or more semesters, depending upon the total time given to the subject. The practices of the junior high school tend to follow those of the high school with regard to length of period, but to devote fewer periods per week to a subject. The average number of periods per week varies from two to six, with the traditional content subjects being assigned the more frequent class meetings.[1]

Studies of time allotment practices are very important in this procedure. Such studies disclose tendencies either to increase or to decrease the amount of time given to various subjects and activities.

The procedure of determining time allotment by present practice may be useful in keeping the allotment practices of a school from getting too much out of line with average practices. Present practice is partly the result of committee reports, such as that of the Committee of Ten; it is partly the result of countless variations due to the pressures of circumstances; and it may be partly the result of numerous judgements made by local school officials and teachers on the basis of ill-considered facts and values.

The judgemental procedure for determining time allotment, like the judgemental procedure for selecting subject matter, has not been clearly formulated.

In the allotment of time by the judgemental procedure, there must be an agreement upon the purposes of the educational program. Since the amount of time allotted to any aspect of the program depends upon what is considered important, agreements upon educational directions are essential to agreement upon time allotment practices.

As agreement upon educational purposes is reached, it becomes possible to bring research findings to bear upon the question of how much time to give to a particular part of the school program. The relevant research findings fall into three categories:

1. There are those studies that show what a given subject matter contributes to the realization of the accepted purposes.

---

1. Loomis, Lide, and Johnson, *The Program of Studies,* pp. 27-28; "Time Use in the Junior High School Program," *Bulletin of the National Association of Secondary School Principals,* Vol. 29, No. 130 (April, 1945), pp. 93-101. Quoted in: B.O. Smith, *Fundamentals of Curriculum Development,* pp. 214-215.

2. There are studies that show the extent to which certain learnings are acquired incidentally.
3. There are studies which show that improved methods and materials of instruction will produce desirable results with a saving of time.

Efforts to reach decisions about time allotment will be ill-considered unless the results of the studies in each of these categories are thoroughly understood.[1]

The length of class periods should be conducive to maximum progress in the subject.

A subject organization is no more bound by its own administrative devices than is any other type of organization. Spelling, for example, has been taught largely by techniques of memorization, and experimentation with these methods has long indicated that the class period should be fifteen to twenty minutes in length. As a consequence, a short period is the general practice when spelling is taught as a subject. On the other hand, many schools have found that the learnings in certain of the science courses can be developed more efficiently in unbroken time intervals as long as ninety minutes, and such periods are fairly common.[2]

Learning takes place only when the individual learner consciously seeks to satisfy a need that he believes is important to him.

Even under the best conditions, *telling* is a highly limited teaching method. Since learners listen in terms of their individual interests and in the light of their individual experiences, what is heard is not identical with each learner.

Transfer of learning is the act of using in one situation something learned in another situation.

The learning transfers because of common components in the learning and using situations, and the learner's ability to make generalizations and see relationships. Facts, concepts, skills, principles, methods, ideals, and attitudes — all can transfer under

1. Smith, *op. cit.*, pp. 219-221.
2. *Ibid.*, p. 240.

proper conditions; but it is the method of study that sharpens the pupils' abilities to reason, memorize, and concentrate.

Remembering is essential to transfer, but memory can not be strengthened simply by memorizing. On the contrary, remembering is made up of many skills. The learners tend to remember best those things that are meaningful, important, and vivid. Teachers can enhance pupils' remembrance of subject matter by emphasizing meanings, generalizations, and by providing plenty of opportunities for review. The secondary-school courses should be designed to induce the maximum amount of transfer, and so should emphasize generalization, applications, thorough meaningfull learning, and attitudes.

The Amount of Homework

The amount and difficulty of homework assignment should naturally vary with individual differences.

For the gifted child, it may involve a review of an article in an encyclopedia in relation to a classroom discussion. For the slow learner, it might simply involve a new way of enhancing or extending previously learned materials. Homework teaches responsibility.

Many kinds of learning require much exercising or drilling of what the child knows, not only an understanding of the problem at hand. Too frequently, children who knew their multiplication tables last year do not remember them this year. There is the opinion that too little attention has been given the matter of homework in the good overall program of education.

Homework can be put to the service of increasing achievement without affecting adversely other important concerns in the educative process.

Drill certainly has a place in education, especially for materials that need to be thoroughly memorized.

The student who reads his lessons three or four times and does not remember what he has read is, in fact, really practicing the wrong conditions for learning.

Drill certainly has a place in education, especially for materials that need to be thoroughly memorized — such as spelling, foreign language vocabularies, verb conjugations, form of speech, etc. The drill should revolve around an opportunity to increase knowledge. Drill should not be used to obtain concentration and focus attention; it depends upon concentration and focus that are already present.

The learner must reach higher orders of insights through his own efforts.

The learner is able to develop insights into the principles of human knowledge by actually working with concrete and abstract materials. The teacher must help him to analyze what he is trying to do, and to consider how best to achieve his goal.

Learners can also be given significant help in developing insights through cooperative evaluation of their own efforts. The development of group feeling and group evaluation is extremely important for the progressive growth of insights. There must be thoughtful identification of good points and friendly discussion of those that are not so good. Teachers should help them to do work of which they can be proud , but too much direction by the teacher will not be drawing out their own conclusions. There may well be times when they should have the opportunity to analyze the work and the techniques used. Obviously, learners must understand the purpose for a lesson, and have ample opportunity to think for themselves about their own problems before they begin to examine other learners' work.

The teacher must be working actively to deepen his own insights, and should be deepening their insights and extending their horizons by the experiences he provides.

The Efficiency of Instruction (Questioning)

The efficiency of instruction is measured, in a large degree, by the nature of the questions asked.

The question technique is difficult and complex. The teacher must not only be prepared to follow up effectively the answer to a question he has asked; he must also be able to analyze quickly an unexpected response, and see its implications.

If a teacher's questions are poor, it means that his knowledge is weak.

Sound ideas and purposes shape questions so that questions become effective. The question-and-answer method can make important contributions, but must be correctly determined at the proper time in the learning.

With the rapid-fire method of questioning, there is no time allowed a pupil to go very far afield in his experience.

The teacher is doing most of the work of the class hour, instead of directing the pupils in the doing. He has no time to cultivate the gentle art of expression. There is little thought given to the needs of individuals.

The large number of questions suggests that the teacher has no time to teach how to study.

He has no time to teach how to organize subject matter, how to judge relative worth of facts studied, or what to memorize. The value of the lesson is likely to be lost sight of in the rapidity and intensity of questioning activity.

The person who has ideas, thoughts, notions of genuine values, real purposes and aims in mind will ask questions in keeping with profitable achievements.

The most important purposes of questions are:
1. To apply information.
2. To develop new ideas.
3. To promote understanding.
4. To test for objectives taught.
5. To stimulate thinking.

Questions are the means to stimulate and direct learning, but the learning itself is individual effort.

In many cases, the aims are neglected because they may be extremely difficult for students to discover without the proper stimulation and direction from the teacher.   The questioning method, if used in accordance with its possibilities, becomes one of the most effective ways of good teaching.

The use of the question under classroom conditions requires some personal equipment on the part of the teacher.

The teacher should have the power of analysis, and the ability to make comparisons and generalizations.   Clear and rapid thinking involves mastery of subject matter, and the power and habit of logical thinking.

The questions or responses of the student may reveal serious deficiencies that must be corrected.

Some questions may well be passed by lightly.   The teacher has to handle questions and responses of the class to the best advantage.

There are distinct difficulties in the formulation of questions.

This difficulty grows out of the very nature of language.   The teacher might be a master of content; he might be schooled in habits of logical thinking, quick in mental reaction, and yet fail through his inability to frame questions skillfully.   The teacher's question should be clear and not too wordy; it should be simple, not complicated; the vocabulary should be suited to the ability of the students; the sequence of questions should lead to better understanding.

It is only fair to the student to word a question so briefly that its meaning can be quickly grasped.   The utmost care in the choice of words and the phrasing of sentences is necessary to insure the clearness of the ideas.

The alert teacher will gauge his questions to the ability of his students.

Questioning should be adapted to the age and ability of the students.

The question should reveal a direct relationship to the objectives of the lesson.

Questions should reflect a definite purpose; they should serve to reenforce other questions, and progressively develop main idea. Questioning develops the value of sequential thinking on the part of the student. Limited response is desirable when drill is the purpose of questioning. The student has to have sufficient time for the formulation of answers.

When a student fails to get the question, pass on to another.

If the class knows the question will be repeated on demand, there is a tendency for students to give less strict attention to the discussion. Ask questions occasionally — it is a good device to handle some disciplinary situations of inattention.

The teacher should use every possible means to get students to participate through questions.

The more certain the teacher can be that education is taking place.

The teacher should be confident in the manner in which the question is directed to the student.

If the teacher is sympathetic, students will free to venture participation at times, though they are in some doubt as to the correctness of their comments.

The teacher should encourage the student to think for himself, not to accept unquestioningly the point of view of the teacher.

Students should be encouraged to ask questions that indicate a sincere disagreement with the teacher.

Illustrations

Any adequate treatment of the learning process and teaching technique must recognize two main forms of aid to the clarification of thought.

These may be classified as *word symbolism* and *concrete materials.* Anecdotes, stories, descriptions, word pictures that stimulate the imagination or recall of incidents of student experience may serve to provide the mental imagery necessary to clarify an abstract idea or principle in learning.

Non-visual illustration (word symbolism) — correct usage of non-visual illustration, however, is dependent upon a full understanding of what are the specific purposes served by non-visual illustrations:

1. *To attract attention* — The value of striking incident, a gripping story, or a humorous anecdote to bring a class to attention.

2. *To facilitate reasoning and understanding.* Oftentimes an incident, a story, or an explanation through comparison of the elements of similarity of the problem at hand with another the student knows, will lead the students to a flash of understanding.

3. *To vivify realization of experience.* A student may know a fact, an axiom or a principle, or some conclusions, but it has not impressed him much. It is therefore likely to have been forgotten quickly. A well-chosen incident or story may make its significance so vivid that it will not soon be forgotten.

4. *To stimulate the imagination and provide for action.* The propagandist knows full well the power of word picture, story, and incident to fire the imagination, arouse the emotions, and incite to action. No more powerful instrumentality lies at hand for the teacher for the development of attitudes and ideals than the use of the vivid imagery of word symbolism to stimulate the imagination and, through it, the effective life of the individual.[1]

---

1. Bossing, Nelson L., *Teaching in Secondary Schools* (Boston: Houghton-Mifflin Co., 1952), pp. 361-371.

How to Use Non-Visual Illustrations

The standards suggested do not apply with equal force in every situation.

1. *Use illustration that actually illuminates the idea.* A story, incident, allusion, or comparison should have one central idea that applies to the situation. Often one thinks he has a good illustration when a little analysis reveals the application as most superficial, and reflection on the part of the student is likely to lead to erroneous deductions.

2. *Use illustrations approximately accurate.* The accuracy of elements in the illustration should be accepted without question. A teacher was desribing a certain geographical spot of interest in a foreign country which he had not visited. For all practical purposes, the description served its purpose, but one student, who had visited this place, immediately called attention to minor inaccuracies in the description.

3. *Use significant illustrations to insure abstraction of essential idea.* The careful guidance of the student, with many illustrations where needed to illuminate trouble spots in his development of thought, is the teaching situation to be devoutly sought. Progress in learning is not to be considered synonymous with the coverage of pages in the textbook, nor the absence of illustrative aid given. The extent to which illustrative aid should be given must remain a matter of dicretion on the part of the teacher.

4. *Use illustrations at times that are vivid and realistic.* Vivid and realistic imagery should be evoked with care. Nonetheless, for purposes of attracting attention, to impress an important point in memory, or to arouse such emotional response as to lead to activity or the formation of attitudes, this form of illustration is most valuable.

5. *Use sparingly illustrations of personal-experience type.* It is natural that one's personal experience should be most vivid and replete in mental imagery. It is most natural that recall should bring to the fore appropriate experiences to fit a given situation. The effectiveness of personal experience as the source for illustrative data differs with different teacher personalities.[1]

1. *Ibid.,* pp. 371-375.

The teacher needs to have all visual aids properly classified and ready for instant use.

The teacher should see clearly a real need for visual assistance, and then select a concrete device that will actually assist the student to overcome his difficulty.

The pupils should be prepared as thoroughly for a broadcast or series of broadcasts.

The educational possibilities inherent in radio and television programs are obvious. Every school can, through radio and television, greatly enrich the existing school program. Almost every event of major importance, regional or national, is now put on the air. The school must undertake seriously the development of listeners who can listen critically.

The pupils should be prepared as thoroughly for a broadcast as for any class activity.

The preparation will be governed by the nature of the subject matter and by the particular broadcast. Preparation must be made less specifically, therefore, than when the general nature of the content of the broadcast is known in advance.

The teacher must insure an environment conducive to listening activity.

The teacher or school may check the radio programs within the reception area of the school which may contribute to some phase of his work, and plan the course to fit into the broadcast schedule. The teacher should make every effort to derive maximum educational values from every broadcast used. The good teacher will consider certain standards to guide him in the selection of radio and television programs.

Types of Testing Programs

The teacher needs to be able to design or select tests which will provide the information he needs.

There are two types of testing programs in operation:

1. A program of teacher-made tests used at appropriate times in all classes.
2. A program of standardized tests administered periodically in only a few areas.

The latter is often set up on a system-wide basis, but in many school systems teachers are free to request additional standardized tests in their areas as the need arises. The teacher needs to be able to design or select tests which will give him the information he requires.

The information yielded by classroom tests differs from day-by-day data-collecting. In the first place, learners know that they are being tested. Then, too, a test calls for responses to the same items from everyone; it provides a basis for comparing learner with learner. In contrast, day-by-day data-collecting tends to be a continuous process done under a variety of circumstances.

Most test items on written examinations can be classified under two main heads:

1. *Selection* items.
2. *Supply* items.

Selection items include true-false, multiple-choice types. Here the learner is asked to select from the two or more alternative answers for the item. Supply items include complete and short answer essays. Here the learner supplies the correct answer from his own background. Selection items — true-false and multiple-choice — are often used to measure a learner's recognition of facts. However, such items, if properly constructed, can be used also to measure a learner's concepts and his ability to apply basic principles. A test made up of true-false items is particularly useful when the teacher wants a quick estimate of his learner's grasp of a number of specific facts. Such items are not as suitable if the teacher wishes to determine whether a learner can apply a generalization to a new situation. They offer, of course, the greatest opportunity for the learner to gain points by shrewd guesses.

Multiple-choice items are more difficult to construct but are preferred over true-false items by most teachers, since a learner must choose among at least three, or at times four or five possible answers. Matching items are similar to multiple-choice items in that the learner must distinguish among several possible answers. They are particularly useful, however, when the teacher wishes to ascertain whether learners have developed clear and precise differentiations among a group of related facts.

When preparing a test using selection items, the teacher should go back to his original objectives and list the facts, generalizations, or skills which he wants to measure. Decide upon the test form that seem most likely to reveal the learnings about which he is concerned. This will help him to decide how many questions to include. With his general pattern for the test determined, he is ready to write specific items to get the information he desires. Be sure also to read his test carefully for ambiguous wording and to make certain that the answer to one question does not hinge on a pupil's ability to answer correctly a preceding question. As a final step, make sure that the directions are clear, and that the method for indicating the correct answer is uncomplicated. If pupils must work from the blackboard, the teacher will need to explain clearly how much is to be copied and how correct answers are to be indicated on their papers.

In many school systems, standardized tests are only given once a year, and then only in a few subjects. The standardized tests are useful only insofar as they are appropriate for a particular course objective.

It is very important, then, to examine the standardized tests being used in a particular school system. They are, after all, designed to challenge the most able learner. The teacher should decide whether the test as a whole stresses objectives he considers to be appropriate for his learners. In the last analysis, the teacher, not his test — standardized or teacher-made — evaluates his learner's progress.

A test — be it commercially produced or one of his own — is simply another sample of a learner's work. It is collected at a given point of time, and subject to all the influences — distractions, tensions, illness — that cause performance on any single job to fluctuate.

The ultimate purpose of a test, as of any other piece of work done by a learner, is to help him grow. Time should be taken to go over some tests, item by item, not only to help learners identify the correct answers, but to determine what caused the original confusion. Also, this should help him gain a better understanding of himself — his needs, interests, strengths, and weaknesses. Tests, then, should provide a learner with a more realistic picture of his abilities, educational progress, and possible vocational choices.[1]

Review

The term "review" connotes not a mere repetition of facts to fix them more firmly in mind, but rather a new view of these facts in a different setting that results in new understandings, changed attitudes, or different behavior patterns.

The student must have factual data upon which to hang his thinking, but the human mind cannot with profit continue to amass these factual data without relating them in some meaningful form.[2]

The review generally comes at the completion of the unit of study.

Any intelligent modification of each of the successive efforts must be conditioned upon some knowledge of the degree of success of each preceding effort. Any repetition tends to fix materials previously studied more firmly in mind.

Evaluation

The teacher must determine the purposes of evaluation in his daily teaching and learn how to use evaluation procedures effectively.

The teacher should be making continuous appraisals of the strengths and weaknesses of his learners as he leads class discussions, listens to reports, checks homework assignments,

1. Carter, William L., and others, *Learning to Teach in the Secondary School* (New York: The Macmillan Co., 1962), pp. 322-330.
2. Bossing, *Teaching in Secondary Schools,* p. 345.

watches demonstrations, reads sets of papers, and watches his learners at work during study periods.

Basically, the purpose of evaluation is to promote growth, as well as to demonstrate at the end of a series of activities that growth has taken place. A skillful teacher does not stop using evaluation procedures — he continues to evaluate by posing questions and setting tasks as the lesson proceeds, in order to identify present levels of understanding.

Evaluation is an integral part of the process, not only for the teacher but for the learners as well. The teacher must bring to each class session his appraisal of the strengths and weaknesses of his group and of the individuals in it.

The mature learner is able to appraise his own strengths and weaknesses realistically. He can analyze a problem for himself, propose the next steps, and carry them out. The teacher helps them to analyze lessons, projects, and assignments, and tries to get them to determine why they went poorly, to look at their errors as well as their successes. Such experiences make a fundamental contribution to two of the most important abilities: self-direction and self-evaluation.

The teacher should make evaluative decisions on the quality of material presented. He should look at content, organization, handwriting, sentence structure, spelling, punctuation. As his learners engage in independent activity, he will be appraising their study and work habits.

The teacher must use evaluation procedures and provide objective data which parents, college admissions' officers, employers, may use. He should put to effective use all the techniques he has developed for working with other teachers and with parents. The evaluation should help him to look at his own effectiveness. He will find a number of provisions in operation in his school system for assisting him in this task. Discussions of promising professional practices can be of help to him in looking at the quality of his classroom work. He should not neglect the professional library, which is another valuable aid.

The principals and the supervisors in his school are to help him. On the basis of his evaluative judgements, he will decide that more help is needed in some areas and with some topics, and he will start to plan the next step. He will determine how much time to allot to topics and problems, each of which seems equally important. He should make these decisions on the basis of his insights into broad educational goals. As he starts to consider how effective his courses have been, he should be looking for growth in specific skills, but he should also be looking for growth in problem-solving skills, for deep interest, for positive attitudes toward learning, for ability to use skills or knowledge in a variety of situations.

The teacher must determine appropriate expectations. He will waste the potentialities of his learners if he sets his sights too low. On the other hand, he will lead to a frustrating year if his standards are too high. Evaluation of learner growth must be concerned with the learner's total progress toward educational objectives, not only with his achievement in a single area. The teacher should examine the course of study for his school system; also look at the standard textbooks published for the grade and subjects he is teaching, and whatever scores on standardized tests are available. They will give him some idea of his learners' abilities and attainments.

The supervisor, other teachers of his subjects, and his own experiences with learners will help him to develop appropriate standards for his classes. It is important to know the experience backgrounds of his learners, as well as their intelligence test scores in determining expectations for their work.

Fundamental Ideas in Grade Placement

The fundamental ideas in grade placement are: maturation, experimental background, prerequisie learning, interest, usefulness, and difficulty. All of these, in one way or another, have been used in the determination of learning sequence in the activity curriculum. The problem is to determine the grade level at which a given phase of a subject is most readily learned.

How to determine the grade in which an objective or the content selected to reach an objective should be placed.

There are only two possible approaches to the solution of problems of grade placement:

1. Adjust the experience to child's level of development.
2. Assume curriculum experiences to be located at a given grade level and provide learnings to adjust the child to these experiences — that is, to get him ready for learning.

The *first* of these approaches studies the child, and adjusts materials and activities to what he is capable of learning at a given period in his growth.

The *second* approach assumes grade placement of materials and activities. The child is then prepared for these potential experiences.

Probably neither of these approaches will be used without consideration for the other. These are the two variables: the child and what is provided for him.

The change of instructional goals is not a different approach to the problem of grade placement. The new materials and activities are then selected to be in keeping with the learner's current stage of development.[1]

Procedures Used to Determine Grade Placement

Two procedures are usually used to determine grade placement on the basis of the foregoing factors: judgemental and experimental.

The *judgemental procedure* is the most commonly accepted procedure, and the grade placement of most skills and content in the current curriculum has been determined by it. One of the serious criticisms of judgemental procedure is that committees too often base their decisions upon the prejudices held by persons disciplined in one field of specialization. As a result, recommendations regarding grade placement too frequently rest upon unexamined assumptions and erroneous judgements of such factors as interest and difficulty.

An examination of the work of the more effective committees reveals the following guideposts:

1. The bases of the committee's judgements should be clearly stated so that the members can better understand their own procedure, and so that other persons may easily

1. Smith, *op. cit.*, pp. 171-173.

evaluate the committee's work.
2. The committee should test all of its choices by the available facts and seek new facts when these are needed.
3. It should examine the extent to which the various factors involved in grade location have been considered and try to use them in its judgements.
4. It should take a broad view of the curriculum and the child, rather than the narrow view usually associated with specialized teachers and subject-matter specialists.
5. It should not be concerned with what should be done at one grade level alone, or with a single activity, topic, or skill, but with all levels of education.

The *experimental procedure* is an attempt to make objective investigations into the placement of activities, skills, and subject matter. There are many different patterns of this procedure, depending upon the criteria of placement employed and the breadth of the study. The usual plan is to select as a guide some factor or set of factors such as child interest, difficulty of content, and mental age. The activities, skills, or content to be located are then selected, and a hypothesis is made as to their probable placement. They are then taught to the children in the selected grade, under specific conditions. The tryout is checked by a-chievement tests.[1]

Scores

Scores on a standardized test must, of course, be interpreted with caution in the case of an individual learner.

Scores on a standardized test are nevertheless helpful in giving the teacher a general idea of what to expect of his class. If his learners are, for the most part, at or beyond their grade expectancy, he should plan to provide activities focused toward a higher level of skill than usually recommended for learners of his subject and grade. If, on the other hand, the class average tends to fall generally below grade expectancy, the teacher will need to build from a more basic level than usually considered appropriate.

Careful observation and listening will be most helpful in

1. *Ibid.,* pp. 190-192.

determining the learners' levels of performance in certain areas. For example, in an algebra class, a teacher may quickly determine a deficiency in understanding a basic skill by asking a learner to explain how he arrived at a particular answer to a problem. Asking learners to explain their work to others is a very good way of discovering the degree of understanding they have achieved.

To make the teaching fully effective, the teacher will need to know individual strengths and weaknesses, as well as the general levels at which his learners are working.

Appraising learner performance and deciding where to begin is certainly not easy. Careful, patient questioning, examination of records, analyses of tests, study of written work, attention to individuals, and sensitivity to the classroom situation — used appropriately, these are the keys to a successful beginning in teaching. Discovering exactly which techniques a pupil is using well or which he is using poorly calls for continuous analysis. Experienced teachers use many techniques to free themselves to work with individuals. These range from planning independent projects with learners to taking a few minutes to walk about the room observing individuals at work.

SUMMARY

Throughout this chapter is emphasized an experimental approach to teaching which recognizes the need of continuous adaptation of educational methods to changing conditions. Systemic methods should be employed in solving such curriculum problems as the grade placement of materials, the identification of child and adolescent needs, and the development of effective methods of teaching. The teacher creates the type of learning situation that will determine the attitudes, understandings, skills, and appreciations that pupils develop.

Education should be interpreted more fully as the dynamic process of guiding the experiences of students so that they will become more adept in achieving important purposes.

This point of view has been expressed here in specific ways by which teachers can work toward improved teaching.

FOR FURTHER STUDY

Alexander, W.M., and P.M. Halverson, *Effective Teaching in Secondary Schools.* New York: Rinehart and Co., Inc., 1956.

American Association of School Administrators. *American School Curriculum.* Thirty-first Yearbook. Washington, D.C.: The Association, 1953.

Anderson, R.H., *Teaching in a World of Change.* New York: Harcourt, Brace and World, Inc., 1966.

Anderson, Vernon, *Principles and Procedures of Curriculum Development.* New York: The Ronald Press Co., 1956.

Association for Supervision and Curriculum Development. *Action for Curriculum Development.* 1951 Yearbook. Washington, D.C.: The Association, 1951.

Barr, A.S., R.A. Davis, and P.O. Johnson, *Educational Research and Appraisal.* New York: J.B. Lippincott Co., 1953.

Bossing, N.L. *Teaching in secondary Schools.* Boston: Houghton Mifflin Co., 1952.

Broudy, H.S., J.R. Palmer, *Exemplars of Teaching Method.* Chicago: Rand McNally & Co., 1965.

Carter, W.L., C.W. Hansen, and M.G. McKim, *Learning to Teach in the Secondary School.* New York: The Macmillan Co., 1962.

Caswell, H.L., and associates. *Curriculum Improvement in Public School Systems.* New York: Bureau of Publications, Teachers College, Columbia University, 1953.

Clark, L.H., R.L. Klein and J.B. Burks, *The American Secondary School Curriculum.* New York: The Macmillan Co., 1965.

Clark, L.H., *Secondary School Teaching Methods.* New York: The Macmillan Co., 1967.

Corey, S.M., *Action Research to Improve School Practices.* New York: Bureau of Publications, Teachers College, Columbia University, 1953.

Cosper, Cecil, *Student-Teaching Theory and Practice.* New York: Greenwich Book Publishers, 1965.

Doll, R.C., A.H. Passow, and S.M. Corey, *Organizing for Curriculum Improvement.* New York: Bureau of Publications, Teachers College, Columbia University, 1953.

Ebel, R.L., *Measuring Educational Achievement.* Englewood Cliff, N.J.: Prentice-Hall, Inc., 1965.

Frymier, J.R., *The Nature of Educational Method.* Columbus, Ohio: Charles E. Merrill Books, Inc., 1965.

Goodlad, J.I., *School, Curriculum, and the Individual.* Waltham, Mass.: Blaisdell Publishing Co., 1966.

Guide to the Study of the Curriculum in the Secondary Schools of Illinois. Springfield, Ill.: State Department of Public Instruction, 1948.

Houston, W.R., F.H. Blackington, and H.C. Southworth, *Professional Growth through Student Teaching.* Columbus, Ohio: Charles E. Merrill Books, Inc., 1965.

Hug, J.H., and P. J. Wilson, *Curriculum Enrichment Outdoors.* New York: Harper and Row, Publishers, 1965.

Inlow, G. M., *The Emergent in Curriculum.* New York: John Wiley & Sons, Inc., 1966.

Kelley, E. C., *The Workshop Way of Learning.* New York: Harper and Brothers, 1951.

Keppel, Francis, *The Necessary Revolution in American Education.* New York: Harper and Row, Publishers, 1966.

Larson, K. G., *Guide to Personal Advancement in the Teaching Profession.* Englewood Cliffs, N.J.: Prentice-Hall, Inc., 1966.

Miel, A. M., *Changing the Curriculum.* New York: Appleton-Century-Crofts, 1946.

National Society for the Study of Education. *In-Service Education for Teachers, Supervisors, and Administrators.* Fifty-sixth Yearbook, part 1. Chicago: University of Chicago Press, 1957.

Oliver, A.I., *Curriculum Improvement.* New York: Dodd, Mead and Co., 1965.

Ovard, G. F., *Administration of the Changing Secondary School.* New York: The Macmillan Co., 1966.

Passow, A. H., M. B. Miles, S. M. Corey, and Dale Draper. *Training Curriculum Leaders for Cooperative Research.* New York: Bureau of Publications, Teachers College, Columbia University, 1955.

Patton, E. D., and D. W. Steiner, *Let's Look at Our Future.* New York: Scarecrow Press, Inc., 1966.

Russell, J. E., *Change and Challenge in American Education.* Boston: Houghton Mifflin Co., 1965.

Saylor, J. G., and W. M. Alexander, *Curriculum Planning for Better Teaching and Learning.* New York: Rinehart and Co., Inc., 1954.

Simpson, R. H., *Teacher Self-Evaluation.* New York: The Macmillan Co., 1966.

Smith, B. O., W. O. Stanley, and J. H. Shores, *Fundamentals of Curriculum Development.* Yonkers-on-Hudson, N.Y.: World Book Co., 1957.

Stratemeyer, F. B., H. L. Forkner, M. G. McKim, and A. H. Passow, *Developing a Curriculum for Modern Living.* New York: Bureau of Publications, Teachers College, Columbia University, 1957.

Thelen, H. A., *Group Dynamics in Curriculum Improvement —* "Educational Leadership," Vol. XI, No. 7, April, 1954.

Vico, G. B., *On the Study Methods of Our Time.* Indianapolis, Ind: The Bobbs-Merrill Co., Inc., 1965.

CHAPTER IV

THE SUBJECT MATTER ORGANIZATION

Ways to Organize the Curriculum

Basically, there are two ways to organize the curriculum:

1. The *experience-centered* curriculum as the true core curriculum, in which course content is built around experiences or problems, and disregards the usual subject matter lines.
2. The *subject-centered* curriculum, in which the courses are organized around fields of knowledge or discipline.

Almost every senior and four-year high school is organized on a subject basis, even though it may offer a core program as part of its program of studies.

Many writers have summarized and reported the claimed advantages and strengths of subject organization.

Hopkins reports, for example, an argument based on objectivity of subject organization:

> This objectivity is best exemplified in the ease with which the program is authoritatively administered. All subjects are isolated. Subject matter is organized in advance of teaching. Persons in authority control the learning situation. Emphasis is placed upon unchanging facts and information. Fixed habits and skills are developed. All children are uniformly exposed to the subject matter. Minimum essentials and grade standards are designated. Credits are determined by the number of class hours of exposure to the subject matter to be covered. The whole organization is governed by a central administrative authority.[1]

The Relationship Between Subjects and Learners

The difference between the subject and experience curriculums

---

1. Hopkins, L.T., *Interaction: The Democratic Process* (Boston: D.C. Heath and Co., 1941), p. 50.

on this point is not that one teaches subjects and ignores learners, or that the other teaches learner and ignores subjects. Each curriculum considers subjects and learners, but in a different way, to a different degree, and with a different emphasis.[1]

The subjects constitute a logical and effective method of organizing learning and of interpreting and systematizing new knowledge and facts.[2]

Systematic organization is essential to the effective interpretation of experience.[3]

Subject organization is an enormous saver of time and energy, a short cut we can all use.

. . . the subject curriculum is most appropriate for developing the intellectual powers of the individual.[4]

The modern claims for subject as means of intellectual development do not rest on formal discipline or the faculty psychology. The contention is rather that each subject worth studying is characterized by a distinctive method or kind of intellectual behavior, some of which are identified in popular speech by such terms as scientific, historical, or philosophical method. It is this uniqueness of method that makes a discipline. The study of such subjects, then, contributes experiences with the important methods of human thought and action and thereby develops intellectual understandings and skills. Furthermore, the method and the organization of subject are seen as complementary to each other.[5]

Every subject-matter field is a potential source of learning products which increase one's capacity to enjoy and to evaluate more worthily the material and immaterial goods of this world, and which lead to efforts to make the everyday environment a source of esthetic pleasure as well as a material utility.[6]

In spite of its secure hold on the secondary schools, the subject-centered curriculum has been criticized severely:

1.   It leads courses becoming out of date and out of touch

---

1. *Ibid.,* p. 21.
2. Saylor, J.G., and Alexander, W.M., *Curriculum Planning for Better Teaching and Learning* (New York: Rinehart & Co., Inc., 1954), p. 253.
3. Alberty, Harold, *Reorganizing the High School Curriculum* (New York: The Macmillan Co., 1953), p. 127.
4. Saylor and Alexander, *op. cit.,* p. 253.
5. Krug, Edward A., *The Secondary School Curriculum* (New York: Harper and Bros., 1960), pp. 212-213.
6. Billet, Roy O., *Fundamentals of Secondary-School Teaching* (Cambridge: The Riverside Press, 1940), p. 169.

with contemporary life.
2. It encourages teaching by "regurgitation."
3. It leads to the proliferation of courses and emphasis on trivia.
4. It results in duplication of course content.
5. It emphasizes the logical at the expense of the psychological.[1]

Some of the characteristics of core classes, furthermore, may be used in a program of classroom studies organized entirely around subjects.

One of these is teacher-student planning of many aspects of classroom work. There is nothing in subject organization that precludes this. True, *it is not desirable in many subjects to invite students to select the topics for study,* but teacher-student planning applies to many other kinds of classroom decisions.

Another core characteristic is that of the larger time block with one teacher. This is brought about by multiple-period scheduling and has the advantage of giving the teacher fewer students to know and work with over the school day. But a multiple-period organization can also be used in the subject organization. A teacher may have the same group of students in English and in social studies. This demands a teacher competent in both fields, and requires daily preparation in two fields instead of one.

The use of multiple-period scheduling opens a *third* possibility of incorporating core characteristics in the subject organization, namely: that of relating classroom instruction and guidance. The multiple-period teacher may assume designated responsibility for guidance. Of course, he does not act alone in this, but neither does the core teacher. Both use the services of guidance specialists if those are available.[2]

Types of Curriculum in American Secondary Schools

Programs of studies in American secondary schools utilize one

1. Clark, *op. cit.,* pp. 421–422.
2. Krug, *op. cit.,* pp. 231–232.

or the other of the following types of curriculum:

1. The single curriculum.
2. The constant-with-variables curriculum.
3. The multiple curriculum.

In the *single curriculum,* all courses are constant; no provision is made for variable courses. It can best be seen in the self-contained classes of the elementary school. Except for very small high schools, some junior high schools, and private preparatory schools, few secondary schools today use the single-curriculum organization.

The *Constant-with-Variables Plan.* Most frequently, secondary schools utilize the constant-with-variables or multiple curriculum patterns. In the former type, certain courses are required of all learners. These subjects are constants, presumably basic to the general education of all youth in the district. In addition, the pupils may select from elective variables to provide the necessary number of units for graduation, and to prepare themselves for their particular goals.

The *Multiple Curriculum Plan.* In the multiple-curriculum organization, different patterns of courses are set up for pupils with different goals. Examples of the curricula or "tracks" that may be found in a multiple-curriculum organization include general, vocational, technical, practical arts, business college preparatory, special education, and fine arts.

College-preparatory Curricula. Usually the requirements include four years of English, two or three of social studies, two of mathematics, one or two of science, and two of foreign language.

General Curriculum. The general curriculum is a pattern of courses that is *not* designed to lead the pupil to college or to any particular vocation. As a rule, it consists of a minimum number of required courses, plus a relatively large choice of electives.[1]

Subject Matter

There is the statement that subject matter is social studies, English, foreign languages, sciences, mathematics, the fine arts, business education, vocational education, health education,

1. Clark, *op. cit.,* pp. 422-424.

physical education.

Social Studies

A group of studies comprised of such subjects as history, geography, civics, anthropology, sociology, political science, problems of democracy, psychology, psychiatry, and sometimes philosophy and ethics.

The purpose of the social studies curriculum:

1. To help learners to understand and appreciate the American way of life.
2. To teach learners the academic skills necessary for effective study.
3. To teach learners how to face up to the problems of modern society.
4. To teach the skills necessary for good human relationships.

Most frequently, the courses in the cycles are:

First Cycle: Grade 4, Geography; grade 5, American History; grade 6, European Backgrounds.

Second Cycle: Grade 7, World Geography, or the Geography of one of the hemispheres; grade 8, American History; grade 9, Civics; grade 10, World History.

Third Cycle: Grade 11, American History; grade 12, Problems of Democracy.

In the typical curriculum, each learner takes a social studies course in at least five of his six secondary-school years. In addition, senior high schools often give electives in such subjects as Latin-American History, the History of the Far East, Contemporary Affairs, Economic Education, and Commercial Law.[1]

History. American History is usually offered in grades 8 and 11, and World History in Grade 10. New history courses are reaching out to include Geography, Economics, Political Science, the behavioral sciences, Literature, and even the sciences. History now touches the common people and the real problems of living. The humane tendency is also reflected in the increased emphasis on biography.

Changes in the content of the history courses are being ac-

1. *Ibid.,* pp. 164-166.

companied by changes of method. Instead of being memory courses, secondary-school courses are beginning to use history as a means for teaching learners to think reflectively.

Geography. Georgraphy has been neglected to the point where it hardly appears at all in many senior high schools, and has only one year—usually grade 7—in the junior high school. As a rule, junior high schools require one year of geography. This course is likely to be either World Geography, or the geography of one of the hemispheres.

Methods — laboratory and problem-solving. Depth is being introduced through the use of regional and area approaches and unit assignments, which induce considerable research and concentrated effort from the pupils. Guests from other lands, moving pictures, television, and firsthand reports by those who have visited the area are bringing the knowledge into the geography classroom.

Contemporary Studies. Contemporary studies do not yet receive emphasis. There are a large number of the areas closed in many secondary schools.

There are relatively few current events courses — instead, current events are usually taught during special periods in other social studies courses.

Some sociology and anthropology is usually included in civics, problems of democracy, and integrated social studies courses.

In many schools, considerable effort has been used to add material about international relations to geography and history.

Sometimes economics courses are offered in the business and commercial curricula.

Psychology has made an entree into the secondary school curriculum and seems to be having steady growth.

English Language Arts

English language arts occupy the central position in the American secondary-school curriculum. Learners must take courses in English up through the eleventh or twelfth grade. The *scope*, basically, consists of four areas: reading, writing, speaking, and listening.

A National Council of Teachers of English commission stated that the English curriculum must be developed in the light of two major principles:

1. Development of language power is an integral part of the total pattern of the child's growth...a curriculum based on a sound scientific inquiry must therefore recognize that a set level of achievement and mastery of a single prescribed content for all individuals within a given grade are impossible of attainment and do violence to the facts of growth (because each child grows at his own pace).

2. Language power is not something in the back of one's head which he thinks long enough: it is the ability to think and to act in the right way at the right moment, and is developed only through a long series of experiences in trying to act in the appropriate way in a similar situation.[1]

The senior high school curriculum is much more traditional than that of the junior high school. Some schools devote the grade 10 to world literature, but this movement has not yet become popular. Where it is offered, English Literature is likely to be either an elective or a required course for college-preparatory learners, rather than a course required for all. Composition in the senior high school seems to be a little less functional than that in the junior high school. English language arts curricula are becoming increasingly concerned with critical thinking and propaganda analysis.

Three different types of reading programs can be found in secondary schools:

1. Provides training for slow learners who need continued coaching in reading to develop their potential.
2. The program for learners who for some reason have not learned to read properly, although their potential ability is average or even better than average.
3. Attempts to improve pupils' already adequate skills and to carry each pupil along to higher competencies.

Usually, reading instruction has entered the secondary school by means of remedial programs for the retarded readers, but the need for developmental programs has become so obvious that these programs are fast gaining popularity in junior high schools. They are more slowly making a place for themselves in

---

1. National Council of Teachers of English, *The English Language Arts* (New York: Appleton-Century-Crofts, Inc., 1952), pp. 12-14.

the senior high schools.[1]

A Good Developmental Reading Program

According to M. J. Weiss:

1. Reading instruction must aim at individual students, taking into account their different backgrounds, abilities, and interests.

2. Flexibility of instruction depends upon the availability of a wide range of reading materials of all kinds and on all sorts of subjects. In an effective program much of the initiative passes to the student and the teacher's role changes to that of a guide, a "listener", a resource person, a critic.

3. Reading instruction means paying attention not only to the basic skills of reading, but also to the general end which education should serve; the widening of the student's intellectual, emotional, and moral horizons.

4. Reading instruction is completely successful only when the student has acquired the habit of active continuous reading and can read with ease in all of the subject areas which, by necessity or choice, he faces.

5. The reading program is not the product of one teacher, but demands the involvement of the entire faculty and administration in a wholehearted and single-minded concentration on drawing the best possible work out of each student.[2]

His first criterion points out the need for individualization of reading instruction. Junior high school developmental reading programs should continue the development of reading skills. Special remedial classes must be provided for learners whose reading is not yet at the high school level.

The Best Approach to the Teaching of Literature

When your purpose is:

1. To acquaint the class with a classic or a type of literature (for example, fable, fairy tale, tall tale) which is part of their heritage — or

2. To have the entire class enjoy a reading or listening experience and the discussion which follows — or

1. Bamman, Henry A., Hogan, U., and Greene, C.F., *Reading Instruction in the Secondary Schools* (New York: Longmans, Greene and Co., Inc., 1961), Ch.2. Quoted in: Clark, *op. cit.*, p. 197.
2. Weiss, M.J., *Reading in the Secondary Schools* (New York: The Odyssey Press, Inc., 1961), p. 10.

3. To provide an opportunity for group guidance through literature — *then do have the entire class read or listen to the same story or poem.*

When your purpose is:

1. To encourage the development of the reading habit — or

2. To give opportunity for meeting individual needs, abilities, and interests — or

3. To raise the level of taste in each individual — *then guided individual reading should be used.*

When your purpose is:

1. To correlate the reading with experiences and activities of interest to the pupil — or

2. To combine general class reading and guided independent reading — or

3. To provide for individual differences within a common class project — *then use the unit approach.*[1]

Many television and radio programs have as much significance to the language arts student.

The secondary school must allow time for units in the use of newspapers, periodicals, radio, television, and moving pictures. Naturally, children should be protected from evil influences. The instruction in the use of mass media is a necessary extension of the study of literature.

The *teaching of composition.* The prescriptive grammatical rules must give way to clear expression. Reviews, analyses, research papers are types of writing activities whose purpose is to help learners become thinkers. Composition classes should tend to place their emphasis on clear communication. The teachers should concentrate on literature, composition, and language. These activities have never been more necessary.

Critical listening. Speech and listening classes should be laboratories in which students learn to present their ideas clearly and logically, and learn to evaluate ideas presented by others. Speech and listening have a definite role in the language arts program. Gifted learners need to develop the same language skills as other learners do. Many secondary schools provide for

1. Curriculum Office, Philadelphia Public Schools, *A Guide to the Teaching of Literature in Grades 7 through 12* (Tentative) (Philadelphia: School District of Philadelphia, 1960), pp. 9-12.

the talented through enrichment programs in the regular class-room. The enrichment program stresses extensive and intensive reading, creative thinking and writing.

Many schools provide modified language arts programs for the slow learners. Course content has been selected to include only the simplest principles of English usage essential to every-day communication. Working at his own level, each learner must progress as he can. The material to be covered varies from individual to individual. Ideally, language development should be continuous and individual.

Remedial and developmental reading programs are gaining acceptance in both junior and senior high schools. Such programs should be individualized so that each learner can learn to read many types of material as efficiently as he can. To share ideas or to provide a basis for discussion or criticism, the learners should read some works together, but the school has to give them reading material they can enjoy and that has some meaning for their own lives.

Foreign Language Arts

In the following few paragraphs, let us examine some of the objectives of foreign language instruction:

1. Proficiency in a foreign language is a sign of man's intelligence.
2. Although English is second in popularity among the world's languages, mastery of at least one additional foreign language is extremely beneficial.
3. A person who knows only one language could be compared with a person who sees only with one eye. His vision of surrounding reality is considerably limited.
4. Knowledge of foreign languages enables students to make rapid progress in scholarship and science.
5. Knowledge of foreign languages is an important medium whereby we acquire friends and achieve our goals.
6. Such knowledge puts us at ease in foreign countries and foreign surroundings and makes us independent in these circumstances.
7. It is an indispensable instrument in foreign trips, assign-

ments, business, research, etc.

8. Knowledge of foreign language opens wide horizons for cultural enrichment, for learning about other people, their culture and civilization.

9. The mastery of one foreign language makes the learning of other languages easier.

Educators recommend continuous developmental sequences extending from the elementary school through the second and collegiate grades into adulthood. Many of them think a ten-year sequence from grades 3 through 12 to be ideal. More recent research indicates that foreign languages can best be learned in childhood, between the ages of four and ten. Under no circumstances should there be any break in continuity. Once started, it should be continued. Secondary school offerings must carefully be articulated with those in both elementary schools and colleges. Large secondary schools can support several foreign language sequences. It is also preferable to offer a full sequence in one foreign language, rather than partial sequences in two languages. By allowing at least full six years in one language and four years in a second language, this plan gives pupils an opportunity to become proficient in both languages.

The Foreign Language Curriculum

The basic ingredient in language teaching and learning is *practice*. Any language is a set of habits that make up the skills of listening, speaking, reading, and writing. To master a language one should first learn to understand it, then to speak it, then to read it, and finally to write it. The learner's first foreign language experiences are audio-lingual, and only as he becomes adept orally are reading and writing introduced. It seems that the proper use of good recorded material can improve the effectiveness of audio-lingual lessons. Many secondary schools are investing in language laboratories. The most of them have several channels, so that different lessons can be played at the same time. A good teacher can teach well by the audio-lingual method. The language laboratory provides voices that the learner can listen to and imitate over and over again. It allows every learner in the class to practice speaking aloud and to listen to himself without disturbing anyone else. Language laboratories are constructed so as to make provision for individual differences easy by allowing the teacher to listen to individuals without interrupting the group. It also gives learners opportunities to hear different speakers.

The goal of reading instruction is to teach learners to read, not to translate.

Principal recommendations:

1. The learners should never be asked to read anything that they cannot understand and say. (The student will develop faulty reading habits; he must understand.)
2. The learner should not have to read childish material and material beyond his maturity level.
3. Some classroom reading should be accompanied by drill and analysis. Too much drill and analysis leads to a tendency to translate instead of read.
4. The learners should discuss what they read. The pattern goes like the following: from repetition to free response questions based on texts, to paraphrasing the text, to resumes, to interpretation, and finally to literary discussion.

The curriculum allows a gradual building up of writing skills.

The learner's first writing experiences should consist largely of copying what he has read. From mere copying he moves up to more complicated exercises, such as writing from dictation, paraphrasing, summarizing, and writing a composition from a prescribed outline, until finally he is writing his own compositions. The sequence is very similar to that recommended for teaching of reading.

Grammatical rules are used only to explain principles.

The students, who already have some knowledge of language principles and how they work, can learn much through a grammatical approach. The educators are recommended to devote beginning instruction to audio-visual experiences without recourse to the textbook. Textbooks will be used later for audio-lingual, reading and writing instruction. Text material must be chosen so as to promote sequential development. The teacher should present and master essential structure patterns through oral drill and meaningful sentences and dialogue, with grammatical explanations when necessary.

In order to develop the cultural values inherent in language study, audio-lingual exercises, discussions, and readings should include material by which the pupils can learn about the country and way of life of the people whose language is being learned.

Use of Latin to improve pupils' understanding of English.

Culturally, the goals of the Latin curriculum are the same as those of modern foreign/ language curricula. Audio-lingual methods are being introduced successfully. Reading materials are extensive and calculated to give learners insights into classical life and history.

Sciences

The schools must give students instruction in the sciences necessary to serve as a base for college and university scientific vocational training.

Through science, man learns about the natural and social world. Scientific thinking is nothing more that critical thinking. The schools, through the study of science, provide the learner with understandings, attitudes and skills. Studying science frequently leads to the developing of interests. Basically, the goals of the science curriculum are to help learners acquire understanding and appreciation of scientific achievements, knowledge concerning his physical and social environment.

The junior high school. In many junior high schools the curriculum is organized into block-of-time programs. Science can also be integrated into true core courses at any level. Science should be part of the general education program because it helps satisfy the requirements for a basic education. General science in the junior high school is conceptual; it provides an effective medium for creating and maintaining science interest. The curriculum attempts to articulate the science of the elementary school with the science of the senior high school. Sometimes this is done by teaching one or more years of general science, sometimes by core curricula or block-of-time courses. Recently there has been a tendency to bring biology, physical science, and earth science into the junior high school as part of the general education.

The senior high school. The usual pattern of senior high school courses includes biology, physics, and chemistry, and occasionally electives in other sciences. Frequently, high schools give advanced work in the sciences in grade 12 as a result of some form of accelerated program.

The following list illustrates one possible placement of various subjects in the science curriculum.

Ninth Grade

Earth Science	Biology
General Science	Physical Science
Chemistry	

Tenth Grade

Biology
Chemistry
Applied Chemistry

Eleventh Grade

Advanced Physical Science	Aviation
Physics	Agriculture
Advanced Chemistry	Advanced Biology
Applied Physics	Meteorology
Astronomy	

Twelfth Grade

Advanced Physical Science	Electronics
Physics	Astronomy
Chemistry	Meteorology
Advanced Physics	Aviation
Advanced Chemistry	Advanced Agriculture
Advanced Biology	Machines and Electricity

Sometimes the advanced courses are inter-disciplinary. Instances in which broad field courses in science have been used to substitute for biology, physics, and chemistry seems to have yielded good academic results.[1]

Mathematics

Mathematics is usually an elective in the upper grades of the high school.

The junior high school. In the junior high school, most learners study arithmetic in grades 7 and 8. The gifted students are not segregated into special sections for mathematics instruction in the seventh and eighth grades. *Special section* means a course of study entirely different from that used for most of the students.

In some schools, able students are members of randomly grouped classes, and enrichment is provided on an individual basis to students who have completed the required assignments; in others, homogeneous grouping is used, plus individual enrichment.

The senior high school. In grade 9 many schools divide the mathematics curriculum into two tracks: 1) for the college-bound, and 2) for the rest. The college-bound course is algebra, and the non-college-bound course, general mathematics—usually a course containing review arithmetic and frequently exploratory work in geometry, arithmetic, and algebra. Several new plans have been proposed: ninth grade Algebra I, tenth grade Algebra II, eleventh grade Geometry, twelfth grade Trigonometry and Solid Geometry.

In addition, mathematics institutes have been held to give the teachers training in both techniques and subject matter. For any kind of an *advanced program* to take place in the twelfth grade, the student must have completed the necessary background work by the end of the junior year.

Some colleges and universities have been quite active in providing programs for high school pupils during the regular school year or during the summer.

One economical way to supplement such a limited offering in mathematics is to encourage the students to enroll in correspondence courses. Students who have had high school corres-

1. Clark, *op. cit.*, p. 250.

pondence courses achieved a higher grade-point average than did students who had not taken such courses. The findings clearly indicate that correspondence study can be a valid way of broadening the curriculum.

Fine Arts

Art and *music* has distinct cultural and educational contributions. The *music* curriculum's purpose should be to develop musical taste, musical skill, and musical knowledge. Good general music courses can help pupils both to develop musical skills and knowledge and to discriminate between good and bad music of all sorts. Music is unique in that the student can gain much through large group instruction and participation in large group activities. Also, large group experiences can give learners aesthetic feelings from playing or singing fine selections.

Secondary-school music develops ability and interest in music for future participation. Performances are an outgrowth of the music program. After studying music for a number of years, individuals need an opportunity to make music.

The music program gives opportunity for pleasure. The individual develops social interests, skills, and habits by participating in a performing group.

The general music course has been in the curriculum for many years, and it can be conceived to be part of basic education. Discrimination of musical qualities is largely intellectual; this means that the music program must develop musical skills and knowledge. General music programs are now organized to develop the intellectual powers of the learner, as well as the emotional.

General music courses are taught both on the junior and senior high school levels.

Junior high school. The general junior high school music course can be a worthwhile educational experience for the adolescent; it can be challenging, interesting, and inspiring under the right teacher using the right materials.

These courses are offered in *both* the junior and senior high schools. The *senior* high school courses differ from those in the junior high school in that they are usually multigrade courses.

Instrumental music is usually restricted to work in performing groups. Small ensembles are more suitable. They also have the advantage of making it easy to provide for individual differences, because to form small groups of fairly homogeneous ability levels is a relatively simple matter.

The music curriculum should have two programs for the talented: one for the musically talented, the other for the academically talented. The school should make every effort to help potentially gifted musicians to make progress. For the others, the program should contain discriminatory activities and musical analysis. The advanced courses in music theory should be available at the senior high school level.

Art, like music, has aesthetic and cultural values; therefore, it should have a privileged place in the program of studies. Undoubtedly, art should be part of the general education of every high school graduate. Aesthetic education in art is concerned with the use and enjoyment of works of art, rather than with the production of visual fine arts. The school is able to instill in the individual the knowledge and experience necessary to develop good taste.

In general, the junior high school art courses are exploratory. In the senior high school, one is more likely to find a variety of distinct art courses of all sorts. At the junior high school levels, art is occasionally included in core curricula and block-of-time courses. In the senior high school may be incorporated fine arts courses and similar interdisciplinary endeavors.

Business Education

The *basic business education* constitutes the business education offerings that contribute to the general education of all learners. The business education curricula, including the distributive trades curricula, are predominantly vocational. They should be based on the realities of the business world. For this reason, the curricula need to be continually brought up-to-date.

In general, high school learners are being prepared for four types of work: stenography, general office work, bookkeeping, and selling.

Typewriting has been offered in grades 7 and 8, as well as in earlier elementary grades. The other course that occurs most frequently at the junior high level is general business, which provides basic business principles, facts of the business world, and simple business skills. In the senior high school, several differentiated business curricula are open to learners. This curriculum is largely concerned with preparing learners to work in the retail and distributive trades.

A partial list of subjects might include:

Typewriting I, II, III	Consumer Education
Shorthand I, II	Keypunch I, II
Introduction to Business —	Machine Accounting I, II
General Business	Bookkeeping I, II, III
Filing	Record Keeping
Secretarial Bookkeeping	Accounting
Retailing	Secretarial Practice
Business Law	Office Practice
Retail Selling	Clerical Practice
Business Arithmetic	Business English
Store Management	Marketing
Salesmanship	Cooperative Store and
Advertising	Office Training
Economics	Economic Geography
Selling and Advertising	Transcription[1]

Vocational Education

Trade and industrial education offers a large variety of programs. In vocational education programs, science, mathematics, and technical subjects that supposedly give learners the background necessary for good understanding of their vocational studies. Vocational mathematics course content is quite similar to that of general mathematics in the general education program. In the vocational program, the courses emphasize applying mathematical skills to occupational and shop problems.

At the ninth grade level, the subject in vocational agricultural courses is general in nature. The work in agriculture is in two areas: 1) farm mechanics, and 2) agricultural science.

Farm mechanics includes a study of farm machinery, farm power, and farm shop skills.

1. *Ibid.*, pp. 314-315.

Agricultural science emphasizes the intellectual aspect of farming. The purposes of vocational agriculture are concerned mainly with productive agriculture.

Junior High School Home Economics is concerned with activities associated with the home. Its subject matter includes many disciplines: art, biology, biochemistry, sociology, chemistry, physics, and economics.

The most common areas covered in homemaking courses are: clothing, foods, family relations, child development, health, home nursing, management, consumer education, housing, etc.

There are two kinds of home economics courses: 1) vocational homemaking (subsidized by the federal government), and 2) nonvocational homemaking (no federal aid). All seventh and eighth grade homemaking courses are considered nonvocational. Some homemaking classes include actual taking care of children in class. In these classes, girls gain the experience of handling young children under guidance of the home economics teacher.

Senior High School Home Economics. In each grade level, *Foods* and *Clothing* receive the greatest portion of time. In senior high school Clothing, two-thirds of the time is spent on the making of clothes. The rest of the time is allocated for child development, family relationships, consumer education, management, and nutrition. In the senior high school, the curriculum is both vocational and nonvocational. At both school levels, home economics courses seem to overemphasize food and clothing at the expense of other important areas.

Industrial Arts. The industrial arts curriculum is defined as part of general education. It includes a study of the materials, processes, and products of manufacturing. The industrial arts program helps the learner gain information about various industrial occupations.

Industrial arts has been divided into several general instructional areas. All industrial arts programs include one or more of the areas listed below:

1. Drawing and Planning
2. Woodworking
3. Metal Working
4. Electricity and Electronics
5. Graphic Arts
6. Transportation
7. Plastics
8. Leather work

9. Ceramics
10. Textiles
11. Home Mechanics

The Junior High School. The goal of industrial arts is to develop an appreciation of good craftsmanship. The industrial arts curriculum in the junior high school varies from state to state and even from district to district.

Today, *coeducational* industrial arts courses and courses for girls are not at all uncommon. Coeducational industrial arts education may also be approached by way of the core curriculum.

The Senior High School. The nonvocational industrial arts subjects offered in the senior high school are:

1. Woodworking
2. Mechanical drawing
3. Metal work
4. Printing
5. Electrical work
6. Handicrafts
7. Automobile mechanics

These courses are commonly offered at multigrade levels. If a learner has taken basic industrial arts courses, and then continues to work in one area for two semesters or more, his work should ordinarily be in the vocational area. Industrial arts offerings in the senior high schools include the following courses:

1. Electricity
2. Power Mechanics
3. Machine Drawing
4. Mechanical Drawing
5. Architectural Drawing
6. Graphic Arts
7. Photography
8. Aeronautics
9. Woodworking
10. Printing
11. Electronics
12. Home Mechanics
13. Plastics
14. Welding
15. Sheet Metal
16. Art Metals
17. General Crafts
18. General Metals
19. Leatherworking
20. Jewelry
21. Ceramics[1]

Driver Education. Driver training usually includes both work in the classroom and time behind the wheel. Topics that may be covered in the classroom include:

1. History of the automobile
2. Psychology of the driver
3. Physical characteristics of the driver

1. Clark, *op. cit.,* pp. 343-344.

4. Study of the automobile
5. Legislative and physical laws
6. Economics of owning and operating an automobile
7. Vocations of the automobile industry
8. Provisions for traffic and its control.

Behind-the-wheel students are taught safety, simple ways to check the car, and control of the automobile.[1]

Health Education

Health education should be a part of the general education of all youth in the secondary school. The health education program must utilize both direct and indirect instruction and guidance services. The health education today is not the province of any one department. Health education functions and responsibilities are carried out by the maintenance crew, the janitorial staff, bus drivers, the guidance staff, medical services personnel, and school lunch workers.

Health Education Courses. In some districts, a semester of health education is one of the senior high school requirements for graduation. In other schools, a separate course is offered only in the junior high school. In still other schools, health education is offered as a six- or eight-week concentrated effort as part of the semester of physical education.[2]

Physical Education

Although many programs emphasize the acquisition of physical skill, physical education must be something more than skill acquisition. Learners need to develop a knowledge of the game — that is, the nuances, strategy, history, and problems of playing. To make physical education worthy of its place in the curriculum, a new emphasis in physical education is needed. The physical education curriculum should be intellectualized. It should include units designed to develop powers of discrimination and greater appreciation of the fine points of play.

Activities included in basic physical education can be divided into the following categories:

1. Adaptive activities.

1. *Ibid.,* p. 353.
2. *Ibid.,* pp. 348-352.

2. Games, sports, athletics, play, and aquatics.
3. Self-testing, combat, and self-defense activities.
4. Out-of-door activities.

Adaptive activities are designed to correct physical defects. They make up what is called corrective education and include the use of mental health measures, as well as physical exercises to correct physical deficiencies.

Games, sports, athletics, play, and aquatics activities are multitudinous. Such activities should include more than just skill development, such as the history of the sport.

Self-testing, combat, and self-defense activities are especially useful for meeting the physical fitness objective.

Out-of-door activities — summer camps for the learners. Other popular out-of-door activities are hiking, the camera hunt, and hunter's safety. These activities are advantageous in that they possess a great amount of carryover value, and can also be tied in with science and social studies.

Intramural activities consist of participation in sports within the limits of the school site. The intramural sports program provides opportunities for pupils to develop skills in sports and games they learned in the basic physical education program.

Extramural Athletics. A logical extension of the intramural program is to have the best team play another school. Extramural sports usually take the form of festivals, play days, sports days, and invitational contests. Play day usually provides many activities in team and individual sports, with a social activity.

Interscholastic Athletics are necessary to provide opportunities for those youths who are highly skilled in athletics. Interscholastic athletics holds too prominent a place in physical education. Frequently, the amount of time and effort spent on these interscholastic teams is way out of proportion to the number of pupils benefiting.[1]

Principles of Subject Matter Selection

Specialized education is the subject matter that particular

---

1. *Ibid.*, pp. 354-361.

learners may want to learn for their own particular reasons.

Its primary function is to provide for differences in the learners, and give each learner a chance to develop in the way that suits him best. It includes vocational, pre-vocational, and even avocational education. A curriculum designed solely to prepare learners to enter college is really specialized education. Its role is to help prepare learners for their roles in life. The school should do all it can to help each youth prepare well for this task, and the latter years of his high school and college life should be devoted largely to vocational preparation. As far as possible, it should provide a wide enough choice of experiences so that each individual learner can pick those experiences best suited to meet his needs. During the upper grades of the secondary schools, specialized education should take an increasingly important part on the learner's time. The learner who wishes to prepare for college entrance will devote almost his entire program to college-preparatory subjects during his last years in the secondary school.

The secondary school must provide many curriculum choices from which learners may choose. The curricula, courses, and units should be differentiated so as to give each child his "own" personal curriculum. With the help of a good guidance program, learners can select their programs with a much greater chance of success.

What is Included in Subject Matter?

Subject matter includes what men know and believe, and their ideals and loyalties.

An institution such as the family is not subject matter, but what is known and believed about the family and the ideals we hold for family life are subject matter. Tools and machines are not subject matter, but knowledge about tools and machines — about how they are made, their operation, and their uses — is subject matter.[1]

1. Smith, B.O., Stanley, W.O., and Shores, J.H., *Fundamentals of Curriculum Development* (Yonkers-on-Hudson, N.Y.: World Book Co., 1957), p. 127.

How Must Subject Matter Be Selected?

Subject matter must be selected in terms of whether or not it is within the experience and ability of the learner.

No matter how desirable it may be for students to study certain subject matter or to engage in cettain activities, these things will be of no avail if the materials of instruction are too far removed from the interests and abilities of the students. The amount of subject matter and the number of problems or activities that will be included in the educational program will depend not only on the ability of the learners but also on the amount of time allotted to the various fields of study, subjects, problems, or activities. How much of the total school time will be allotted to a given field or subject depends in part upon what is deemed to be important, and in part upon a judgement of how long it will take the "average" individual to do what is expected of him.[1]

The subject matter of a school subject is what man has learned about that subject — whether it be agriculture, biology, economics, mathematics, health, or what not.

It is selected from the vast stock of facts, ideas, and values that man has accumulated from his collective and specialized endeavors.

Descriptive subject matter consists of facts and principles.

Facts are reported in statements about things that can be perceived directly or in principle. If someone says that the thermometer reading is 70°, he is making factual statement which can be directly verified by observing and counting.

Descriptive principles are laws, rules, and theories, such as scientific laws and theories.

They indicate how to proceed when in doubt.

Normative subject matter consists of the rules of the game, norms, or standards by which individuals make moral and aesthetic

1. *Ibid.*, p. 106.

choices.

Normative content and descriptive content may be further distinguished by relating them to the kinds of questions that might be asked about an event.[1]

Standards for Subject-Matter Selection

The ultimate basis of subject-matter selection should rest with the determination of objectives.

In question form, the following five standards for subject-matter selection are presented:

1. Is the subject-matter significant to an organized field of knowledge?
2. Does the subject matter stand the test of survival?
3. Is the subject matter useful?
4. Is the subject matter interesting to the learner?
5. Does the subject matter contribute to the growth and development?

It should be understood that these are not criteria to be applied as standards for all subject matter by anyone engaged in content selection. These are simply five different single criteria that have been used. However, it is hoped that knowledge of these currently used criteria will help the curriculum worker in his approach to the problem of content selection.

The curriculum should consist of subject matter that is needed in solving pupil problems or in fulfilling pupil purposes or plans.

The subject matter must satisfy the needs of the learner. The subject matter included in the curriculum must be important to the learner. Although interests vary from individual to individual, investigations indicate that some interests are more or less common and can, therefore, be employed in the selection of content.

The criterion of interest has been most persistently and thoroughly embraced by those who hold intelligent self-direction to be the major aim of education. The capacity of self-direction

1. *Ibid.*, pp. 129-131.

is best developed according to this view, by engaging in activities of concern to the individual. As the individual seeks goals to which he feels committed, he learns to think for himself, to weigh and use knowledge, and to be self-dependent.[1]

Both experiences and materials will be most effective if they involve the learner as an increasingly independent, mature participant in the learning process.

The selection of materials is the result of careful analysis and study. Material for learning derives its validity primarily from the curriculum. Each material should have its definite part to play in the curriculum. No one kind of material — books alone or newspapers or motion pictures alone — can be expected to provide the means to accomplish all objectives. With each objective, it is important to ascertain just what concepts, skills, attitudes, and appreciations each material can best further.

Learning materials should be a spur to student initiative, and should be chosen to fit into a planned, continuing program of instruction.

Disciplinary subjects constitute only one aspect of the humanist's program of secondary education.

It is important that education should include an intensive study of the great classics of western literature. These books represent the noblest and best thought, and hence any complete education must include a mastery of them. A continuation of the ancient ideal of the cultivated gentleman, the study of the councils of government, and the mind, character, and taste are best developed through intimate and sustained contact with the great literary products of the past.

The humanist argues that a true understanding of human values and the basic principles of right conduct can be acquired only by a rigorous literary discipline. The correct thinking in these important matters is a product of the absorption into the personality of the values and principles embedded in the classics.

There is an intimate relationship between thought and language. The clear expression in written form is always a mark of

1. *Ibid.*, pp. 142-145.

clear thinking. There remains the contention that the study of the classics is the supreme vehicle for the cultivation of character and taste.

The spirit of the classics is the spirit of aristocracy; the virtues they inculcate are the virtues of a ruling class. In its literary form it was unquestionably the expression of great and noble ideals. The values that may be lost with its passing, the fact that the social order out of which this spirit grew, and whose standards it beautifully formulated — has passed from the stage of history. The study of the present by means of the classics represents, in an extreme form, an abstract and bookish procedure of doubtful validity for the great majority of students. For it is a fact that many who lack the highly specialized interest and ability required to master the literary tradition can achieve a general understanding of the problems that affect their daily lives.

The restoration of order and clarity in education requires a knowledge of the tradition, but in relationship to the problems and conditions of the modern world. This knowledge cannot be secured from a curriculum composed in major part of a study of the classics.

The school should strive to familiarize its students with the above-mentioned literature because acquaintance with it definitely increases the student's intelligence. This does not mean, however, that other modern languages as well as other subjects such as mathematics should be neglected at the expense of this ancient language.

The nature of the subject determines the content of the curriculum in most American secondary schools.

In general, the curriculum in American secondary schools is subject-centered. The curriculum is chosen by the faculty members and administrative officers on the basis of subject matter and presumed adult needs.

In the seventh and eighth grades, the subjects are usually common to all learners, although sections may be differentiated according to ability. In the ninth grade and in the senior high school grades, the offering is usually differentiated into various types of curricula designed to lead to different specialized goals.

The curriculum of today must not consist of merely covering a certain body of content.

Subject matter is valuable for teaching processes, principles, attitudes, ideals, appreciations, and skills. To teach these important learnings does not depend so much on what subject matter one teaches as how one teaches it. Facts and information are very important. By studying more deeply, learners could concentrate their learning so that it would really function. Any subject matter is essential for every secondary-school learner; presumably some learnings are valuable for everyone — no matter what their longings or abilities. These learnings make up general education. It consists of those things that generally would be well to learn but not prepare one for any particular vocation.

Selection of Centers for Extended Study

The centers for extended study should be selected in the light of the general maturity of learners.

The primary responsibility of the teacher will be to decide how to approach the proposed topics so that they are purposefull for his learners; to identify the point of contact where the experience backgrounds touch the area to be studied. The teacher should use all his techniques for studying learners in order to identify problems of potential educative value, and which are both appropriate for the maturity level of his learners and of genuine concern to them. How many learners are concerned with this particular problem? Which seem most apt to stimulate growth? Which are likely to be the most effective assignments for homework?

In fact, if the teacher is uncertain about the centers for study that he has selected, it might be helpful to glance over a well-planned course of study from another school system. In courses of study, the topics will be logically related to each other, and the sequence planned so that each new one adds systematically more information. Curriculum designs under which teachers are free to work in terms of the particular need of the group are not proposed merely to make school easier; it has been because serious educators see them as the most effective way of achieving a comprehensive education for learners. Only careful study of the capacity and background of learners can determine the level to which the teacher should gear his work. The broader his own insights into the implications of learners' questions, the more possible ways of exploration he will uncover.

As a guide in deciding how extensively to explore a topic with his learners, the teacher should ask himself what sub-topics they can recognize as clearly related to the general problem. If the learners cannot see the new aspect of the sub-topic as purposeful, their work at this point becomes a blind following of his suggestions. The questions of learners and expressed interests can be valuable guides to areas in which further study can be worthwhile, but they must be helped to appraise them thoughtfully.

In some instances, too, side issues will represent problems which the learners, at their present levels of maturity, cannot explore very far. Other topics will be well worthy of extended study. It can be provided in several ways. Some of the important problems may be assigned for homework. All such arrangements call for careful pupil-teacher planning. Opportunities to develop the understanding can come through classroom problems and student-council activities. The teacher can proceed to other topics, safe in the knowledge that he will have many opportunities before the year is out to stress similar concepts, and his approach from a new side will result in a better understanding.

Procedures of Content Selection

Experimental Procedure

All experimental procedure of content selection tries to determine by actual test whether or not subject matter satisfies a particular criterion.

All experimentation follows the same general pattern:

1. Tentative selection of subject matter in accordance with a criterion.

2. Hypothesis that the tentatively selected subject matter meets the conditions of the criterion (that it is interesting or useful).
3. Prescribed conditions of the tryout (description of children, teacher, classroom, methods of teaching, materials to be used, and other factors affecting the experiment).
4. Objective techniques for determining the results (tests, other observations, and records).
5. Checking the results against the hypothesis to find whether or not the subject matter satisfies the criterion.

This procedure has not been used extensively, but its findings have been generally respected. It has been used, for example, in ascertaining the interests of children in poetry and other forms of literature, in music, and in color combinations and arrangements.[1]

Analytical Procedure

The analytical procedure of content selection consists of the application of certain techniques of fact-finding to the activities under investigation.

Therefore, the *first* step is the selection of the area of human concern, the specific function, or the specialized occupation to be investigated. After one of these has been selected, it is broken down into more specific elements, and an appropriate technique is chosen for collecting facts about these various elements. There are six such techniques in general use:

1. *Interviewing.* The interviewer requests a person on the job to name the duties for which he is responsible.
2. *Working on the job.* The investigator works on the job, studying the operations required and making a list of them.
3. *Analysis of the job or activity by the worker.* A person who has become familiar with a job or activity is asked to list his duties or the operations he performs. This differs from the preceding technique primarily in the amount of familiarity with the work on the part of the persons involved, the worker being more familiar than the investi-

1.   Jordan, Arthur M., "Children's Interests in Reading," *Teachers College Contributions to Education,* No. 107. See also: G. La V. Freeman and R.S. Freeman, *The Child and His Picture Book;* B.E. Mellinger, "Children's Interests in Pictures," *Teachers College Contributions to Education,* No. 516; B.O. Smith and others, *Fundamentals of Curriculum Development,* 1957, pp. 156-157.

gator.
4. *Questionnaire.* The duties or operations involved in a job or activity are sought by means of an inquiry blank sent to the workers or persons whose activities are under investigation.
5. *Documentary analysis.* The investigator makes an analysis of magazines, correspondence, public records, and the like, and tabulates the information, skills, or principles found in these documents.
6. *Observing the performance of people.* This may be concerned with the daily activities of people or it may involve analysis of individuals or groups in certain situations.

The application of these six techniques yields a list of performances or "needs."[1]

The consensual procedure is a way of collecting people's opinions about what they believe the curriculum should be.

The results of the consensual procedure are expressed in terms of the number of persons, or percentage of persons, of a particular community or group who believe that such and such should be taught in the schools.[2]

Specific Preparation of the Teacher

The teacher needs a very broad concept of the role of resources in learning.

A task in which teachers need specific preparation and experience is the proper selection and use of resources for learning. The possible number of resources is almost infinite. The practices of teaching have glorified the textbook as the one resource for learning. Since learners vary widely in their experiential background and abilities, they do not make uniformly good use of the same resource. Here the teacher's planning is very important — it must include careful examination of materials recommended by the teacher for pupil use. Reading materials in particular lack utility because of the variations in individual

1. Haines, Aleyne C., *Children's Perception of Membership Roles in Problem-Solving Groups.* Quoted in: Smith, *op. cit.,* pp. 161-163.
2. Smith, *op. cit.,* p. 166.

reading levels. Therefore application of the criterion of availability means considerable study on the teacher's part of the potential resources. The textbooks are frequently selected by persons other than the teacher, but he must be acquainted with possible inaccuracies in their content. The teachers must be careful in selection of materials, especially inexpensive pamphlets and visual aids. In such situations, teachers will find very helpful some of the various services available as guides to free and inexpensive materials, in addition to the frequent listing of pertinent materials to be found in the professional journals of various curriculum areas. In many cases the cost of resources is a determining factor in their selection.

If the teacher has the advantage of lists of resources, his day-to-day planning regarding resources consists primarily of selecting appropriate resources from a list in the unit and arranging for their use.

The teacher will need to be careful if he is expected to select his own topics without the guidance of a course of study or a textbook.

Textbooks and courses of study should be utilized only as guides to content selection. An inexperienced teacher must be careful if he is expected to select his own topics without the guidance of a course of study or a textbook. It takes a few years of experience before the teacher is sufficiently secure in his work with secondary learners to be certain that his choice of topics will result in greater understanding on the part of the learners. Even though he is an expert in his field, he will be forced to re-learn some of his material before he can teach it.

Whatever the basis in his school for selecting general content to be stressed, he may be permitted to plan some units of work centered around the major areas designated for study. Even if his course of study prescribes the general direction of his work, he will still have many choices to make. What particular aspects of the designed topics are likely to be the most meaningful centers for extended study for my learners? How deeply should they be encouraged to explore?

SUMMARY

The primary function of the subject matter organization is to provide for differences in the learners and give each learner a chance to develop in the way that suits him best. It includes vocational, pre-vocational, and even avocational education.

Specialized education is the subject matter that particular learners may want to learn for their own particular reasons. A curriculum designed solely to prepare learners to enter college is really specialized education.

Specialized education's role is to help prepare learners for their roles in life. Any subject matter is essential for every secondary school learner; presumably some learnings are valuable for everyone — no matter what their longings or abilities. These learnings make up general education. It consists of those things that generally would be well to learn but not prepare one for any particular vocation.

FOR FURTHER STUDY

Adler, Alfred, *Education of the Individual.* New York: Philosophical Library, 1958.

Alberty, Harold, *Reorganizing the High School Curriculum.* New York: The Macmillan Co., 1953.

Berman, Louise M., ed., *The Humanities and the Curriculum.* Washington, D.C.: Association for Supervision and Curriculum Development, 1967.

Billett, R. O., *Fundamentals of Secondary-School Teaching.* Cambridge: The Riverside Press, 1940.

Clark, L. H., R. L. Klein, and J.B. Burks, *The American Secondary School Curriculum.* New York: The Macmillan Co., 1965.

Curriculum Office, Philadelphia Public Schools, *A Guide to the Teaching of Literature in Grades 7 through 12* (Tentative). Philadelphia: School District of Philadelphia, 1960.

Dallmann, Martha, *Teaching the Language Arts in the Elementary School.* Dubuque, Iowa: W. C. Brown Co., 1967.

French, Will, *Behavioral Goals of General Education in High Schools.* New York: Russell Sage Foundation, 1957.

Hock, Louise, and T. J. Hill, *The General Education Class in the Secondary School.* New York: Holt, Rinehart and Winston, Inc., 1960.

Hopkins, L. T., *Interaction: The Democratic Process.* Boston: D. C. Heath and Co., 1941.

Krug, E.A., *The Secondary School Curriculum.* New York: Harper and Brothers, 1960.

Leonard, J. P., *Developing the Secondary School Curriculum.* New York: Holt, Rinehart and Winston, Inc., 1953.

National Council of Teachers of English, *The English Language Arts.* New York: Appleton-Century-Crofts, Inc., 1952.

Olson, W. C., *Child Developing.* Boston: D.C. Heath and Co., 1959.

Saylor, J. G., and W. M. Alexander, *Curriculum Planning for Better Teaching and Learning.* New York: Rinehart and Co., Inc., 1954.

Smith, B. O., W. O. Stanley, and J. H. Shores, *Fundamentals of Curriculum Development.* Yonkers-on-Hudson, N.Y.: World Book Co., 1957.

Weiss, M. J., *Reading in the Secondary Schools.* New York: The Odyssey Press, Inc., 1961.

Wiles, Kimball, *Teaching for Better Schools.* Englewood Cliffs, N. J.: Prentice-Hall, Inc., 1959.

CHAPTER V

LESSON PLANNING

Lesson Planning is the First Essential of Good Teaching

Lesson planning is a complex process demanding a high level of knowledge and skill. Lesson plans must be modified from class to class. Teachers often start to plan by trying to remember lessons they have seen in other classes or have read about. Plans work out better if the teacher forgets these and starts with an analysis of his class, and what the learners actually need. Furthermore, the function of the school is to provide for the maximum growth of each individual in the classroom. Therefore, each plan will require modifications as the teacher puts it into operation. The teacher must be able to establish objectives and identify necessary areas of progress for the entire year. He also needs to know how to plan effectively the details of a lesson for a single period.

One of the first responsibilities of a teacher will be to become thoroughly acquainted with curriculum guides and specific courses of study in which is established the curricular pattern for his school. The general areas suggested in the course of study will reveal the curriculum design guiding the choice of learner experiences in his school system. The lists of objectives for each area or subject, the concepts and generalizations considered to be of major importance in setting up long-term goals. Each teacher must know something of the experience which the learners have had in the preceding years, and the experience they are likely to have in grades which follow. The general goals outlined in the course of study must always be modified in terms of the capacities and needs of individuals. Textbooks have always served as aids in achieving the aims of the course of study. Even though the teacher does not follow the sequence of the adopted text exactly, he will find that the textbooks are very helpful.

"Lesson Plan" is the title given to a statement of the achievements to be realized and the specific means by which these are
to be attained as a result of the activities engaged in day by day
under the guidance of the teacher.[1]

Two kinds of lesson planning are recognized: the *memorized
and the written.* The *first* visualizes the expected activities of
the classroom, and plans for the situations as it is believed they
will arise. The *second* kind of lesson planning requires the same
imagery and vigorous reflection as does the first. It does not,
however, depend upon memory to be the sole depository for
lesson plans, but commits these reflections to writing in the form
of a well-organized plan.[2]

Six Essential Elements

The six elements enumerated are those most universally recognized as essential to any complete lesson plan.
   1. *The plan should evince a clear understanding of the outcomes to be achieved.* This involves a recognition both of the
immediate results of the lesson and of the relationship of the
immediate to the more remote inclusive objectives of the
course.
   2. *The plan should definitely relate the lesson to the previous
work of the course.* Unless the teacher provides for this conscious
recognition of the connection between past and present experiences, pupil progress will be impeded.
   3. *The plan should provide for the selection and organization
of subject matter, materials, and activities.* Materials may involve
subject matter as found in textbooks, library references, etc.
These materials require very careful consideration by the teacher.
Activity, too, is increasingly being recognized as an effective
medium of education.
   4. *The plan should indicate the application of appropriate
teaching procedures to the lesson.* There are different types of
learning which require different techniques for efficient development. The lesson plan should reveal discernment in analysis of the learning types involved and the application of approved
teaching techniques to each.
   5. *The plan should provide for the proper evaluation of suc-*

1. Bossing, *Teaching in Secondary Schools* (Boston: Houghton Mifflin Co., 1952),
p. 283.
2. *Ibid.*, p. 285.

cess in the realization of the objectives. Intelligent teaching
requires such evaluation. The lesson plan is defective if it does
not provide for it.

6. *The plan should project today's lesson into tommorow's
situation.* The student should have his attention focused upon
and prepared for the next step.

Certain Features of Lesson Planning

The features that, in general, should be observed in lesson-
planning are as follows:

1. Well-formulated aim.
2. Good assigment.
3. Good summary.
4. Provision for individual differences.
5. Inclusion of pivotal questions.
6. Inclusion of important illustrations.
7. Review.
8. Content materials.
9. Motivation techniques.
10. Evaluation techniques.
11. Rough allocation of time to each phase of the lesson.
12. Attention to apperceptive learning—the new related to
   the old.[1]

Precautions to be Observed in Making Lesson Plans

1. *Avoid overcompleteness.* The main items should be present in the plan, together with whatever details may be necessary
to insure proper development of the lesson.

2. *Avoid too fragmentary a plan.* The teacher should work ·
out lesson plans in considerable detail, even though it is found
best to brief them before use in the class.

3. *Avoid sameness in plans.* One of the principles of motivation is the use of variety in classroom technique.

4. *Avoid undue reverence for the printed text.* The competent teacher will exercise the freedom consonant with the administrative limitations placed upon him in the choice of textbook
material and in the reorganization of content for better teaching

1. *Ibid.*, pp. 287-289.

purposes.[1]

If a person is to make competent decisions, he must have a healthy respect for accuracy and the necessity for thorough information, so that he can be certain he has reached the correct conclusion.

The individual who arrives at sound conclusions does not act on half-truths — he has acquired objectivity and the habit of withholding judgement until he has the information he needs. Most of the significant information the learners must acquire calls for similar depth of understanding.

When the teacher plans to help learners to acquire accurate information, he is not working for memorization of isolated details or the precisewording of the textbook. The teacher's task is to provide the experiences that insure precise and accurate meanings appropriate to his learners' levels of maturity. It is quite possible for an individual to possess accurate information about a topic and yet not be able to apply it to a new situation.

The individual who has developed effective understanding has organized his information in such a way that he can use it. Furthermore, the individual who solves effectively his day-by-day personal or vocational problems habitually seeks to apply his knowledge as he faces a new situation. If learners are to use their knowledge in new situations, they must have worked with teachers who are broadly educated and informed in many areas of knowledge.

The person who brings effective understanding to bear upon his problems possesses the basic techniques for acquiring new information. He knows how to interpret what he reads in newspapers. He is skilled in distinguishing fact and opinion, propoganda and information. The more limited a person's intellectual ability, the more likely it is that he will need to rely on the guidance of others.

Planning of a Skill Development Program

Many skills needed in adult life can be identified and taught in

---

1. *Ibid.*, pp. 289-290.

regular classroom settings.

Planning a program in terms of those activities that learners see as purposeful certainly demands much more of a teacher than merely following an adopted text or standard course of study. Many skills needed in adult life can be identified and taught in regular classroom settings. There must be many things to read — books, magazines, papers. There should be motivation for communication — school newspapers, debates and discussions, reports to be written and presented orally, and planning sessions.

Any program responsive to the problems being faced by a particular class must be planned by the teacher assigned to that class. The teacher will need to familiarize himself with the plan currently in operation in his secondary school. Sound plans need to be made in order to know where to begin, and how to locate specific strengths and weaknesses of learners. With able learners, the problem often is to capitalize upon the learners' own sense of direction and to provide them with the materials they need to pursue their interests. For learners needing extended remedial help, it is particularly important to choose materials which are easy enough to allow the pupils to proceed with confidence. The better informed learners are about the work that is ahead, and the more meaningful the assigned homework, the better is the guarantee that the learning will fit the needs and abilities of learners.

If the program of skill development is planned in the light of pupil needs revealed through on-going classroom activities, the teacher will have no difficulty in helping his learners to see the value of more expertise.

The teacher must plan carefully to help his learners acquire insight into the new skills he introduces, and must plan for practice activities on these and other skills that will make maximum contributions to their proficiency. He must develop the kind of understanding that makes a person able to handle a new situation competently, and to use practices in the learning process at the point where it is most likely to be effective. If the teacher tries to develop the abstraction too soon, he is likely to have his learners memorizing and reciting principles they do not understand.

One of the most important educational principles is that understanding grows from a concrete experience.

The teacher, in making a new technique meaningful to his class, must think about the concrete experiences that might serve for illustrative purposes. It is easy enough, for example, to drill until a desired verbal response is elicited. If, however, a learner is to understand what he is saying, he will need many and varied experiences where the response is encountered in real situations. In helping learners achieve a higher level of performance, the teachers will depend in large measure upon his choice of illustrative material to introduce new ways of working. The inductive process contributes to independent study. Experience shows that learners gain satisfaction from making their own discoveries. A learner who finds out something for himself retains this knowledge longer. The inductive process is a necessary method for gaining and extending knowledge.

The lesson plans, in order to develop proficiency in skills, must include ample opportunities to try out newly learned techniques.

Teachers should allow time for some demonstrations following the introduction of a new technique, in order to make sure that everyone understands. Explanations should accompany these demonstrations. The objective is to show the correct response, so that the learner's practice is directed toward correct procedures at the very beginning. Practice activities concluding the lesson that develops a new principle are frequently followed with additional practice for several sessions, or assigned as homework until the new way of working is thoroughly established.

Effective practice contributes to many facets of the skill and requires learners to apply general principles in many types of situations. The material chosen and the tasks to be accomplished in practice sessions should be suitable to the purposes of the teacher.

Teachers often develop and conclude a lesson with some individual work. This may be in the form of examples prepared by the teacher or found in a textbook, or it may be a classroom problem in which the new technique is needed. For the most part, however, the teacher will be teaching skills which he hopes learners may use in new situations.

At the times when the teacher and his learners are checking a series of practice exercise, valuable opportunities are provided to help learners identify errors and see where more practice is indicated. Learners should be actively involved in identifying where they are wrong and, even more important, in arriving at the correct answer by themselves.

The practice should include day-by-day opportunities to use the new skills as well as the special assigntents. The richer his total program, the more will the teacher find himself using on-going classroom activities as realistic sources of practice, instead of setting up special exercises. For maintaining a needed skill that is not used daily in classroom work, teachers should plan for out-of-class practice, spaced widely throughout a semester or school year.

Many teachers do not realize how many details must be thought through if the activities for a period are to go well.

An essential part of the teacher's preparation should be to get his teaching aids ready before a period begins. It is a great help to check on the number of books available to determine whether or not he will have to mark in his text any pages or passages that he will want to discuss with learners. Pausing while the teacher looks for materials, the class must wait while he puts work on the board — such delay always leads to unnecessary confusion and to trouble. The more thorough the preparation, the more secure the teacher. Learners respect and like to work with the teacher who knows his subject.

A systematic way of using equipment should be worked out.

The more policies that can be clearly established before the occasion arises, the easier classroom routines can be performed. A routine way of taking attendance saves confusion.

Talking things over is important in building self-control.

Through discussions, the teacher can help his learners to take joint responsibility for setting standards for their own behavior. Learners should work with the teacher on the establishment of many of the necessary routines.

Written Curriculum Guides

Once the teacher's study of his teaching assignment has resulted in a statement of purposes for each class, the next step is an over-all organization of framework of instruction.

The teacher's job may be facilitated by written curriculum guides of the school. These guides may be classified as follows:

1. Guides to curriculum planning.
2. Guides (courses of study) to learning experiences for specific areas and levels.
3. General guides to the framework of the curriculum.
4. Descriptions of practices in the school, etc.

Any general guide should indicate whether the organization is subject, broad field, core, or some other type. How to organize instruction, how to plan units of 'work, how to evaluate pupil progress, and how to select resources for learning — for these the teachers will find suggestions in specific bulletins. Such bulletins give local illustrations pertinent to these problems, and list persons, places, and materials available for the teacher. Such materials are almost indispensable in a core curriculum organization. With good guides, the job of the teacher is primarily one of selection and adaptation of materials.

There are two fundamentally different bases for organizing instruction:

1. The logical pattern of subject matter.
2. The psychological pattern of the learner's own purposes.

Although the core organization facilitates the use of the learner's purposes, they may also be consulted in a subject organization. Regardless of the instructional pattern, each learner develops his own organization of purposes and learning experiences.

The chief utility of patterns of curriculum organization other than the subject one lies in their lack of an inherent logical organization and hence their ready adaptation to an instructional organization based on the learners' own problems. Thus, the teacher planning an organization of instruction within a core curriculum or for a new problem-type course is not faced with the dilemma of whether to follow the logic of the subject.

Each subject area has its own logical organization. Thus, the logical organization of history is around chronology; of literature around literary types; of chemistry around chemical elements; of agriculture around products; etc. But learners in the history class may not be interested in chronological periods as such, but in current or unusual events or problems, etc.[1] Hence, effective planning of instructional organization in a subject area needs to work out a set or organizing centers that represents the best reconciliation possible of the logic of the subject and the interests of learners.[2]

Good Rapport

A good rapport is a prerequisite before cooperative planning is undertaken.

Several kinds of general measures of intelligence, achievement level, personality, and interest may have been used to give the teacher more insight into the nature of the pupils with whom he is working. The school environment, too, in and out of the classroom, has been studied for its potentialities for learning. The setting for cooperative problem-solving must be warm, friendly, and comfortable for teacher and learners alike.

The first important step is to make some decisions about the size and appropriateness of the problem.

The following criteria developed by a group of ninth-graders bear testimony to the fact that even this age level is capable of doing some constructive thinking about choice and clarification of problems:

1. Facts must be explained in terms of their causes, and such explanation must be undertaken even against the expressed opposite wishes of students. Learning definitely gains from such explanation.
2. Alexander and P.M.H., *Effective Teaching in Secondary Schools*, pp. 445-448.

1. Knowledge of the topic should be useful now.
2. Knowledge of the topic should be useful in later life.
3. A topic should be interesting.
4. Knowledge of the topic should help in understanding the world.
5. Students should be able to find enough material on the topic.
6. It should be a subject not studied before.[1]

The teacher's guidance is necessary to bring the students to the point of recognizing differences in facts and opinions, and a clarification of what the problem really is.

This is moving the group to an orderly problem-solving approach. The skillful teacher puts the class interest and motivation in the setting of orderly problem-solving.

The major curriculum goals are properly set by the cooperative planning of all groups involved in the school operation.

Actually, the first steps in curriculum planning are logically taken by groups of professional and lay persons before the classroom teacher individually sets up plans for instruction of specific learning groups.

In most schools, some statement of purposes of instruction as a whole, if not for particular departments or courses, is usually valuable.

These statements may be in the form of educational purposes for the system as a whole or for the individual school or for subject departments.

The purposes of instruction in particular subject fields, even individual courses, are also frequently to be found in written form, usually in courses of study or other curriculum guides. A course of study is usually an outline of instruction in a particular field, and more general curriculum guides simply suggest various principles and plans of organizing instruction. These publications may be issued by the state departments of education,

1. Faunce, Roland C. and Bossing, N.L., *Developing the Core Curriculum* (New York: Prentice-Hall, Inc., 1951), p. 115.

the city or county school system, or the individual school. If the statements are already prepared, the teacher can review these at the beginning of the year with other teachers to determine which seem applicable for students to be taught this particular year.

Some purposes are fixed and must be predetermined and plann-ed for by the teacher.

Although the major purposes may be the same, it is unlikely that each learning group will have sufficient identity of previous experience to justify uniform instructional purposes. The total list of purposes should include all the skills, understandings, and behaviors which the teacher hopes learners will achieve in the total school year, or semester. The list should reflect the teach-er's analysis of purposes which are fixed by requirements or general expectations.

Practice in stating instructional purposes in terms of pupil per-formance will help in the process of refining objectives.

A great many statements of educational purposes seem very idealistic and unattainable when viewed in relation to the learn-ers, teachers, and resources involved. Such statements are of little worth in educational planning. Purposes that are realistic are based on thorough understandings of the learners as well as of the subject matter.

The statement should be so prepared and used as to have a high degree of flexibility.

An initial statement must be prepared at the beginning of the year, and many circumstances may develop in the school to make it desirable to eliminate or add purposes. The teachers work to-gether in curriculum planning; there may be need to experiment with the attainment of different purposes from those originally anticipated. The initial statement is primarily a working guide to give direction to teacher-pupil planning activities and to the development of unit plans.

Planning from Day to Day

Six Suggestions

The teacher should keep at least six suggestions in mind for the intelligent use of the lesson plan.

1. The lesson plan should more and more be looked upon as a guide to stimulate thought and not as something to be slavishly followed.

2. The plan, once used, should become the basis for extended development. There is a real danger that the indolent teacher will place undue dependence upon a lesson plan once carefully prepared.

3. In the use of lesson plans, one should use rather detailed plans at first but, as experience is gained, a briefer form may be employed.

4. It is impossible to predict the line of development of the lesson. The more freedom one attempts to use in teaching, the greater the possibilities of divergence from the plan formulated.

5. No two pupils react exactly alike. Outside of pivotal questions and some illustrative data, there must be a readiness to capitalize on the opportunity of the moment with a repertoire, as it were, of well-selected questions and illustrative materials.

6. It is very difficult to estimate the exact time required to complete the task laid out in a daily plan. With the uncertain factors that enter in, time approximations only can be determined.[1]

The purposes of the lesson should be made clear to learners.

Learners need to know why they are being asked to listen to information or to engage in an activity; there is no guarantee that they will learn what the teacher believes is important.

A good plan for a single lesson needs to include some questions, examples, or other opportunities for group reaction that will survey the aspects of present status. Obviously, the longer the teacher has worked with a class, the more accurate he will be in judging present and future needs.

1. Bossing, *op. cit.*, pp. 291-292.

The teacher plans how to secure the best thinking of every-body. Much variety can be planned within the limits of a short period. Learners should share in considering the plans for the best use of a single period. They can help to sharpen specific problems or identify skills they lack or special techniques they need to learn.

The purpose of cooperative planning is not to reduce all in-sights to a common level of thinking. It is to develop problem-solving skills at the level at which the group can operate. Co-operative problem-solving involves careful evaluation of pro-posals.

Evaluation of Each Lesson

If day-by-day activities are to be effective, the teacher must learn to make a continuous evaluation of each lesson taught.

If he is a mathematics teacher, he will be deciding which topics in algebra should be given priority, and looking ahead to related content which could make a special contribution to ad-vanced mathematics. In any case, as he walks from group to group during a work session, he should be alert for difficulties in locating information, inaccurate concepts, problems in human relationships. When he starts to make his plans for tomorrow, he will have to think though in detail how best to handle each of the problems. The amount of detail he actually puts on paper will depend on the nature of the lesson to be taught. There are certain details the teacher needs to think through, even for the simplest plan.

1. The teacher has to consider his goals. What does he hope to accomplish in his work today? What new skills does he aim to develop? What understandings does he hope to clarify?

2. It is to decide what kind of leadership is needed if a par-ticular set of goals is to be achieved. If the goal is to help learn-ers arrive at a clear understanding of a new process in mathe-matics, the function will probably be to guide an inductive reason-ing process.

The teacher will need some means of evaluation — what ques-tions could help to discover how much his learners have actually learned.

A *summary* is important — it need not be a tedious review of all that has gone before. Sometimes the activity he plans in order to evaluate new learnings will serve as his summary.

Records

The teachers who build the most comprehensive records have learned to use effectively the rich and varied sources of evidence residing in ongoing classroom activities.

The possibilities for classroom records that help learners to appraise their own growth and yet yield the evidence needed for reporting to parents and building cumulative records are numerous. Among those commonly used are:

1. Theme folders (or folders for written work) in which sample papers collected at intervals are filed.
2. Personal check lists of typical English errors.
3. Inventory tests on basic facts for a course.
4. Lists of current library books read, briefly annotated.
5. Logs or diaries of special activities completed.
6. Special notebooks kept on a course or for a unit of work.
7. Personal biographies.

The record-keeping devices for personal guidance to ongoing activities can be filed and analyzed for information regarding progress:

1. Lists of committees can give the teacher a picture of the specific parts of projects on which individuals worked.
2. Teachers can keep flow charts, recording the contributions and questions of class members during group discussions.
3. Pupils' preferences for working partners on cooperative projects can be studied for sociometric data.
4. Plans filed by committees can be consulted if details are needed on a pupil's experiences in connection with a unit.
5. Lists of standards established for some phase of work can be checked against present performances.
6. Teacher's plans can reveal objectives for groups and for individuals, special assignments provided for individuals,

and activities provided for the class as a whole.[1]

A *resource unit* is a compilation of suggested learning experiences and resources related to some broad area. From this compilation, teachers can choose ideas, materials, and procedures to be used in their plans.

Every teacher needs a set of vertical files, even if the school system provides teacher-prepared resource units, and the school library has a comprehensive vertical file.

Teachers who have their own files of resource materials usually find them meaningful and usuable. The preparation and maintenance of a vertical file of resource materials is not very difficult and only takes a little extra time for the teacher who reads and studies.

The teacher should keep certain types of evidence in his own daily record book. This should contain more than a series of numbers or grades. He should record ratings for special papers and assignments, notes about special strengths or weaknesses. For some classes, a place in the record book to check off assignments completed on time may be useful. Since the space for notes in most printed record books is limited, the teachers should maintain folders for learners. Samples of written work and tests are filed in such folders and evaluated periodically.

Many schools keep files of some type of evaluation record of different resources.

Such a guide for selecting can be of great help to the individuals. The card files, giving more data regarding addresses and phone numbers, can be very useful.

The problem of identifying community resources is of consequence only in the larger communities where teachers cannot easily be acquainted with all the resources. Many teachers have to rely on the advice of persons who are more familiar with community resources. In larger high schools, some persons may be charged with the responsibility for maintaining this information.

---

1. Carter and others, *op. cit.*, pp. 320-321.

The obvious way of identifying library resources is to use the school library.

Services provided by the librarian in regard to reading lists, reserves, locating materails, teaching library usage, etc. are items of information needed by teachers.

Improvement is much more likely to come when learners are given specific criticisms and suggestions on their products.

The teacher challenges pupils to do various kinds of work — essays, outlines, summaries, reviews, drawings, maps, charts, and many kinds of products.   Without criticism and suggestions learners may simply be permitted to continue to make the same errors. It is better to expect less work and make good use of it for improvement purposes.   A frequent mistake in teaching is the use of pupils' work for marking purposes only. Overlooked are such basic purposes as discovering one's errors and how to overcome them.   Each piece of work examined and returned with constructive suggestions means the possibility of improvement.

Evaluation check lists and tests are frequently needed.

Teaching involves the preparation of various materials, such as unit outlines, lists of readings, suggested learning activities, and other items relating to each unit of work which are very helpful to pupils.

Teachers on the job have the need to review the information being sought by their pupils.

Teachers should be expected to have considerable understanding of most problems dealt with by learners.   Teachers need to review the information, to check for additional information that may be needed, and to look up particular questions that were asked and could not be answered at the time.

Unit Organization of the Curriculum in the Classroom

Unit organization of the curriculum is considered here as refer-ring to the organization of activities, experiences, and subject matter around a central problem or purpose of a group of pupils.

The unit is a recognizable advance to be made by the pupils in some concepts, skills, ideals, attitudes, or appreciation.

The units of work will probably be more effective in such courses as English, history, social studies, general science, and science. If the teacher does not use a unit plan which extends over several periods, he will obviously be faced with the details of planning a single lesson.

Unit Activity

Unit activities offer many occassions for encouraging individual learners to pursue special interests.

The most extensive opportunities to encourage individual exploration come at the point where small groups assume re-sponsibility for various aspects of the problem. However, many important learnings can come from working with others, and many all-class activities planned to enrich concepts can also serve to stimulate individual interests.

Able learners can secure valuable experiences in leadership, as well as learn much about clarifying a problem through group discussion. It should be obvious that learners of different abil-ities can contribute from different levels of insight and experi-mental background. The teachers must help able learners to develop an independent approach to new information, and must make the most of classroom opportunities to explore fields of knowledge extensively.

The suggestions that cannot be incorporated into the plans for a unit may often be the centers of special research by learn-ers. Many of the most worthwhile activities connected with a unit of work in the hands of the more able learner indicate almost unlimited possibilities.

Special emphasis must be given to interesting learners in current happenings. Occasionally a period may be set aside to discuss topics of unusual interest. For an able learner they may open the doors to independent exploration. The success of the teacher in stimulating broad interests in his learners will depend as much on his attitude toward knowledge as it will on his scholarship.

Helping learners to develop and maintain effective skills will create a number of major problems for the teacher regardless of his teaching field. First and most important, the teacher must clearly see his ultimate goals. He must also know how to adjust his plans for skill development to the other activities of his classes, and to decide where to begin and what sequence of experiences to provide. The teacher must help his learners maintain proficiency in basic skills, while introducing special skills in such a way that the learners will understand the principles underlying the new techniques they are learning. He should be just as concerned with the way his learners are working as with the end results of their efforts. The teacher should remember this as he is introducing a new skill or is seeking to help his learners reach higher proficiency levels.

The effectiveness of the teacher will depend, in large measure, upon his analysis of his learners' present performances. The teacher should provide situations in his classes that call for flexibility in applying skills, opportunities created to help his students learn to adjust their skills to the demands of ongoing classroom activities. The learner should be able to recognize success and failure, and he needs to grow in his understanding of the basic principles governing the skill he is learning.

Learners need to enjoy what they are doing, to feel successful with it, and to want to participate in it.

The Essence of Unit Acitivity

The essence of unit activity is a problem-solving approach to learning in which teacher and learner are jointly involved.

Together, they explore a problem of mutual concern; they then plan cooperatively a way of working that will provide the required information or enable them to take other steps needed to solve problems. Next, they carry out their plans, checking on progress from time to time, and revising the plans. Often, they plan followup activities in order to make use of what they have learned — whether the total job is simple or complex, involves the class as a whole, small groups, or individualized work — ends in an elaborate exhibit of projects or a simple class discussion. All depend on the original problem and the plans to solve it.

To plan effectively for a unit, a teacher needs to work at three levels:

1. He makes out a *preliminary plan* that explores the possibilities of the unit.
2. He plans how and at what points learners should be involved.
3. He revises his preliminary plan and expands it into day-by-day plans as the unit develops.

The Preliminary Plan

The preliminary plan should not be an exact outline — it is rather a broad exploration. The order in which the teacher outlines specific topics depends upon how much he needs to put down for his own security. In any event, the teacher will have to develop a preliminary plan for himself, not once, but several times, before he finds the pattern that works most effectively for him.

A preliminary plan should also include possible pupil activities. These cannot be included in detail prior to planning sessions with the class, but possibilities can be thought through, and at least a tentative selection of activities proposed.

A preliminary plan can usefully contain a survey of teaching aids. Many teachers have discovered that examining the teaching aids available with care is a very practical means of reviewing in detail the educative possibilities of an area to be studied.[1]

1. Carter, *op. cit.*, 161-164.

Unit Assignments

*The selection of learning experiences so as to provide for in-
dividual differences among students is another aspect in curriculum development.*

The psychological studies which have identified the extent of
differences among schools, classes, and students in the same
class — differences which affect interests, meanings, efforts, and
outcomes in school work.

Typical devices to provide for differences among students
have involved adaptations in the time given to completing learning exercises. The first type of adaptation requires a plan for
students to work at varying rates. Among the early developments
were the San Francisco, Dalton, and Winnetka plans — all of
which involved organizing the school day in two parts — one for
group activity, and the other for individual work. These plans
also required the development of a series of assignments, so that
the students could work as individuals on different assignments
at the same time.

The use of individual projects is also a means of adapting to
the individual student's interest and ability. The projects themselves could differ in the rigor of their intellectual demands
among students. In the small group, they could adapt further to
the abilities and interests of the individual.

Most curriculum guides include a discussion of how to select
from among the large number of learning experiences suggested
in the course of study those which are likely to be most effective
for students with varying backgrounds and abilities.

*The unit assignment is a planned series of situations through
interaction with which the pupil will achieve advancement.*

The statement of the unit requires the teacher to study carefully the pupil's present experimental level. It is made accessible
to all pupils by the teacher in whatever way seems best.
Usually, certain parts are best presented orally, other parts by
way of the blackboard — still other parts through demonstrations,
etc.

The assignment should indicate careful planning to the end that these required activities are likely to be challenging to pupils of the experiental level for which they are intended.

The assignment should enable the student to see the purpose for his study.

The ability of students to perform their tasks depends upon the degree of clarity with which the assignment designates definite goals.

The assignment should arouse interest in the advance work.

The assignment should be motivated by the hope of worthwhile achievements. The introduction of new materials, or using old materials in different ways arouses interest.

An assignment might be misunderstood because the language used is not suited to the experience of the students.

The use of concrete illustrations and physical materials will help the teacher. The list of guide questions might well be used to clarify the assignment further.

The assignment should be made by the close of the hour.

In a developmental lesson, the advance work necessarily must wait until conclusions have been reached, inasmuch as it may have direct bearing on the intelligibility of the next assignment.

There is an opportunity for varied experiences, with different pupils doing the things most suit to their abilities and interest, and using materials of varied difficulty.

A variety of instructional material must also be planned, because not everyone in the class comes equipped to learn the same thing in the same way.

The assignment definitely must provide for individual differ-

ences in aptitudes, abilities, interests, aims, and needs.

The assignments should be differentiated qualitatively as well as quantitatively. It has to permit the brighter pupils not only to accomplish more work than the slower ones, but also to use different methods even in the required situations.

The assignment has to provide better work even for the slowest pupils.

The assignment must be such that slow pupils may have the advantage of relatively specific directions and problem situations encouraging the establishment of relatively specific goals.

The assignment has to be accompanied by plans for securing appropriate evidence of the actual growth of each pupil in the field represented by the unit.

There has to be individual organization or summarization by each pupil of his work with the assignment — situations in which pupil behavior in the field of the unit may be carefully observed and the test properly objectified.

The unit provides for constant evaluation of progress.

The effective teacher will take equal note of how well the student worked in his group, what pictures he collected for the bulletin board display, and the quality of the questions asked.

In the very nature of the practical situation in which most teachers are working, they must advance by fairly easy steps from courses as they now are to courses as they will be when they are well organized.

The extent to which the unit of work provides for continuity in learning must be determined by evaluation of its results for different learners.

Good unit planning anticipates a variety of experiences that may have been had by different learners in terms of their needs and interests. The unit plan must then assume varying situations, different subgroups for specific purposes, different written conversations for study, and other alternatives to meet the needs of students.

The length of time given to the assignment must be determined by the nature of the subject or problem, and the relative difficulty of the advance work.

An assignment should require a maximum of ten minutes of the sixty-minute class period.

The plan of unit learning experiences should take cognizance of the long-term goals of the high school.

The unit assignment should provide for pupil activity which can be effectively guided and supervised, and which will lead to definite growth.

Progressive development is secured by the kind of planning along the instructional route that is sensitive to pupil interests, and alert to the needs of students for related information.

The assignment should make optimal use of challenging questions, difficulties, and problems growing out of the preceding assignment in the course.

Questions should stress concrete problems. Problems can be made concrete if conceived in terms of everyday applications. The pupils should have a chance to participate in setting their own goals. It is good technique to help students phrase their purposes in the form of questions.

The assignment should be an integral part of the experiential sequence which constitutes the course.

The assignment should involve to an optimal degree the use of previously mastered units and should lead as naturally as possible to the next assignment.

If assignments are used to carry the day's work forward, they should make clear what to do, how to do it, and why to do it.

Assignments must be made at the right time, on the basis of inadequacies in discussion, when they will lead to further learning.

The assignment should emphasize logical memory and the thought process, rather than rote memory.

The assignment has to lead the pupils into experiences by means of which the educational advance represented by the unit may be most economically and effectively achieved. The assigment has to be so organized and planned that its several parts can each be presented to the pupils in the effective way, whether by lectures, discussions, excursions, demonstrations, blackboard work, charts, films, or other devices in common use.

The students must learn to adjust their reading skills flexibly to the particular assignment they face.

Each content field has its own special vocabulary. These are the concepts which the teacher will need to make meaningful through a variety of activities. In the areas of science and mathematics there will be an increasing number of symbols and abstractions to handle.

The students need to be able to locate exact information and to pull together several items of information in order to arrive at a conclusion. It is also helpful to thik about the difficulties that are apparent in previous assignments and to identify opportunities in the present unit for additional practice. With a survey of needed skills as background, the teacher can then decide what to do for specific lessons. He must ask himself what the trouble might be when he hears an inaccurate answer, watches a learner handling reference books aimlessly, etc. These are indications that reading skills are not functioning effectively.

The Role of Chairman

The chairman comes with an agenda for each of his planning sessions.

The chairman will ask his group to consider his agenda and add to it, but he has done some preliminary thinking about the most important problems and what points must be considered in laying effective plans to solve them.

The chairman must learn to think about the topics the learners need to consider in planning sessions. As preparation for the planning sessions that initiate the new unit, the chairman should consider precisely how to introduce the problem to the class. This activity should be developed in detail in *preliminary planning* prior to any sessions with the learners.

An important step in outlining the agenda for the discussion that initiates a unit is to consider how much can reasonably be accomplished in this planning period. An opening session should strive for a clarification of sub-problems and some specific suggestions about how to work — or might it be better to plan for some preliminary exploration of the total problem? The chairman has an obligation to help learners reach thoughtful decisions and a right to suggest that final plans be delayed until the possibilities of a proposal are completely explored.

Planning is a continuing process involving evaluation of progress, determination of new problems, and proposals of the next steps. The chairman and learners should think about the topics to be explored. Exact ways of working will develop as the chairman and learners think through such problems. In the light of this preliminary exploration, the chairman is then ready to expand the appropriate sections of his preliminary plan into precise detail.

Nothing the teacher can do by way of lecture, discussion, or recitation lessons based on a single text can equal the quality of the learning that comes when learners are involved in unit activities. Units of work can, however, be wasteful of time, if there is not intelligent leadership and careful preplanning by the teacher.[1]

---

1. *Ibid.*, 165-169.

Class Meetings

Each class meeting should be devoted to a phase, part, problem, or other division of the unit work.

The meeting must be devoted to such related purposes as: planning a unit work; organizing committees to undertake study of questions involved in the unit work; using library materials related to particular questions; seeing a film; discussing a particular topic or problem; hearing committee reports; writing papers under direction; discussing errors made in some papers; carrying on laboratory experiments; working as committees, etc. The daily outline should show the central thing to be accomplished.

If the procedure is a class discussion, it may be desirable to list specific questions that may stimulate the discussion.

The teacher may need to list specific directions to be given for study, as well as introductory and followup questions. If there is to be committee work, suggested resources for the committees are needed. If the teacher feels more at ease with a detailed outline of what to do, then such an outline should be available. Some teachers find it desirable to prepare a detailed outline and go over it carefully in advance of the class meeting, but to conduct the class meeting from memory as much as possible, with only occasional reference to the notes when memory fails.

A summary of the discussion, plans, understandings, or agreements reached is desirable at the end of all meetings.

If the meeting is planned as a discussion, a summary by the recorder, by the teacher, or the entire class is important. If the meeting is devoted to committee work, a one-minute summary by each committee may serve to end the meeting constructively. The teacher's outline may desirably list questions to be asked, or questions to which pupils are to respond in writing.

Usually some things happen in the interim, or were overlooked at the previous meeting that need to be covered. Good teachers find it desirable to jot them down in the outline.

Records of Observation

Accurate records of observation are important.

The extent to which the teacher will have to work with learners in recording depends upon the experience they have had in previous grades. Recording and reporting information are among the most difficult language skills for pupils to acquire. There are also a host of problems related to presenting information in logical order, even when reports are written in a single paragraph. The students must learn to select their means of reporting in terms of their purposes.

Flexibility is an important attribute of good recording and reporting. In improving these skills, it is better to help learners individually. When learners face the complex task of pulling together information into several related paragraphs, or of organizing an oral presentation, it is important that they are taken logically from topic to topic.

Reports to the class as a whole should be primarily for sharing new information. It is important to appraise the purposes for which the learners are working. One of the problems is the tendency of some learners to copy directly the words of a reference book. Most copying occurs when pupils with limited skill in written expression are assigned a report too elaborate for their capabilities. If this is the case, the teacher should ask his learners to read the material, discuss it with them, and then suggest important points which he records for them on the blackboard.

The teacher who sees planning as an essential phase of his job will keep records that will make future related units of work easier and more successful.

The teacher may mark up his original unit plan, if written, to show changes from time to time. He may keep records of materials used, tests given, interviews, trips, and pupils' achievements; and he may collect samples of pupils' work, newspaper and magazine clippings, pamphlets and other materials. All these materials become his *unit record*, which also usually contains some notes by the teacher regarding learners' reactions and progress and, perhaps, evaluative papers or check list, or a summary thereof.

All members of the learning group have an opportunity to participate in planning; it also shows that leadership is necessary.

Someone must guide the inexperienced and immature members of the learning group. The teacher may involve learners in many phases of planning, but his is the responsibility for leadership.

Service Courses

Courses are added as work in the core programs suggest the need for special help.

What service courses should be offered?

In considering what service courses should be offered, the faculty has to decide how to plan a program sufficiently flexible to provide for growth in ability to deal with life situations as the students actually face them. The teachers also determine, in their preplanning, subject areas and sequences most likely to provide for the needs of youth. Each teacher of a service course is also responsible for guidance.

Classes are organized and scheduled to meet specific student needs.

Service courses meet two, three, or four periods a week, depending on the nature of the problems being studied. Flexible use of personnel and material resources to provide certain kinds of learning experiences mark the program in this school.

Group Work

*Group work is justified as an approach to building understandings
only if it contributes to effective learning.*

Group work should enable the teacher to individualize his
teaching. Once groups have been organized and have developed
a plan of work, it is likely that they will be self-directing for
several class periods. This means that the teacher is free to give
help as needed — to aid one pupil in locating information, to work
on reading problems with another, or to proof-read a report
with a third.

Small-group activities also make it possible for the teacher
to provide more effectively for individual talents, needs, and
interests. When the teacher directs the activities of the class as
one large group, he must, of necessity, hold everyone to the same
subject matter. When, however, the teacher works within a
small-group situation, it is possible for *special groups* or individuals to investigate aspects of the total problem of particular
concern to them, and to explore these sub-problems as deeply
as their maturity will allow.

Small-group activities need not always be used in the infor-
mation-getting process. Sometimes the limited experience of
learners may make it highly desirable for the teacher to work
with the class as a whole during most of the activities leading
to development of new understandings. The teacher must be able
to decide when group work is appropriate, and what kind of
group organization will best achieve his objectives.

The number of groups at work and their size will depend upon
the way the problem develops, and on the maturity of the learners.
There may be times when more groups, smaller in size, will
achieve smoother working relationships.

There is no way of assigning learners to groups. Learners
should share in decisions on how they will work, but this does
not mean that friends always work together. The teacher should
use an all-class planning session to assign priorities to certain
jobs or topics, and arrive at some agreement about the number
of learners needed for specific jobs. The maturity of learners,
the problem, and the needs of learners should be the guide for
the teacher.

Committees and pupils undertaking individual projects need a clear sense of purpose.

They need to visualize how their work fits into the total plan, and they must know precisely what they are expected to accomplish. If the teacher meets briefly with each committee to hear a report of its plans and to give help when problems of interpersonal relationships have arisen, the group work is usually off to a much smoother start. It is helpful to take a few minutes at the beginning of each session to make sure that plans are clear and needed material is at hand. Equally valuable is the policy of asking for brief progress reports at the end of the session.

The Teacher's Help

The teacher must help with needed reference skills, to solve problems of interpersonal relationships, to work on summarizing and reporting skills.

The teacher must not go back to his desk once he is sure that plans are understood and the committees are at work. Here is his opportunity to get better acquainted with learners. Once he is sure that everyone is at work, he can give his attention to special problems — one group at a time. His help will be particularly valuable at the points where his committees are facing the more complex aspects of their work. The teacher can also be helpful if he makes notes regarding the major understandings to which the report is likely to contribute.

Part of the help the teacher gives may be on the problems of how to work cooperatively. Such problems need to be talked through, disagreements and difficulties brought out into the open, and plans suggested for the next steps.

It can also be helpful, at the end of the period, to ask for an evaluation of how well the group work went, and to identify special aspects of the cooperative process.

Teaching Aids

It is important to remember that the textbook is not only teaching aid.

Films, pictures, collections, exhibits, excursions, learners' out-of-school experiences, and the skill of the teacher provide other means for building understanding. These should be used to make concepts meaningful for all learners, but they are very important when reading skills are limited. Observing and listening seem to be an inborn means of securing information. Learners need to become accurate in identifying the distinguishing characteristics of the objects they observe. They must learn to use a variety of aids to accurate observation: scales, rulers, compasses, microscopes, thermometers, etc. They must grow increasingly skillful in recognizing where confusion still exists. The more mature the learners, the more likely they are to face problems.

Good listening or observing involves active participation. The teacher must help his learners to understand that it is important to give their undivided attention to the speaker or to whatever is being observed. There is an incentive for careful observing or listening when learners know they are to have an opportunity to discuss or write a short report. In planning for observing and listening sessions, the teacher must, therefore, be sure that the quality of the presentations is appropriate for the maturity of his learners.

Location of Needed Resources

High school students must learn to locate needed resources and to be able to comprehend the information contained therein.

They will need to take notes and keep records; they will need to make reports — both written and oral. Any skills is best developed when related to the actual situation in which it is needed. The teacher must give help on skills in a number of ways and at many points, as the study of an extensive problem develops. The entire class may take time to discuss how to locate accurate information in various references, practice note-taking, or draw up criteria for a good report. The situation that provides the most effective practice of these skills is often the one in which the learners actually need to use the reference texts which are available as valuable teaching aids.

SUMMARY

In this chapter the role of planning in the teaching-learning process is indicated. The unit of learning is examined as a concept of great usefulness in planning classroom work. The fundamental roles of teacher and learners have been described.

Since the curriculum is defined in terms of experiences of learners, this chapter on common and specialized learnings is a discussion of the kinds of experiences youth have in their classes. The description of the experiences also reveals how life situations are likely to recur in the lives of learners.

For teachers planning to develop experiences with learners in relation to life situations, the concept that growth in dealing with these situations can come in many ways is important.

FOR FURTHER STUDY

Alberty, Harold, *Recognizing the High School Curriculum.* New York: The Macmillan Co., 1953.

Alexander, W.M., and P.M. Halverson, *Effective Teaching in Secondary Schools.* New York: Rinehart & Co., Inc., 1956.

Anderson, V.E., and W.T. Gruhn, *Principles and Practices of Secondary Education.* New York: The Ronald Press Co., 1951.

Bayles, E.E., *Pragmatism in Education.* New York: Harper & Row, Publishers, 1966.

Benne, Kenneth, and Bozidar Muntyan, *Human Relations in Curriculum Change.* New York: The Dryden Press, Inc., 1952.

Bossing, N.L., *Teaching in Secondary Schools.* Boston: Houghton Mifflin Co., 1952.

Carter, W.L., W.H. Care, and M.G. McKim, *Learning to Teach in the Secondary School.* New York: The Macmillan Co., 1962.

Faunce, R.C., and N.L. Bossing, *Developing the Core Curriculum.* New York: Prentice-Hall, Inc., 1951.

Giles, H.H., *Teacher-Pupil Planning.* New York: Harper & Brothers, 1941.

Grambs, J.D., and W.J. Iverson, *Modern Methods in Secondary Education.* New York: The Dryden Press, Inc., 1958.

Green, J.A., *Fields of Teaching and Educational Services.* New York: Harper & Row, Publishers, 1966.

Karmel, L.J., *Testing in Our Schools.* New York: The Macmillan Co., 1966.

Klausmeier, H.J., *Principles and Practices of Secondary School Teaching.* New York: Harper & Brothers, 1953.

Krug, E.A., *Curriculum Planning.* New York: Harper & Brothers, 1950.

Murray, L.J., and L.D. May, *The Child and His Curriculum.* New York: Appleton-Century-Crofts, Inc., 1950.

Rasey, M.I., *This Is Teaching.* New York: Harper & Brothers, 1950.

Saylor, J.G., and W.M. Alexander, *Curriculum Planning for Modern Schools.* New York: Holt, Rinehart & Winston, Inc., 1966.

——————, *Curriculum Planning for Better Teaching and Learning.* New York: Rinehart & Co., Inc., 1954.

Spears, Harold, *The Emerging High-School Curriculum.* New York: American Book Co., 1948.

Umstattd, J.G., *Secondary School Teaching.* New York: Ginn and Co., 1953.

Walton, John, *Toward Better Teaching in the Secondary Schools.* Boston: Allyn & Bacon, Inc. 1966.

BIBLIOGRAPHY*

VOLUME II

Adams, G.S., and others, *Measurement and Evaluation for the Secondary School Teacher*. New York: The Dryden Press, Inc., 1956.

Adams, J.F., *Counseling and Guidance*. New York: The Macmillan Co., 1965.

Alberty, Harold, *Reorganizing the High School Curriculum*. New York: The Macmillan Co., 1953.

Alexander, W.M., and J.G. Saylor, *Secondary Education*. New York: Holt, Rinehart and Winston, Inc., 1950.

——————, and P.M. Halverson, *Effective Teaching in Secondary Schools*. New York: Rinehart and Co., Inc., 1956.

American Association of Colleges for Teacher Education, *Evaluative Criteria for Accrediting Teacher Education*. Washington, D.C.: 1967.

——————, *The Future Challenges to Teacher Education*. Oneonta, N.Y.: 1958.

——————, *Bulletin*. Washington, D.C.: 1963.

American Council on Education, Council on Cooperation in Teacher Education, *The Preparation of Secondary School Teachers*. Washington, D.C.: The Council, 1956.

Anderson, R.H., *Teaching in a World of Change*. New York: Harcourt, Brace & World, Inc., 1966.

Anderson, V.E., and W.T. Gruhn, *Principles and Practices of Secondary Education*. New York: The Ronald Press Co., 1962.

Armstrong, W. Earl, "The Teacher Education Curriculum," *The Journal of Teacher Education,* September, 1957.

Association for Student Teaching, *Improving Instruction in Professional Education*. Lock Haven, Pa.: The Association, 1958.

Audio-Visual Materials of Instruction, Forty-eighth Yearbook, Part I. National Society for the Study of Education. Chicago: University of Chicago Press, 1949.

* This Bibliography gives publication data for all references mentioned in the text, the footnotes, and FOR FURTHER STUDY.

Baumgartner, B.B., *Guiding the Retarded Child.* New York: John Day Co., Inc., 1965.

Baxter, Bernice, *Teacher-Pupil Relationships.* New York: The Macmillan Co., 1941.

Bayles, E.E., *Pragmatism in Education.* New York: Harper & Row, Publishers, 1966.

Beery, John R., *Professional Preparation and Effectiveness of Beginning Teachers.* Coral Gables, Fla.: University of Miami, 1960.

Beggs, D.W., *A Practical Application of the Trump Plan.* Englewood Cliffs, N.J.: Prentice-Hall, Inc., 1964.

Belth, Marc, *Education as a Discipline.* Boston: Allyn & Bacon, Inc., 1965.

Bent, R.K., and H.H. Kronenberg, *Principles of Secondary Education.* New York: McGraw-Hill Book Co., 1949.

Bereday, G.Z.F., and J.A. Lauwerys, *The World Year Book of Education, 1967 — Editor's Introduction.* New York: Harcourt, Brace & World, Inc., 1967.

Berkowitz, P.H., *Public Education for Disturbed Children in New York City.* Springfield, Ill: Charles C. Thomas, Publishers, 1967.

Bigelow, K.W., *Teachers of Our Times.* Washington, D.C.: American Council on Education, 1944.

Billett, R.O., *Fundamentals of Secondary-School Teaching.* Cambridge: The Riverside Press, 1940.

Bode, B.H., *How We Learn.* Boston: D.C. Heath and Co., 1940.

Borrowman, Merle L., *The Liberal and Technical in Teacher Education.* New York: Bureau of Publications, Teachers College, Columbia University, 1956.

Bossing, N.L., *Principles of Secondary Education.* Englewood Cliffs, N.J.: Prentice-Hall, Inc., 1955.

——————————, *Teaching in Secondary Schools.* Boston: Houghton Mifflin Co., 1952.

Bottrell, H.R., *Teaching Tools.* Pittsburgh: The Boxwood Press, 1957.

Bradley, Gladyce H. "A Survey of Field Experiences in Institutions in A.A.C.T.E.," *Journal of Educational Research,* 52, May, 1959.

Brameld, T.B.H., *Education as Power.* New York: Holt, Rinehart & Winston, Inc., 1965.

Brandfield, J.M., and others, *Measurement and Evaluation in Education*. New York: The Macmillan Co., 1957.

Brown, J.F., *The American High School*. New York: The Macmillan Co., 1909.

Brownell, Baker, *The Human Community*. New York: Harper and Brothers, 1950.

Butler, F.A., *The Improvement of Teaching in Secondary Schools*. Chicago: University of Chicago Press, 1954.

Callahan, S.G., *Successful Teaching in Secondary Schools*. Chicago: Scott, Foresman and Co., 1966.

Carter, W.L., C.W. Hansen, and M.G. McKim, *Learning to Teach in the Secondary School*. New York: The Macmillan Co., 1962.

Childs, J.L., *Education and Morals*. New York: John Wiley & Sons, Inc., 1967.

Clark, L.H., R.L. Klein and J.B. Burks, *The American Secondary School Curriculum*. New York: The Macmillan Co., 1965.

Colman, J.E., *The Master Teachers and the Art of Teaching*. New York: Pitman Publishing Co., 1967.

Combs, A.W., *The Professional Education of Teachers*. Boston: Allyn & Bacon, Inc., 1965.

Conant, James B., *The Education of American Teachers*. New York: McGraw-Hill Co., Inc., 1963.

Cooper, Herman, "Teacher Education in the State University," *New York State Education,* 45, May, 1958.

Cooper, James, and H.M. Elesbree, "A Comparison of Two Plans of Teacher Education," *Journal of Educational Research,* 51, May, 1958.

Cosper, Cecil, *Student-Teaching Theory and Practices*. New York: Greenwich Book Publishers, 1965.

Cottrell, Donald P., ed., *Teacher Education for a Free People*. Oneonta, N.Y.: Association of Colleges for Teacher Education, 1956.

Council on Cooperation in Teacher Education. "Report of Conference on preparation of Secondary School Teachers," *Educational Record,* 38, July, 1957.

Craig, R.C., *The Psychology of Learning in the Classroom*. New York: The Macmillan Co., 1966.

Crow, L.D., W.T. Murray, and H.H. Smyth, *Educating the Culturally Disadvantaged Child.* New York: David McKay Co., Inc., 1966.

Cunningham, Ruth, and others, *Understanding Group Behavior of Boys and Girls.* New York: Bureau of Publications, Teachers College, Columbia University, 1951.

Cyphert, F.R., and E. Spaights, *An Analysis and Projection of Research in Teacher Education.* Columbus, Ohio: The Ohio State University Research Foundation, 1964.

Devor, J.W., *The Experience of Student Teaching.* New York: The Macmillan Co., 1964.

Douglass, H.R., *Secondary Education.* New York: The Ronald Press Co., 1952.

Downey, L.W., *The Secondary Phase of Education.* New York: Blaisdell Publishing Co., 1965.

Dunn, L.M., *Basic Principles of Special Education.* "The Exceptional Pupil — A Challenge to Secondary Education," *Bulletin of the National Association of Secondary-School Principals,* Vol. 39, January, 1955.

Ebel, R.L., "Measurement Applications in Teacher Education: A Review of Relevant Research," *Journal of Teacher Education,* 17:15-25, 1966.

Eby, Frederick. *The Development of Modern Education.* Englewood Cliffs, N.J.: Prentice-Hall, 1952.

Eye, G.G., and L.A. Netzer, *Supervision of Instruction.* New York: Harper and Row, Publishers, 1965.

Faunce, R.C., and M.J. Clute, *Teaching and Learning in the Junior High School.* San Francisco: Wadsworth Publishing Co., Inc., 1961.

—————————, *Secondary School Administration.* New York: Harper and Brothers, 1955.

Figueroa, J.P., "Postgraduate Teacher Education: Some Experiments in the United States," *Universities Quarterly,* 13, November, 1958.

Flaum, L.S., *The Activity High School — The Principles of Its Operation.* New York: Harper and Brothers Publishers, 1953.

Frandsen, A.N., *Educational Psychology.* New York: McGraw-Hill Book Co., 1967.

Frankel, M.G., F.W. Happ, and M.P. Smith, *Functional Teaching of the Mentally Retarded.* Springfield, Ill.: Charles C. Thomas, Publishers, 1966.

Frederick, Robert, *The Third Curriculum.* New York: Appleton-Century-Crofts, Inc., 1959.

French, Will, *Behavioral Goals of General Education in High School.* New York: Russell Sage Foundation, 1957.

Fretwell, E.K., *Extra-Curricular Activities in Secondary Schools.* Boston: Houghton Mifflin Co., 1931.

Full, Harold, *Controversy in American Education.* New York: The Macmillan Co., 1967.

Gabriel, John. *Analysis of the Emotional Problems of the Teacher in the Classroom.* Melbourne: F.W. Cheshire, 1957.

Gardner, R.S., "Media Facilities at the State University of New York at Albany," *Action for Improvement of Teacher Education,* edited by E.C. Pomeroy. Washington, D.C.: The American Association of Colleges for Teacher Education, 1965.

Garrett, H.E., *The Art of Good Teaching.* New York: David McKay Co., Inc., 1964.

Gauerke, H.J., and A.K. Cardew, "Teacher Training via TV," *Modern Language Journal,* 1963, 47:69-70.

Gelinas, P.J., *So You Want to Be a Teacher.* New York: Harper & Row, Publishers, 1965.

Glaser, R., ed., *Training Research and Education.* Pittsburgh: University of Pittsburgh Press, 1962.

Glennon, Vincent J., *The Road Ahead in Teacher Education.* New York: Syracuse University Press, 1957.

Goodland, J.T., "An Analysis of Professional Laboratory Experiences in the Education of the Teachers," *The Journal of Teacher Education,* 1965. 16:263-270.

Gordon, T.J., *The Teacher as a Guidance Worker.* New York: Harper & Brothers, 1956.

Grambs, J.D., and others, *Modern Method in Secondary Education.* New York: The Dryden Press, 1958.

Grant, Bruce, G.D. Demos, and Willard Edwards, *Guidance of Youth.* Springfield, Ill.: Charles C. Thomas, Publisher, 1965.

Gronlund, N.E., *Measurement and Evaluation in Teaching.* New York: The Macmillan Co., 1965.

Gruber, F.C., and T.B. Beatty, *Secondary School Activities.* New York: McGraw-Hill Book Co., 1954.

Gruhn, W.T., and H.R. Douglass, *The Modern Junior High School.* New York: The Ronald Press Co., 1956.

Guided Study and Homework, by Ruth Strang. From the NEA Journal, October, 1955.

Haag, J.H., *School Health Program.* New York: Holt, Rinehart & Winston, Inc., 1965.

Hahn, R.O., and D.B. Bidna, *Secondary Education.* New York: The Macmillan Co., 1965.

Hall, H.O., "Professional Preparation and Teacher Effectiveness," *The Journal of Teacher Education,* 1964. 15: 72-76.

Harden, E.L., *How to Organize Your Guidance Program.* New York: The Macmaillan Co., 1951.

Hart, J.K., *Education in the Humane Community.* New York: Harper and Brothers, 1951.

Haskew, Laurence D., "The Real Story in Teacher Education," *Journal of Teacher Education,* 9. June, 1958.

Herrick, Virgil E., "Our Future in Teacher Education," *Teachers College Record,* 57. February, 1956.

Herriot, M.E., and others., "History and Objectives of Junior High School Education in California," *The Bulletin of the National Association of Secondary School Principals, XXXV,* December, 1951.

Hill, G.E., *Management and Improvement of Guidance.* New York: Appleton-Century-Crofts, 1965.

Hillman, Arthur, *Community Organization and Planning.* New York: The Macmillan Co., 1950.

Hodenfield, G.K., and T.M. Stinnett, *The Education of Teachers.* Englewood Cliffs, N.J.: Prentice-Hall, 1961.

How to Pass Graduate Record Examination; Advanced Test: Education. New York: College Publishing Corp., 1967.

Hudgins, B.B., *Problem Solving in the Classroom.* New York: The Macmillan Co., 1966.

Hunt, E.C., *Education of Teachers.* Columbia, S.C.: University of South Carolina Press, 1944.

Jenkins, D.H., and Ronald Lippitt, *Interpersonal Perceptions of Teachers, Students, and Parents.* Washington, D.C.: The

Division of Adult Education, National Education Association 1951.

Jersild, A.T., *In Search of Self.* New York: Bureau of Publications, Teachers College, Columbia University Press, 1952.

Johnston, E.G., and R.C. Faunce, *Student Activities in Secondary Schools.* New York: The Ronald Press Co., 1952.

Johnston, E.G., and others, *The Role of the Teacher in Guidance.* Englewood Cliffs, N.J.: Prentice-Hall, 1959.

Jones, A.J., *Principles of Guidance.* New York: McGraw-Hill Book Co., 1951.

Jones, R.M., *Contemporary Educational Psychology.* New York: Harper & Row, Publishers, 1967.

Kagan, N.D., R. Krathwohl, and R. Miller, "Simulated Recall in Therapy Using Video Tape — A Case Study," *Journal of Counseling Psychology,* 1963. 10:237-243.

Kelley, J.A., *Guidance and the Curriculum.* Englewood Cliffs, N.J.: Prentice-Hall, 1955.

Kilzer, L.R., H.H. Stephenson, and H.O. Nordberg, *Allied Activities in the Secondary School.* New York: Harper & Brothers, 1956.

Kinder, J.S., *Audio-Visual Materials and Techniques.* New York: Chanticleer Press, 1949.

King, Clarence, *Organizing for Community Action.* New York: Harper & Brothers, 1948.

Kirkendall, L.A., and F.R. Zeran, *Student Councils in Action.* New York: Chartwell House, 1953.

Koenker, R.H., "Sixth Year Programs in Teacher Education: A Survey," *Journal of Teacher Education,* 9, March, 1958.

Koerner, James, *The Miseducation of Teachers.* Boston: Houghton Mifflin Co., 1963.

Krug, E.A., *The Secondary School Curriculum.* New York: Harper & Brothers, 1960.

Laing, J.J., "Search of Reputability for Disreputable Supervision," *National Association of Secondary Principals Bulletin,* 42, March, 1958.

Larson, K.G., *Guide to Personal Advancement in the Teaching Profession.* Englewood Cliffs, N.J.: Prentice-Hall, 1966.

Lee, F.H., *Principles and Practices of Teaching in Secondary Schools*. New York: David McKay Co., Inc., 1965.

Lieberman, Myron, *Education as a Profession*. Englewood Cliffs, N.J.: Prentice-Hall, 1956.

Lindsey, Margaret, and W.T. Gruhn, *Student Teaching in the Elementary School*. New York: The Ronald Press Co., 1957.

Lueck, W.R., *Effective Secondary Education*. Minneapolis, Minn: Burgess Publishing Co., 1966.

Martin, T.D., "Code of Ethics for Teachers," *Encyclopedia of Education*. New York: The Macmillan Co., 1941.

Maslow, A.H., *Motivation and Personality*. New York: Harper & Brothers, 1954.

Mayer, Martin, *The Schools*. New York: Anchor Books, 1963.

McConnell, T.R., and others, "General Education," *Encyclopedia of Educational Research*. New York: The Macmillan Co., 1950.

McDaniel, H.B., *Guidance in the Modern School*. New York: The Dryden Press, 1956.

McGuire, Vincent, R. B. Myers, and C. L. Durance, *Your Student Teaching in the Secondary School*. Boston: Allyn & Bacon Inc., 1959.

McKown, H. C., *Extra-Curricular Activities*. New York: The Macmillan Co., 1952.

——————, *Home-Room Guidance*, second edition. New York: McGraw-Hill Book Co., 1946.

Melby, E. O., *The Education of Free Men*. Pittsburgh: University of Pittsburgh, 1955.

Menge, J. W., and R. C. Faunce, *Working Together for the Better Schools*. New York: American Book Co., 1953.

Miller, C. H., *Guidance Service*. New York: Harper & Row, Publishers, 1965.

Miller, F. A., J. H. Mayer, and R. B. Patrick, *Planning Student Activities*. Englewood Cliffs, N. J.: Prentice-Hall, Inc., 1956.

Miller, Richard, *Perspectives on Educational Change*. New York: Appleton-Century-Crofts, Inc., 1967.

Mills, H. H., and H. R. Gouglass, *Teaching in High School*. New York: The Ronald Press Co., 1957.

Morris, Van Cleve, *Existentialism in Education*. New York: Harper & Row, Publishers, 1966.

National Association of Student Councils, *Student Councils Handbook*. Washington, D. C.: National Association of Secondary School Principals, 1949.

National Commission on Teacher Education and Professional Standards. *Working Papers for Participants in Kansas Conference*. Washington, D.C.: National Education Association, 1959.

Newsome, G. L., "Sixth Year Programs in Teacher Education: Some Questions." *Journal of Teacher Education,* 9 March, 1958.

Noar, Gertrude, *Freedom to Live and Learn*. Philadelphia: Franklin Publishing Co., 1948.

Oliva, P.F., and R. A. Scrafford, *Teaching in a Modern Secondary School*. Columbus, Ohio: Charles E. Merrill Books, Inc. 1965.

Oliver, G. E., *A Study of Pre-Service Teacher Education in the Use of Media of Mass Communication for Classroom Instruction*. Athens, Georgia: University of Georgia, 1962.

Pai, Yound, *Philosophic Problems on Education*. Philadelphia: J. B. Lippincott Co., 1967.

Parrish, B. M., *Education of the Gifted*. New York: Twayne Publishers, Inc., 1965.

Patterson, C. H., *The Counselor in the School*. New York: McGraw-Hill Co., 1967.

Phillips, E. L., D. N. Wiener, and N. G. Haring, *Discipline, Achievement, and Mental Health*. Englewood Cliffs, N. J.: Prentice-Hall, Inc., 1960.

Pierce, P.R., *Developing a High School Curriculum*. New York: American Book Co., 1942.

Plath, K. R., *Schools within Schools*. New York: Bureau of Publications, Teachers College, Columbia University, 1965.

Riessman, Frank, *Helping the Disadvantaged Pupil to Learn More Easily*. Englewood Cliffs, N. J.: Prentice-Hall, Inc., 1966.

Rivlin, H. N., *Teaching Adolescents in Secondary Schools*. New York: Appleton-Century-Crofts, Inc., 1948.

Robb, Felix C., "The Academic Preparation of Teachers: Conant's Proposals," *Science,* Vol. 141, pp. 1166-1168, September 20, 1963.

Ross, C. C., and others, *Measurement in Today's Schools.* New York: Prentice-Hall, Inc., 1954.

Rosser, N. A., *Personal Guidance.* New York: Holt, Rinehart & Winston, Inc., 1964.

Rothney, John, *The High School Student: A Book of Cases.* New York: Dryden Press, 1953.

Rourke, Robert E. K., "Some Implications of Twentieth Century Mathematics for High Schools," *The Mathematics Teacher,* 51, February, 1958.

Rubin, E. Z., C. B. Simson, and M. C. Betwee, *Emotionally Handicapped Children and the Elementary School.* Detroit: Wayne State University Press, 1966.

Ruediner, W. C., *Teaching Procedures.* Boston: Houghton Miflin Co., 1932.

Ryans, D. G., *Characteristics of Teachers.* Washington, D.C.: American Council on Education, 1960.

Sanders, J. T., *Making Good Communities Better.* Lexington, Ky.: University of Kentucky Press, 1950.

Sarason, Seymour B., Kenneth Davidson, and Barton Blatt, *The Preparation of Teachers: An Unstudied Problem in Education.* New York: John Wiley, 1962.

Saylor, J. G., and W. M. Alexander, *Curriculum Planning for Modern Schools.* New York: Holt, Rinehart & Winston, Inc., 1966.

Schueler, Herbert, *Teacher Education and the New Media.* Washington: American Association of Colleges for Teacher Education, 1967.

Sheviakov, G. V., and F. Redl, *Discipline for Today's Children and Youth.* Washington, D.C.: Department of Supervision and Curriculum, N.E.A., 1944.

Simpson, R. H., *Teacher Self-Evaluation.* New York: The Macmillan Co., 1966.

Smith, B. O., and others, *Fundamentals of Curriculum Development.* Yonkers-on-Hudson, N.Y.: World Book Co., 1957.

Smith, Elmer R., ed., *Teacher Education: A Reappraisal.* New York: Harper & Row, Publishers, 1962.

Smith, Eugene R., and R. W. Tyler, *Appraising and Recording Student Progress.* New York: Harper & Brothers, 1942.

Smith, G. E., *Principles and Practices of the Guidance Program.* New York: The Macmillan Co., 1951.

Smolensky, Jack, and L. R. Bonvechio, *Principles of School Health.* Boston: D. C. Heath & Co., 1966.

Sprinthall, N. A., J. J. Whitely, and R. C. Mosher, "A Study of Teacher Effectiveness," *The Journal of Teacher Education,* 1966, 17:93-106.

Steffre, Buford, *Theories of Counseling.* New York: McGraw-Hill Book Co., 1965.

Stiles, L. J., "Maintaining High Certification Standards," *Virginia Journal of Education,* 50, April, 1957.

Stiles, Lindley J., A. S. Barr, H. R. Douglass, and H. H. Mills, *Teacher Education in the United States.* New York: The Ronald Press Co., 1960.

Stinnett, T.M., "Crucial Problems in Teacher Education," *Partners in Education. Forty-fifth Annual Schoolmen's Week Proceedings.* Philadelphia: University of Pennsylvania, 1958.

Stoller, N., and G. S. Lesser, "A Comparison of Methods of Observation in Pre-Service Teacher Training," *AV Communication Review,* 1964, 2:177-197.

Stone, James C., *The Graduate Internship Program in Teacher Education.* Berkeley: University of California Press, 1959.

Stone, J. C., and F. W. Schneider, *Commitment to Teaching.* New York: Crowell Collier, Inc., 1955.

Strang, Ruth, *How to Report Pupil Progress.* Chicago: Science Research Association, Inc., 1955.

——————, *Reporting to Parents.* New York: Bureau of Publications, Teachers College, Columbia University, 1947.

——————, *Guided Study and Homework.* From the NEA Journal, October, 1955.

Stratemeyer, F. B., H. L. Forkner, M. G. McKim, and A. H. Passow, *Developing a Curriculum for Modern Living.* New York: Bureau of Publications, Teachers College, Columbia University, 1957.

Telford, C. W., and J. M. Sawrey, *The Exceptional Individual.* Englewood Cliffs, N. J.: Prentice-Hall, Inc., 1967.

Tevens, A. C., *Techniques for Handling Problem Parents.* Englewood Cliffs, N.J.: Prentice-Hall, Inc., 1966.

Thatcher, A. W., *The Teacher Education Program: Basic Principles and Issues.* Washington, D.C.: National Commission on Teacher Education and Professional Standards, National Education Association, 1958.

The Junior High School Program. Atlanta: The Southern Association of Colleges and Secondary Schools, 1958.

The Shape of Education for 1967-68. Washington, D.C.: National School Public Relations Association, 1967.

Thomas, G. T., and Joseph Crescimbeni, *Guiding the Gifted Child.* New York: Randome House, Inc., 1966.

Thomas, R. M., *Social Differences in the Classroom.* New York: David McKay Co., Inc., 1965.

——————, *Aiding the Maladjusted Pupil.* New York: David McKay Co., Inc., 1967.

Thompson, N. Z., *Vitalized Assemblies.* New York: E. P. Dutton & Co., Inc., 1953.

Torrance, E. P., and R. D. Strom, *Mental Health and Achievement.* New York: John Wiley & Sons, Inc., 1965.

Travers, Robert, *How to Make Achievement Tests.* New York: Odyssey Press, 1950.

Trow, W. C., *Teacher and Technology.* New York: Appleton-Century-Crofts, 1963.

Vaizey, J. E., *Education for Tomorrow.* Baltimore: Penguin Books, Inc., 1966.

Walhquist, J.T., *An Introduction to American Education.* New York: The Ronald Press Co., 1947.

Walters, Everett, *Graduate Education Today.* Washington, D.C.: American Council on Education, 1965.

Walton, John, *Toward Better Teaching in the Secondary Schools.* Boston: Allyn & Bacon, Inc., 1966.

Washburne, Carleton, *Adjusting the School to the Child.* Yonkers, N.Y.: World Book Co., 1932.

Wesley, E.B., *Teaching the Social Studies.* Boston: D.C. Heath & Co., 1950.

Westby-Gibson, Dorothy, *Grouping Students for Improved Instruction.* Englewood Cliffs, N.J.: Prentice-Hall, Inc., 1967.

Wiles, Kimball, *Teaching for Better Schools.* Englewood Cliffs, N.J.: Prentice-Hall, Inc., 1953.

——————, *Supervision for Better Schools.* Englewood Cliffs, N.J.: Prentice-Hall, Inc., 1967.

Williams, J.P., "Comparison of Several Response Modes in a Review Program," *Journal of Educational Psychology,* 1963. 54:253-260.

Williams, P.P., *Techniques for Studying Certain School-Community Relationships.* Gainesville, Fla.: College of Education, University of Florida, 1953.

Woodring, Paul, *New Directions in Teacher Education.* New York: The Fund for the Advancement of Education, 1957.

Worcester, D.A., *The Education of Children of Above-Average Mentality.* Lincoln: University of Nebraska Press, 1956.

Wrenn, C.G., and W.E. Dugan, *Guidance Procedures in High School.* Minneapolis: The University of Minnesota Press, 1950.

Yeager, W.A., *School Community Relations.* New York: Dryden Press, 1951.

Young, M.D., *Innovation and Research in Education.* London: Routledge & K. Paul, 1965.

VOLUME III

Adler, Alfred, *Education of the Individual.* New York: Philosophical Library, 1958.

Alberty, Harold, *Reorganizing the High School Curriculum.* New York: The Macmillan Co., 1953.

Alexander, W.M., and Paul Halverson, *Effective Teaching in Secondary Schools.* New York: Rinehart & Co., Inc., 1956.

American Association of School Administrators, *American School Curriculum.* Thirty-first Yearbook. Washington, D.C.: The Association, 1953.

Anderson, R.H., *Teaching in a World of Change.* New York: Harcourt, Brace & World, Inc., 1966.

Anderson, V.E., and W.T. Gruhn, *Principles and Practices of Secondary Education.* New York: The Ronald Press Co., 1951.

Anderson, Vernon, *Principles and Procedures of Curriculum Development.* New York: The Ronald Press Co., 1956.

Arons, L., and M.A. May, *Television and Human Behavior.* New York: Appleton-Century-Crofts, 1963.

A Sound Core Program — What It Is and What It Isn't, by Harold Alberty. From the NEA Journal, January, 1956.

Association for Supervision and Curriculum Development. *Preparation of Core Teachers for Secondary Schools.* Washington, D.C.: National Education Association, 1955.
——————, *Action for Curriculum Development,* 1951 Yearbook. Washington, D.C.: The Association, 1951.

Baldwin, Orrell, *The Way We Live.* New York: Noble & Noble, Publishers, Inc., 1964.
Barr, A.S., R.A. Davis, and P.O. Johnson, *Educational Research and Appraisal.* New York: J.B. Lippincott Co., 1953.
Bayles, E.E., *Pragmatism in Education.* New York: Harper & Row, Publishers, 1966.
Beck, R.H., W.W. Cook, and N.C. Kearney, *Curriculum in the Modern Elementary School.* Englewood Cliffs, N.J.: Prentice-Hall, Inc., 1953.
Bellack, A.A., *Theory and Research in Teaching.* New York: Teachers College, Columbia University, 1963.
Benne, Kenneth, and Bozidar Muntyan, *Human Relations in Curriculum Change.* New York: The Dryden Press, Inc., 1952.
Berman, Louise M., *The Nature of Teaching: Implications for the Education of Teachers.* Milwaukee, Wis.: School of Education; University of Wisconsin, 1963.
——————, ed., *The Humanities and the Curriculum.* Washington, D.C.: Associations for Supervision and Curriculum Development, 1967.
Biddle, B.J., and W.J. Ellena, editors, *Contemporary Research on Teacher Effectiveness.* New York: Holt, Rinehart & Winston, 1964.
Billett, R.O., *Fundamentals of Secondary-School Teaching.* Cambridge: The Riverside Press, 1940.
Bossing, N.L., *Teaching in Secondary Schools.* Boston: Houghton Mifflin Co., 1952.
——————,*Principles of Secondary Education.* Englewood Cliffs, N.J.: Prentice-Hall, Inc., 1955.
Broudy, H.S., and J.R. Palmer, *Exemplars of Teaching Method.* Chicago: Rand McNally & Co., 1965.
Brown, J.W., and J.W. Thornton, Jr., *New Media in Higher Education.* Washington, D.C.: Association for Higher Education and the Division of Audiovisual Instructional Service, National Education Association, 1963.

Bruner, J.S., *The Process of Education.* Cambridge, Mass.: Harvard University Press, 1960.

——————, and R. Tagiuri, "The Perception of People," *Handbook of Social Psychology,* Volume 2. Cambridge, Mass.: Addison-Wesley, 1954.

Butler, F.A., *The Improvement of Teaching in Secondary Schools.* Chicago: University of Chicago Press, 1954.

Campbell, D. T., "Factors Relevant to the Validation of Experiments in Social Settings," *Psychological Bulletin,* 1957. 54:297-312.

——————, and J. C. Stanley, "Experimental and Quasi-Experimental Designs for Research on Teaching," *Handbook of Research on Teaching.* Chicago: Rand McNally, 1963.

Caswell, H.L., and Associates, *Curriculum Improvement in Public School Systems.* New York: Bureau of Publications, Teachers College, Columbia University, 1953.

——————, and A.W. Foshay, *Education in the Elementary School.* New York: American Book Co., 1957.

Cay, D.F., *Curriculum: Design for Learning.* Indianapolis: The Bobbs-Merrill Co., Inc., 1966.

Clark, L.H., *Secondary School Teaching Methods.* New York: The Macmillan Co., 1967.

——————, R.L. Klein, and J.B. Burks, *The American Secondary School Curriculum.* New York: The Macmillan Co., 1965.

Corey, S.M., *Action Research to Improve School Practices.* New York: Bureau of Publications, Teachers College, Columbia University, 1953.

Cosper, Cecil, *Student-Teaching Theory and Practices.* New York: Greenwich Book Publishers, 1965.

Coulson, J.E., "Programmed Instruction: A Perspective," *The Journal of Teacher Education,* 1963. 14:372-378.

Curriculum Office, Philadelphia Public Schools, *A Guide to the Teaching of Literature in Grades 7 through 12* (tentative). Philadelphia: School District of Philadelphia, 1960.

Dallmann, Martha, *Teaching the Language Arts in the Elementary School.* Dubuque, Iowa: W.C. Brown Co., 1967.

Doll, R.C., A.H. Passow, and S.M. Corey, *Organizing for Curriculum Improvement.* New York: Bureau of Publications, Teachers College, Columbia University, 1953.

Douglass, H.R., *Secondary Education.* New York: Ronald Press Co., 1952.

Ebel, R.L., *Measuring Educational Achievement.* Englewood Cliffs, N.J.: Prentice-Hall, Inc., 1965.

Eye, G.G., and L.A. Netzer, *Supervision of Instruction.* New York: Harper & Row, Publishers, 1965.

Faunce, R.C., and N.L. Bossing, *Developing the Core Curriculum.* New York: Prentice-Hall, Inc., 1951.

Fearing, F., "Toward a Psychological Theory of Human Communication," *Journal of Personality,* 1953. 22:71-88.

Flanders, N.A., "Teacher Influence in the Classroom," *Theory and Research in Teaching.* New York: Teachers College, Columbia University, 1963.

————, *Helping Teachers Change Their Behavior.* Ann Arbor: University of Michigan, 1963.

French, Will, *Behavioral Goals of General Education in High Schools.* New York: Russell Sage Foundation, 1957.

Frymier, J.R., *The Nature of Educational Method.* Columbus, Ohio: Charles E. Merrill Books, Inc., 1965.

Gage, N.L., "A Method of 'Improving' Teacher Behavior," *The Journal of Teacher Education,* 1963. 14:261-266.

————, ed., *Handbook of Research on Teaching.* Chicago: Rand McNally, 1963.

Gagne, R.M., *The Conditions of Learning.* New York: Holt, Rinehart & Winston, 1965.

Gelinas, P.J., *So You Want to Be a Teacher.* New York: Harper & Row, Publishers, 1965.

Gerlach, V.S., and J.P. Vergis, "Self-Instructional Motion Pictures," *AV Communication Review,* 1965. 13:196-204.

Giles, H.H., *Teacher-Pupil Planning.* New York: Harper & Brothers, 1941.

Goodland, J.T., *School, Curriculum, and the Individual.* Waltham, Mass.: Blaisdell Publishing Co., 1966.

Gordon, T.J., "The Assessment of Classroom Emotional Climate by Means of the Observation Schedule and Record," *The Journal of Teacher Education,* 1966.

Grambs, J.D., and W.J., Iverson, *Modern Methods in Secondary Education.* New York: The Dryden Press, Inc., 1958.

Green, J.A., *Fields of Teaching and Educational Services.* New York: Harper & Row, Publishers, 1966.

Gropper, G.L., *A Behavioral Analysis of the Role of Visuals in Instruction.* Pittsburgh: American Institutes for Research, 1963.

——————, *Learning from Visuals: The Application of Programming Principles to Visual Presentations.* Film Report. Pittsburgh: American Institute for Research, 1963.

——————, and A.A. Lumsdaine, *The Use of Student Response to Improve Televised Instruction: An Overview.* Pittsburgh: American Institutes for Research, 1961.

Guide to the Study of the Curriculum in the Secondary Schools of Illinois. Springfield, Ill: State Department of Public Instruction, 1948.

Gulliksen, H., and S. Messick, editors. *Psychological Scaling: Theory and Applications.* New York: Wiley, 1960.

Gwynn, J. Minor, *Curriculum Principles and Social Trends.* New York: The Macmillan Co., 1960.

Haines, A.C., editor, *Concern for the Individual in Student Teaching.* Dubuque, Iowa: William C. Brown, 1963.

Handbook on Curriculum Study, Curriculum Series, Bulletin No. 1. State of Oregon, Department of Education, December, 1937.

Herrick, V.E., D.W. Andersen, and J.B. Macdonald, *Strategies of Curriculum Development.* Columbus, Ohio: Charles E. Merrill Books, Inc., 1965.

Hoban, C.F., *Implications of Theory for Research and Implementation in the New Media: Conference on Theory for the New Media in Education.* Lansing, Mich.: Michigan State University, 1962.

Hock, Louise, and T.J. Hill, *The General Education Class in the Secondary School.* New York: Holt, Rinehart & Winston, Inc., 1960.

Holland, J.G., and B.F. Skinner, *The Analysis of Behavior*. New York: McGraw-Hill Book Co., Inc. 1961.

Hopkins, L.T., *Interaction: The Democratic Process*. Boston: D.C. Heath & Co., 1941.

Houston, W.F., F.H. Blackington, and H.C. Southworth, *Professional Growth through Student Teaching*. Columbus, Ohio: Charles E. Merrill Books, Inc., 1965.

Hug, J.H., and P.J. Wilson, *Curriculum Enrichment Outdoors*. New York: Harper & Row, Publishers, 1965.

Hughes, Marie M., *Development of the Means for the Assessment of the Quality of Teaching in Elementary Schools*. Salt Lake City: University of Utah Press, 1959.

Hunt, M.P., and L.C. Metcalf, *Teaching High School Social Studies*. New York: Harper, 1955.

Hunter, Elizabeth, *The Cooperative Teacher at Work: Case Studies of Critical Incidents*. New York: Teachers College, Columbia University, 1962.

Hurley, B.D., *Curriculum for Elementary School Children*. New York: The Ronald Press Co., 1957.

Inlow, G.M., *The Emergent in Curriculum*. New York: John Wiley & Sons, Inc., 1966.

Insel, S.A., K. Schlesinger, and W. Desrosiers, "Dependency Responses to Televised Instruction," *Journal of Applied Psychology*, 1963. 47:328-331.

Karmel, L.T., *Testing in Our Schools*. New York: The Macmillan Co., 1966.

Kazamias, A.M., "A Note Concerning Practice in Teaching," *Harvard Educational Review*, 1961. 31:449-451.

Kelley, E.C., *The Workshop Way of Learning*. New York: Harper & Brothers, 1951.

Keppel, Francis, *The Necessary Revolution in American Education*. New York: Harper & Row, Publishers, 1966.

Klausmeier, H.J., *Principles and Practices of Secondary School Teaching*. New York: Harper & Brothers, 1953.

Kress, G.C., and G.L. Gropper, *Individual Differences in Learning from Self-Paced Programmed Instruction*. Pittsburgh: American Institutes for Research, 1964.

Krug, E.A., *The Secondary School Curriculum*. New York: Harper & Brothers, 1960.

——————, *Curriculum Planning.* New York: Harper & Brothers, 1950.

Larson, K.G., *Guide to Personal Advancement in the Teaching Profession.* Englewood Cliffs, N.J.: Prentice-Hall, Inc., 1966.

Leonard, J.P., *Developing the Secondary School Curriculum.* New York: Holt, Rinehart & Winston, Inc., 1953.

Lieberman, Myron, *The Future of Public Education.* Chicago: University of Chicago Press, 1960.

Lindquist, E.F., *Design and Analysis of Experiments in Psychology and Education.* Boston, Mass.: Houghton Mifflin, 1953.

Lumsdaine, A.A., and S.M. Roshel, *Experimental Research on Educational Media.* Los Angeles: University of California, 1962.

Mager, R.F., *Preparing Objectives for Programmed Instruction.* San Francisco, Cal.: Fearon, 1962.

Macomber, F.G., and L. Siegel, *Final Report on the Experimental Study in Instructional Procedures.* Oxford, Ohio: Miami University, 1960.

Mayer, Martin. *The Schools.* New York: Harper & Row, Inc., 1961.

Mays, A.B., *Principles and Practices of Vocational Education.* New York: McGraw-Hill Book Co., Inc., 1948.

Miel, A.M., *Changing the Curriculum.* New York: Appleton-Century-Crofts, 1946.

Mills, H.H., and H.R. Douglass, *Teaching in High School.* New York: The Ronald Press Co., 1957.

Murray, L.J., and L.D. May, *The Child and His Curriculum.* New York: Appleton-Century-Crofts, Inc., 1950.

Nason, L.J., *How to Study the Right Way.* New York: Cornerstone Library, Inc., 1965.

National Council of Teachers of English, *The English Language Arts.* New York: Appleton-Century-Crofts, Inc., 1952.

National Society for the Study of Education, *In-Service Education for Teachers, Supervisors, and Administrators.* Fifty-sixth Yearbook, Part I. Chicago: University of Chicago Press, 1957.

Oberholtzer, E.E., *An Integrated Curriculum in Practice.* New York: Bureau of Publications, Teachers College, Columbia University, 1937.

O'Donnell, Mabel, *Real and Make-Believe.* New York: Harper & Row, 1966.

Oliver, A.T., *Curriculum Improvement.* New York: Dodd, Mead & Co., 1965.

Olson, W.C., *Child Developing.* Boston: D.C. Heath & Co., 1959.

Orme, M.E.J., F.J. McDonald, and D.W. Allen, *Effect of Modeling and Feedback Variables on the Acquisition of a Complex Teaching Skill.* Stanford, Cal.: Stanford University, 1966.

Ovard, G.F., *Administration of the Changing Secondary School.* New York: The Macmillan Co., 1966.

Passow, A.H., M.B. Miles, S.M. Corey, and Dale Draper, *Training Curriculum Leaders for Cooperative Research.* New York: Bureau of Publications, Teachers College, Columbia University, 1955.

Patton, E.D., and D.W. Steiner, *Let's Look at Our Future.* New York: Scarecrow Press, Inc., 1966.

Plath, K.R., *Schools within Schools.* New York: Bureau of Publications, Teachers College, Columbia Universtiy, 1965.

Rasey, M.T., *This Is Teaching.* New York: Harper & Brothers, 1950.

Rosenthal, R., "The Effect of the Experimenter on the Results of Psychological Research," *Progress in Experimental Personality Research.* Edited by B.A. Maher. New York: Academic Press, 1964.

Russell, J.E., *Change and Challenge in American Education.* Boston: Houghton Mifflin Co., 1965.

Saylor, J.G., and W.M. Alexander, *Curriculum Planning for Better Teaching and Learning.* New York: Rinehart & Co., Inc., 1954.

——————————, *Curriculum Planning for Modern Schools.* New York: Holt, Rinehart & Winston, Inc., 1966.

Schramm, W., *Programmed Instruction: Today and Tomorrow.* New York: Fund for the Advancement of Education, 1962.

Shaplin, J.T., "Practice in Teaching," *Harvard Educational Review,* 1961. 31:33-59.

Simpson, R.H., *Teacher Self-Evaluation.* New York: The Macmillan Co., 1966.

Sleeper, W.R., and H.E. Tefler, "Planning Orientation to Student Teaching," *The Journal of Teacher Education,* 1962. 13:50-54.

Smith, B.O., W.O. Stanley, and J.H. Shores, *Fundamentals of Curriculum Development.* Yonkers-on-Hudson, N.Y.: World Book Co., 1957.

Smith, Paul, *Creativity — An Examination of the Creative Process.* New York: Hastings House, 1960.

Spears, Harold, *The Emerging High-School Curriculum.* New York: American Book Co., 1948.

Strang, Ruth, "How Guidance Relates to the Curriculum," *The Personnel and Guidance Journal,* January, 1954.

Strategy for Curriculum Change, Edited by Robert R. Leeper. Washington, D.C.: Association for Supervision and Curriculum Development, 1965.

Stratemeyer, F.B., H.L. Forkner, M.G. McKim, and A.H. Passow, *Developing a Curriculum for Modern Living.* New York: Columbia University, Teachers College, Bureau of Publications, 1957.

Thelen, H.A., *Group Dynamics in Curriculum Improvement — Educational Leadership,* Vol. XI, No. 7, April, 1954.

Townsend, E.A., and P.J. Burke, *Learning for Teachers.* New York: The Macmillan Co., 1962.

Travers, R.M., *Essentials of Learning.* New York: The Macmillan Co., 1963.

Umstattd, J.G., *Secondary School Teaching.* New York: Ginn & Co., 1953.

Vico, G.B., *On the Study Methods of Our Time.* Indianapolis: The Bobbs-Merrill Co., Inc., 1965.

Walton, John, *Toward Better Teaching in the Secondary Schools.* Boston: Allyn & Bacon, Inc., 1966.

Weiss, M.J., *Reading in the Secondary Schools.* New York: The Odyssey Press, Inc., 1961.

Wiles, Kimball, *Teaching for Better Schools.* Englewood Cliffs, N.J.: Prentice-Hall, Inc., 1959.

Wright, G.S., *Core Curriculum Development: Problems and Practices,* U.S. Office of Education Bulletin, 1952, No. 5. Washington, D.C.: Government Printing Office, 1952.

INDEX